HONORING THEIR PATHS

African American Contributions
· ALONG THE ·
Journey Through Hallowed Ground

Deborah A. Lee, Ph.D.

Deborah A. Lee

The Journey Through Hallowed Ground Partnership
Waterford, Virginia

2009

This book was manufactured in the United States of America.
Printing by Better Impressions, Sterling, Virginia.

Lee, Deborah A. (1955-   ).
          Additional authors: United States Department of the Interior, National Park Service.

          Honoring Their Paths: African American Contributions
          Along the Journey Through Hallowed Ground.

          Includes index.
          ISBN 978-0-615-30241-6

Cover and book design by Keith Damiani/Sequoia Design
Maps by Watsun Randolph/Piedmont Environmental Council, and Keith Damiani/Sequoia Design

Cover photographs by Kenneth L. Garrett; copyright The Journey Through Hallowed Ground Partnership.

Contents

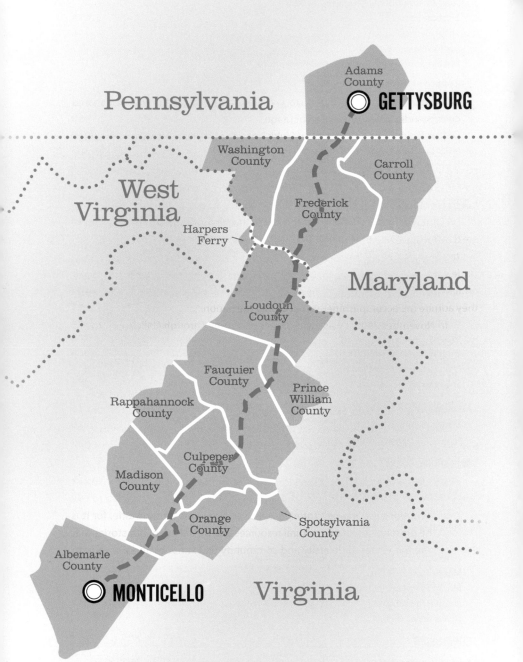

Pennsylvania

Adams
County

GETTYSBURG

Washington
County

Carroll
County

West
Virginia

Frederick
County

Harpers
Ferry

Maryland

Loudoun
County

Fauquier
County

Prince
William
County

Rappahannock
County

Culpeper
County

Madison
County

Orange
County

Spotsylvania
County

Albemarle
County

MONTICELLO

Virginia

Foreword

I t has been said that "without history, there is nothing." So it is with our shared understanding of our American heritage.

Our history is a story often told with images of sewing: a patchwork quilt in which each piece has a special story but the full effect is only achieved when they are sewn together. Our heritage is a tapestry of interwoven strands representing every hue and color, which form the patterns of our great heritage. I like those images because they tell the story of America.

The Journey Through Hallowed Ground is where "America Happened." Here are the stories of educational, political, cultural, business and civil rights leaders. Here are the way stations on the routes of a dynamic, expanding nation, along with the Underground Railroad. Here are the places that help us learn and understand our human experience, so that citizens may avoid repeating grievous mistakes even as they admire the accomplishments that glorify the nation.

In November 2006, I was invited by the Journey Through Hallowed Ground Partnership to address a newly formed Advisory Council of African American historians and representatives from historical organizations from four states: Pennsylvania, Maryland, Virginia and Harpers Ferry, West Virginia. This group was convened to begin the arduous and critically important work of chronicling the contributions of African Americans throughout the Journey Through Hallowed Ground.

What I saw that day was electrifying. Research was shared and stories were told. As the day moved forward, it became apparent that while this region may cover 180 miles, there was a unique richness of shared history in this place.

The product of that seminal meeting and the subsequent three years of research is what you are holding in your hands. *Honoring Their Paths: African American Contributions Along the Journey Through Hallowed Ground* is a fitting title, for it is through the preservation of our cultural resources and the telling of our stories that demonstrate the values of diversity and community which honor and link us with the heritage of our predecessors, and represents our individual and collective legacy to our successors.

I am honored to have been a part of this inspiring and important publication.

— *Dr. Robert G. Stanton*

DEPUTY SECRETARY OF THE UNITED STATES DEPARTMENT OF THE INTERIOR
FORMER DIRECTOR OF THE NATIONAL PARK SERVICE (1997-2001)

Introduction

Understanding the African American experience lends new dimensions to the phrase "hallowed ground." Most of the earliest black settlers in the historic landscape of The Journey Through Hallowed Ground National Heritage Area—from Gettysburg, Pennsylvania to Monticello in Virginia—were enslaved. Yet they contributed their knowledge, skills, and creative genius to help shape the land and its culture.

African Americans resisted, undermined, and fought slavery in myriad ways, most notably through organizing and utilizing the Underground Railroad and participating in the Abolition movement. Leonard Grimes, for example, a free black man born near Leesburg, Virginia, used his hackney carriage business to aid freedom flights in and around the Nation's Capital until his arrest and imprisonment in 1839. Later, he was a pastor at Twelfth Baptist Church in Boston—known for aiding freedom seekers. During the Civil War he lobbied the Massachusetts governor to allow black soldiers, recruited for the 54th Massachusetts Regiment, and met with President Abraham Lincoln to obtain protection for black ministers working in Union lines in the South. James W.C. Pennington of Washington County, Maryland, escaped from slavery and helped others do so as well. Additionally, he attended classes at Yale, received an honorary doctorate of divinity from the University of Heidelberg, and helped lead the international abolition movement. Hundreds of African American men from the region fought in the Union Army during the Civil War—forty-three from Gettysburg alone.

The period following the Civil War was a time of institution building in the black community. African Americans created religious congregations and fraternal organizations. They pooled their resources and built homes, schools, churches, and meeting halls. They cultivated farms and organized horse shows and baseball leagues and Emancipation Day celebrations. These communities supported their members during Jim Crow segregation. Their men continued to fight in the military for freedom even when it was denied to them at home. They fought consistently for better education, exemplified by the stories of schoolhouses and high schools that dot the region, including Jennie Dean's founding of the Manassas Industrial School in Prince William County, Virginia, in 1894.

Together, in such communities and institutions, African Americans laid a foundation for the civil rights movement of the twentieth century. They set the cornerstone at Harpers Ferry in 1906, during the second meeting of the Niagara Movement. Leader W.E.B. Du Bois understood the symbolic power of place, asked members to remove their shoes and socks as they tread upon the "hallowed ground" at the site of John Brown's "martyrdom" and to reconsecrate themselves to the full "emancipation of the race." Jessie Vann from Gettysburg used her roles as newspaper publisher and national board member of the National Association for the Advancement of Colored People (NAACP) to advance the cause during the Roosevelt and Eisenhower administrations. The civil rights movement played out in small communities throughout the region as much as in the big cities of the nation and helped the United States to more completely fulfill its founding ideals of freedom and equality.

African Americans from the Journey Through Hallowed Ground also shaped our national cultural traditions. Billy Pierce took black dance moves from the Loudoun County countryside to New York City, where he helped popularize the Charleston and Black Bottom. John Jackson of Rappahannock County shared Piedmont blues with the world and achieved recognition as a National Heritage Fellow. Through his virtuoso trumpet playing, Lester Bowie added soul and humor from Frederick County, Maryland, to contemporary jazz music. Edna Lewis of Orange County, Virginia, elevated rural southern cooking to a recognized cuisine and helped launch the culinary movement that celebrates regional cooking with farm-fresh seasonal foods.

We owe gratitude to the many African Americans, famous and anonymous, who have enriched our world in so many ways. Through their lives and work, their struggles and achievements, they hallowed this ground. Through this project, and through visits to the places they knew, we seek to honor their paths.

— *Deborah A. Lee, Ph.D.*

About this Book

This remarkable book is the culmination of a three-year effort to research and incorporate the history of African Americans who lived within the Journey Through Hallowed Ground as part of the intrinsic culture of our American Heritage. In 2006, as the Journey Through Hallowed Ground Partnership began documenting the history in what would become the 38th National Heritage Area our research revealed an abundance of information on the contributions of European Americans, but little on the contributions of African Americans. Accordingly, under the invaluable leadership of Beth Erickson, our Vice President, we sought the funding and the expertise to remediate this inexcusable void.

The African American history in the Journey Through Hallowed Ground encompasses the realities of slave life, the countless stories of people who risked everything to escape and navigate the Journey on the Underground Railroad to freedom, lives of freed slaves after emancipation and their struggle for survival and equality. Generation after generation, the people of this remarkable region have been called upon to define what it means to be an American. Yet, many of these stories were untold.

In 2006, we sought and received a grant from the Virginia Foundation for the Humanities to do the necessary primary source documentation research of the African American experience within this region. In November 2006, we brought together 75 African American historians from the 4-state Journey Through Hallowed Ground Partnership Area to begin sharing information and identifying 100 key sites and stories to be researched, and shared. This work was then further supported by additional grants from the Virginia Foundation for the Humanities, the Pennsylvania Museum and Historical Commission, the Loudoun Restoration and Preservation Society, the Virginia Department of Historic Resources, and individual supporters including Mr. and Mrs. James Moorman, Mr. and Mrs. Donald Pongrace, and Mr. and Mrs. David Williams.

We are eternally thankful to our remarkable group of expert Advisors, who formed the JTHG African American History Committee, each of whom contributed their considerable expertise, acumen and time over the past three years to contribute both to this research as well as to the overall efforts of the Journey Through Hallowed Ground Partnership. *(For a list of our Advisors, please see the Acknowledgments starting on page 243.)* On every step of this project Dr. Deborah Lee was guided by these regional and national advisors, including the National Park Service, to ensure the integrity of this research.

We are proud to share the incredible contributions of African Americans within the Journey Though Hallowed Ground—from Colonial times to today. And through compelling stories and archival images, it is our hope that readers will gain a better understanding of our collective American story. Sites and stories are profiled from every county within our 4-state region. Each chapter begins with a map to invite readers to explore and visit while having a better understanding of the people who made these places historic.

There are far more stories of African American contributions and historic sites than are included in this volume, each worthy of honor and remembrance. We encourage additional research and engagement and ask each reader to share your knowledge with us. We ask each reader to spend time with professionals in the museums, resource centers, and organizations that document and share African American heritage. It is our hope that this work will encourage the preservation and conscientious stewardship of these often fragile cultural resources. Finally, on behalf of all who have worked on this invaluable research, I invite you to *Take the Journey*™ with your families so that current and future generations will benefit from these inspiring stories and remarkable places within our shared Journey Through Hallowed Ground National Heritage Area.

— *Cate Magennis Wyatt*
PRESIDENT , THE JOURNEY THROUGH HALLOWED GROUND PARTNERSHIP

Adams County
PENNSYLVANIA

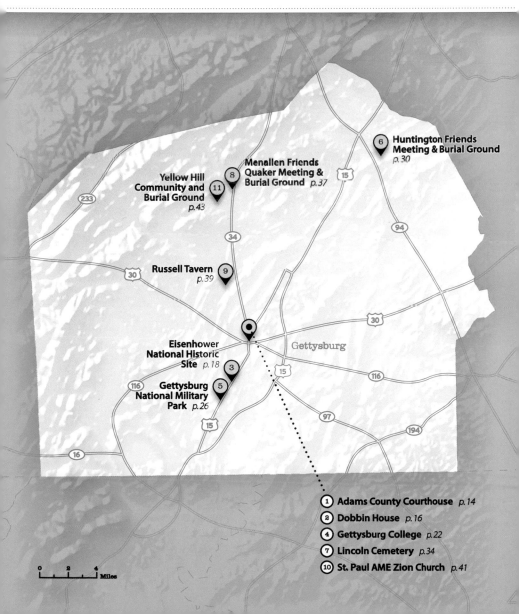

0 2 4 Miles

Margaret (Mag) Palm, demonstrating how her wrists were bound during an attempted kidnapping.
(Adams County Historical Society)

1

Adams County Courthouse

The Adams County Courthouse, at this site and its prior locations nearby, is known locally for its role in three stories about African American freedom during the time of enslavement.

HISTORIC SITE	Open to the public
LOCATION	111 Baltimore St. Gettysburg, PA
CONTACT INFORMATION	(717) 337-9820
ON THE WEB	www.adamscounty.us/adams

On October 3, 1831, Clem Johnson became free, manumitted by Francis Scott Key, author of the Star Spangled Banner. Both men were from Maryland, so it is unclear why Key filed the papers at the Gettysburg Courthouse. At the time, however, a significant number of African Americans migrated to the town from Maryland. Gettysburg was growing so work was plentiful, slavery was dying out due to the 1780 gradual abolition act, and educational opportunities were available. Perhaps Johnson wanted to settle there. Researchers can find no other records of him, so his fate is unknown.

Two court cases involving black women and kidnapping drew a good deal of public attention. One of the most compelling stories is that of Catherine "Kitty" Payne, a woman who was kidnapped, along with her young children, and imprisoned for almost a year in Rappahannock County, Virginia *(see profile, p. 35)* in 1846. One of their abductors, a local man named Thomas Finnegan, was tried, convicted, and sentenced to five years in jail.

In 1858, Margaret Devitt, later known widely as Mag Palm, was abducted by three men but managed to escape by crying out, fighting with her bound hands, and allegedly biting one man's thumb off. The court indicted the three men for the kidnapping attempt. Only one was found and arrested, but he was released after the court accepted his alibi. Around the same time on Breckinridge Street, a group of several women and children assaulted a black man suspected of playing a role in the kidnapping attempt. A police officer rescued him.

Resources

For Clem Johnson manumission, see Adams County Bicentennial Committee, "Adams County Bicentennial Tidbits." (Sept. 1999) *www.gettysburg.com/adams200/tidbits/sept.htm*

Dobbin House

Dobbin House

2

Reverend Alexander Dobbin, an early settler in the area that became Adams County, played a major role in the founding of Gettysburg. In 1774, Dobbin purchased 300 acres of land in and around what is now the town of Gettysburg and commenced construction of a farm and the Dobbin House, for use as their dwelling and as a Classical School, today's equivalent of a secondary school.

HISTORIC SITE	Open to the public
THINGS TO DO AND SEE	Restaurant is open daily from 5 PM. Reservations Advised.
DESIGNATIONS	National Register of Historic Places National Historic Landmark
LOCATION	89 Steinwehr Ave. Gettysburg, PA Business Route 15 South from Gettysburg
CONTACT INFORMATION	(717) 334-2100
ON THE WEB	www.dobbinhouse.com

Alexander Dobbin, like many of the early Scots-Irish immigrants to Adams County, held slaves. But on March 1, 1780, in the wake of the American Revolution, Pennsylvania lawmakers passed an "An Act for the Gradual Abolition of Slavery." It required that everyone born into slavery after that date become free at age twenty-eight. Alexander Dobbin recorded the following births: Becky and Eliza in 1800, Sall in 1803, and Amy in 1805. Unfortunately, their fates are unknown. Until his death in 1809, Alexander Dobbin was a minister in the Associate Reformed Presbyterian Church, which eventually endorsed antislavery. His son was also a devout member of the church and took over the farm after his father's death. In 1820 Matthew Dobbin worked his farm with four free people of color, probably a family consisting of a man and a young woman and a boy and a girl under age fourteen. By 1825, however, Dobbin sold the farm for financial reasons and became a teacher. In 1837 he took a teaching position in Franklin County where he was active in the Underground Railroad. It is possible that he aided freedom seekers in Adams County and was apparently part of the larger interracial antislavery network.

According to local legend, the Dobbin House served as a safe house for enslaved people traveling north in search of freedom. The National Geographic Society featured the site and its hidden crawl space in an article on the Underground Railroad in 1984.

John and Delores Moaney lived and traveled with the Eisenhowers for more than thirty years
(Gettysburg Times)

Eisenhower National Historic Site

3

D
wight and Mamie Eisenhower enjoyed life at their restored farmhouse in Gettysburg; it was the only home they ever owned. But they did not live there alone—two members of their domestic staff, John and Delores Moaney, were their constant companions. In fact, the Moaneys' presence was so strong and important there that the Eisenhowers' son John called them "the soul of that place."

HISTORIC SITE	Open to the public.
THINGS TO DO AND SEE	Enjoy the farm exhibit and grounds
DESIGNATIONS	National Register of Historic Places National Historic Landmark
LOCATION	Visitors Center 1195 Baltimore Pike Gettysburg, PA
CONTACT INFORMATION	(717) 338-9114 john_joyce@nps.gov
ON THE WEB	www.nps.gov/eise

John and Delores Moaney's lives became intertwined with the Eisenhowers well before they purchased the Gettysburg Farm or moved to the White House. Drafted into the Army in 1942, John Moaney served General Dwight Eisenhower on his personal staff and after the war his wife Delores cooked and served as a housekeeper and personal assistant to

Mamie Eisenhower beginning in 1947. The two couples traveled together, with the Eisenhowers insisting on the same first class level of accommodations—usually an adjacent room—even in the segregated South. John Moaney loved the Gettysburg farm and vegetable gardening there. Moaney and "Ike" were frequent companions—together they fished in the pond, prepared vegetable soup, and grilled steaks rolled in salt and pepper. Moaney prepared breakfasts for Eisenhower, cared for his clothing and personal items, and served meals and beverages to guests. Delores cooked delicious

Delores Moaney with Eisenhower grandchildren, Anne and Susan Eisenhower. *(Eisenhower National Historic Site)*

meat and potato meals and she and Mamie doted over their own and one another's grandchildren.

President Eisenhower advanced civil rights in the nation, but he moved cautiously and focused on areas in which he had clear jurisdiction. He first ordered Attorney General Herbert Brownell to end segregation in the District of Columbia. Powell did so by resurrecting and enforcing Reconstruction-era legislation known as "the Lost Laws." Eisenhower then directed the completion of desegregation in the military. He appointed the first African American, Frederic Morrow, to an executive position on the White House staff. He also selected African American newspaper publisher and civil rights advocate Jessie M. Vann for governmental advisory boards and diplomatic positions. Eisenhower ordered the 101st Airborne to enforce school desegregation in Little Rock Arkansas, for him a difficult decision. Eisenhower then supported and signed the Civil Rights Act in 1957, the first civil rights legislation in eighty-two years. In 1959 he hosted the entire White House staff at a picnic at the Gettysburg farm. His warm and respectful relationship with the Moaneys also illuminates his quiet progressivism.

Resources

"A Valet and His President." *Christian Science Monitor* (June 12, 1957), 6.

David A. Nichols. *A Matter of Justice: Eisenhower and the Beginning of the Civil Rights Revolution.* New York: Simon & Schuster, 2007.

Kasey S. Pipes. *Ike's Final Battle: The Road to Little Rock and the Challenge of Equality.* New York: World Ahead Publishing, 2007.

Eisenhower National Historic Site

John A. Moaney Jr. (1914–1978) **and Delores Moaney** (1917–)

Dwight D. Eisenhower with
John A. Moaney

John A. Moaney was one of Dwight D. Eisenhower's closest friends. During the war, Moaney served on General Eisenhower's personal staff in Africa and Europe. Among his other duties, he tended Eisenhower's two beloved Scotties, Telek and Caacie (Khaki), and their puppies. After the war, Eisenhower retained Staff Sergeant Moaney as his valet and the two men remained together until Eisenhower's death in 1969. At his funeral, Master Sergeant Moaney served as an honorary pallbearer with Eisenhower's two brothers and brother-in-law and six military commanders from World War II; he was the first African American to serve as a presidential pallbearer. Moaney retired from the Army shortly thereafter. He and his wife Delores continued to work for Mamie Eisenhower at the farm in Gettysburg. The couple retired to their home in Washington, DC in 1977. John Moaney died the following year. When Susan Eisenhower, granddaughter of Ike and Mamie, moved to Washington in 1986, she turned to Delores Moaney, whom she considered family, for support in caring for her three children. Now fully retired, Delores Moaney maintains a close relationship with the extended Eisenhower family.

John and Delores Moaney both hailed from the Eastern Shore of Maryland, near Easton. They were childhood sweethearts, but each married another, moved away, and were widowed. They reunited in Washington, D.C. in 1945 and married the following year. As a girl who loved preparing food from the time she could stand, Delores dreamed of one day cooking for a famous person, earning $18 a week, and riding a train a long distance. Acknowledging those were big dreams, she felt satisfaction in their spectacular realization. The Moaney's home community took great pride in them. One special day at the White House, the Eisenhowers hosted thirty-two members of Moaney's Methodist church on the Eastern Shore of Maryland, including John's 67-year-old mother. The *New York Times* reported, "No foreign or domestic dignitaries ever received a warmer White House welcome than the one President and Mrs. Eisenhower extended today."

Resources

Oral history transcriptions at the Eisenhower National Historic Site.

"White House Valet, His Family and Friends Call on His Boss." *Washington Post* (June 13, 1957), B1.

PEOPLE IN THE PLACES **Jessie Mathews Vann** (1885–1967)

essie Mathews Vann grew from a poor orphan girl to a businesswoman who managed national and international affairs. Jessie was the granddaughter of underground railroad activists Edward and Annie Mathews from the Yellow Hill community of Adams County, Pennsylvania (see p. 44). Her father William and his two brothers served in the U.S. Colored Troops during the Civil War. Both parents died before Jessie turned six and she grew up among extended family.

Jessie Vann, left, beside the Liberty ship *Robert L. Vann* in 1943. *(Carnegie Museum of Art, Pittsburgh; Heinz Family Fund)*

In 1910, Jessie Ellen Mathews married attorney and civil rights activist Robert Lee Vann, editor and publisher of the *Pittsburgh Courier*, an African American newspaper. In 1940, after thirty years of marriage, Robert Vann died, and Jessie Vann became publisher/treasurer of the *Pittsburgh Courier*. Under her tenure it reached circulation of 400,000 and became the most popular black newspaper in the country. Its success was due in part to its World War II "Double V" campaign, meaning victory for democracy at home and abroad—over prejudice and discrimination in the U.S. and against foreign enemies abroad. In 1943 the Navy named the USS Robert L. Vann Liberty ship in Vann's honor and Jessie christened it with a bottle of champagne.

Jessie Vann's effective leadership and human rights advocacy earned her major roles in business, politics, government and international diplomacy. She served on boards such as the NAACP and Urban League. President Dwight Eisenhower appointed her to his International Development Advisory Board and another that set retirement tables for the Armed Forces. In 1944 she represented the United States at President William Tubman's inauguration in Liberia. Eisenhower asked Vann to serve as an alternate delegate to the United Nations, but she declined, citing business duties. She visited Gettysburg periodically and spoke in 1950 at the National Military Park in a memorial service to honor African Americans killed in battle. Well known and highly regarded in her day, she appeared on the popular television show, *This is Your Life*, and wrote an essay for Edward R. Murrow's radio program, *This I Believe*. She affirmed that "if you give to the world the best that you have, the best will come back to you."

Resources

Jessie M. Vann. "This I Believe."
www.thisibelieve.org/dsp_ShowEssay.php?uid=17068&themelist=death&yval=0&start=560

Debra McCauslin. *Yellow Hill: Reconstructing the Past.* Gettysburg, Penn.: For the Cause Productions, 2005. 17-19.

Gettysburg College

Gettysburg College

4

Daniel Alexander Payne, after studying at the Lutheran Theological Seminary from 1835-37 and operating a school for black children at Gettysburg College, had a special place in his heart for Gettysburg. As an ordained Lutheran minister, he returned for a visit in 1838 and sent an open letter to the Colored American newspaper with news

HISTORIC SITE	Open to the public
THINGS TO DO AND SEE	The Gettysburg College campus is available for walking tours. Call ahead for information. Historic Marker, Tours, Self-Guided Walking Trails
DESIGNATIONS	Historical Highway Marker, "Daniel Alexander Payne."
LOCATION	300 North Washington St. Gettysburg, PA
CONTACT INFORMATION	(717) 337-6000
ON THE WEB	www.gettysburg.edu

of his warm welcome and experiences. He listened to an antislavery speech by Dr. Simon Schmucker, founder of Gettysburg College and the Lutheran Theological Seminary; visited a Sunday School taught by students; and distributed "a goodly number of antislavery publications among the students." Payne expressed the opinion that "the colored people of Gettysburg have more means for mental and moral improvement than any community of colored people with which I am acquainted." He added that "the professors in the College and the Seminary, and also the students of both institutions, stand ready to counsel, assist and instruct them, both night and day." He lamented that few took advantage of the opportunity, mainly because of their frequent movement between Gettysburg, Carlisle, Chambersburg, and York (perhaps for economic and familial reasons), and of religious divisions among them. A historical highway marker on the Gettysburg College campus commemorates Payne's presence and contributions.

Before and during the Civil War, some students, faculty, and staff at Gettysburg College sympathized with refugees from slavery and a few gave direct aid. In particular, its highly regarded African American custodian, John "Jack" Hopkins, and the Beta Delta fraternity of white students known as the "Black Ducks," assisted freedom seekers in finding safe passage through Pennsylvania.

Among the distinguished alumni of Gettysburg College, Bruce Gordon graduated in 1968 and returned in 2006 to deliver the commencement address. A noted businessman and then president of the NAACP, he told students that when he arrived for his first day of college, he just wanted to fit in, but due to his education and national events such as the assassinations of Malcolm X and Martin Luther King Jr., he left determined to be "a social change agent." In words that would have pleased forbears Schmucker and Payne, he said that he "learned that change was not just good; it was necessary." He warned that growing economic disparities led "too many people to have nightmares instead of dreams," and affirmed that "finding your purpose includes the fuel to carry that purpose out."

Bruce Gordon
(Gettysburg College)

Resources

Origen [Pen name of Daniel Alexander Payne]. "To the Church and Congregation at T[roy]," *The Colored American,* October 13, 1838.

Gettysburg College. "Bruce Gordon." *www.gettysburg.edu/podium/gettysburg_gallery/bruce_gordon.dot*

PEOPLE IN THE PLACES

Daniel Alexander Payne

(1811–1893)

Daniel Alexander Payne

Daniel Alexander Payne became the most influential African American Christian of the nineteenth century, and Gettysburg played a key role in his rise. Born free but orphaned at age nine in Charleston, South Carolina, Payne obtained an education there from prominent free black men. He operated a school himself until 1835, when the state made it illegal to teach slaves to read and write. He migrated north, where Lutheran Theological Seminary officials offered him higher education in theology so that he might minister among African Americans. He graduated and was ordained as a Lutheran minister, but in 1842 he joined the African Methodist Episcopal (AME) Church. Payne valued intellectual rigor over emotionalism and championed education. In 1848 Bishop Paul Quinn appointed him historian of the AME Church, and four years later he was elected Bishop.

In 1856, Bishop Payne was a founding trustee for Wilberforce University in Ohio. The private college educated African Americans, many from the South. Payne and the college played important roles in the Underground Railroad by spreading information and aiding freedom seekers. The university closed during the Civil War until, under Payne's leadership, the AME Church purchased and reopened it in 1863. Daniel Alexander Payne then became the first African American college president, serving Wilberforce in that office until 1877. He published his memoir in 1888 and The History of the AME Church in 1893.

Frederick Douglass and Alexander Payne had high regard for one another. In 1851 the Anti-Slavery Committee invited Payne to become a lecturer as Douglass had been, but Payne declined. "When God has a work to be executed he also chooses the man to execute it," Payne remarked, and "qualifies the workman for the work." He and Douglass, he noted, each were specially suited to their respective roles. Both men, however, served African Americans and the nation well as public intellectuals.

Resources

PBS, "Daniel Payne," This Far by Faith. *www.pbs.org/thisfarbyfaith/people/daniel_payne.html*

Daniel Alexander Payne. *Recollections of Seventy Years* (Nashville: A. M. E. Sunday School Union, 1888). *docsouth.unc.edu/church/payne70/menu.html*

> **PEOPLE IN THE PLACES**
> ## John "Jack" Hopkins
> (1806–1868)

From his appointment as custodian of Gettysburg College in 1847 to his death in 1868, John Hopkins won the affection and esteem of students and faculty. Known for his fidelity, integrity, and "gentlemanly deportment," students called him "vice president" of the college. Born in Maryland in 1806—unknown whether enslaved or free—Hopkins moved to Pennsylvania and married Julia Ann, a native of the state. Son John Edward was born in 1842 followed closely by Wilson and Mary. In 1857 Hopkins purchased a home at 219 South Washington Street in Gettysburg from Abraham Brian, when Brian bought a farm on Cemetery Ridge.

John Hopkins (Courtesy of Special Collections/Musselman Library, Gettysburg College, Gettysburg, Pennsylvania.)

In 1860 the Hopkins family moved to a house on college grounds, but kept the one on Washington Street. On July 4th of that year, the couple hosted a "Grand Fancy Dress Ball." *The Star and Sentinel* reported that it was "attended by all the colored aristocracy of the town, with specially invited guests from York, Harrisburg, Columbia, and Chambersburg." Hopkins's status and social network supports other evidence that he was active in the Underground Railroad. The caption of an old railroad cut photograph stated that freedom seekers traveled the route from Thaddeus Stevens's Maria Furnace to Gettysburg College, where "Jack Hopkins notified the BDs who took them to Wrights." The BDs were the Black Ducks, an unofficial antislavery fraternity also known as Beta Delta. Gettysburg College Professor and alumnus J. Howard Wert published an account of their aid to freedom seekers in 1904.

Since college administrators and faculty opposed slavery, Hopkins may have had support among them for such activities. Upon his death in 1868, the college processed as one to attend his funeral—an extremely rare occurrence.

During the Civil War, son John Edward enlisted and served in Company F of the 25th U.S. Colored Troops, attaining the rank of sergeant. He returned to Gettysburg after his tour, and suffered the rest of his life from service-connected illnesses while continuing to support his family. In 1870 he lived in the house at 219 South Washington Street with his wife Margaret, two children, and his mother. The privately owned house still stands and is marked with an interpretive sign.

Resources

Peter C. Vermilyea. "Jack Hopkins' Civil War." *Adams County History* 11 (2005): 4-21.

Abraham Brian's house on Cemetery Ridge as it appears today.

Gettysburg National Military Park

5

B y the time the Civil War came to Gettysburg, three decades of growth and economic development had attracted African American workers from Maryland and beyond. In Pennsylvania, north of the Mason-Dixon line, slavery had

HISTORIC SITE	Open to the public
THINGS TO DO AND SEE	Self-guided tours Licensed battlefield guides Visitor center
LOCATION	97 Taneytown Rd. Gettysburg, PA
CONTACT INFORMATION	(717) 334-1124
ON THE WEB	www.nps.gov/gett

been gradually abolished by legislation adopted in 1847 and black children could attend school. Still, life was often hard—they coped with social and economic segregation and slave catchers who hunted freedom seekers and sometimes kidnapped free people of color. Nonetheless, some African Americans purchased their own homes and farms. Abraham Brian, for example, (also spelled Bryan or Brien) owned property on Cemetery Ridge at the time of the battle, including a dwelling and barn that still stand, along with a house near Emmitsburg Road he rented to Mag Palm in 1860. James and Sarah Warfield owned a small farm on Seminary Ridge, where

James also maintained a blacksmith shop.

When rumor reached Gettysburg of the Confederate invasion in 1863, most black citizens evacuated Adams County. They had more to fear than white residents did, including enslavement. After the war, returning property owners found their farms severely damaged and their homes ransacked. Some, such as Basil Biggs, helped move hastily buried bodies of fallen soldiers to the newly established National Cemetery. The Sons of Goodwill established Lin-

Abraham Brian's house just after the battle. *(Library of Congress)*

coln Cemetery *(see p. 34)* in 1867 for black citizens, including those who served in the U.S. Colored Troops.

African Americans also contributed to the Park Service. When Franklin D. Roosevelt took office during the Great Depression, he quickly established the Civilian Conservation Corps (CCC) in 1933 as part of the New Deal. Two African American units, Companies 385 and 1355, improved and maintained Gettysburg National Military Park. Most of the men hailed from the region, including Gettysburg, and Maryland. The Gettysburg units built roads and fences, laid pipe, and groomed the forests and fields of the 26-acre National Military Park. Company 1355 produced an outstanding camp newspaper, the *Battlefield Echo.*

Staff members of the Civilian Conservation Corps camp at Gettysburg National Military Park. *(National Archives)*

Gettysburg was also distinguished among CCC camps because of its black leadership. At first, only white officers and foremen supervised the camps. Under pressure to allow black leadership, in 1935

President Roosevelt issued an executive order mandating the change. The War Department and Park Service complied by making Gettysburg a model program with all black leadership. Over the next five years, they appointed African American men as camp commander and staff, superintendent, and engineers that designed CCC projects. The program was deemed successful and black leadership was established in other units as well.

Resources

Margaret S. Creighton. *The Colors of Courage: Gettysburg's Forgotten History.* Basic Books, 2005. *books.google.com/books?id=fMdq1YHh2FAC*

Gettysburg National Military Park. *War for Freedom: African American Experiences in the Era of the Civil War.* *www.nps.gov/gett/forteachers/warforfreedom.htm*

John C. Paige. *The Civilian Conservation Corps and the National Park Service, 1933-1942: An Administrative History.* See especially, "Black Enrollment," in chapter 3, "The National Park Service Camps." National Park Service, Department of the Interior, 1985. *www.nps.gov/history/history/online_books/ccc/ccc3e.htm*

PEOPLE IN THE PLACES | **Basil Biggs** | (1819–1906)

Basil and Mary Biggs *(Adams County Historical Society)*

Born free near Pipe Creek Quaker Meeting in Carroll County, Maryland *(see p. 50)*, Basil's mother died when he was four and he was bound out to perform hard labor. As an adult he became a teamster, hauling goods and carrying large sums of money between Carroll County and Baltimore. He married Mary J. Jackson, a free black woman raised by white Presbyterian families in nearby New Windsor. In 1858 the Biggs sold their three-acre farm and moved with their children—Hannah, Eliza, Calvin, and William—to Adams County where their children could be educated. The parents could not read or write, but the three eldest children entered school and learned to read. Basil and Mary Biggs had three more children and helped found and build Asbury M.E.

Church in Gettysburg.

People fleeing slavery on the underground railroad found safe refuge on the Biggs farm. They rested by day and at night Biggs took them twelve miles north to the black community of Yellow Hill overlooking the Quaker Valley *(see p. 43)*. From there, Edward Mathews helped them connect with Quakers active in assisting freedom seekers in Adams County and beyond. Biggs's eldest daughter Hannah married Mathews's son Nelson.

When hearing of the approaching Confederate Army, Biggs sent his family away, but did not leave himself until Confederates marched into the town from the west. Biggs borrowed a horse and rode east to York. Confederate forces used his home as a field hospital. He returned to find the graves of forty-five Confederates, the house and garden damaged, and crops, livestock, and household goods taken or destroyed.

With contributions from the northern states whose troops fought at Gettysburg, the Commonwealth of Pennsylvania established a National Cemetery in 1863. Biggs and others exhumed, moved, and reburied over 3,000 dead from makeshift graves to the new cemetery. Biggs used his two-horse team and carried nine coffins at a time. In 1868 he submitted a claim for $1,507 in war damages and was awarded $1,357 but the state never allocated funds to pay. Nonetheless, he bought farmland on Cemetery Ridge, near the field of Pickett's Charge. A historian persuaded him not to remove the famous copse of trees there. In 1892, Biggs purchased a home at the corner of Washington and High Streets in Gettysburg. For at least thirty years before his death in 1906 he was a licensed veterinary surgeon, in business with his son. He was one of the most renowned and respected citizens of the region.

Resources

Margaret S. Creighton. *The Colors of Courage: Gettysburg's Forgotten History.* Basic Books, 2005.

Peter C. Vermilyea. "The Effect of the Confederate Invasion of Pennsylvania on Gettysburg's African American Community." *www.gdg.org/Gettysburg%20Magazine/gburgafrican.html#_ftnref65*

Huntington Friends
Meeting House with
Wright gravestones
in the foreground
(Photo by Deborah Lee)

Huntington Friends Meeting & Burial Ground

6

Quakers, members of the Religious Society of Friends, established Huntington Meeting in 1746, first gathering in private homes. In 1750 they erected a log meetinghouse and established an adjacent burial ground. In 1790 they built a stone meetinghouse still used for silent worship. Along with meetings in Pennsylvania, Maryland, and northern Virginia, they participated in the Baltimore Yearly Meeting. Quakers advocated human equality and denounced slavery, though they varied on the appropriate level of activism. Quakers often hired free African American workers, many assisted them in legal matters, and some aided freedom seekers. A few Huntington Quakers vigorously worked to oppose

HISTORIC SITE	Viewable from the road
THINGS TO DO AND SEE	Operating Quaker Meeting House
DESIGNATIONS	National Park Service Underground Railroad Network to Freedom Site
LOCATION	300 Quaker Church Rd. York Springs, Pennsylvania
CONTACT INFORMATION	Debra Sandoe McCauslin, historian, author, and meeting member: (717) 528-8553 dmccauslin@gettysburghistories.com
ON THE WEB	www.freedomliesnorth.org/ index.php?option=com_content& task=blogcategory&id=15&Itemid=28

and undermine slavery, utilizing their networks with African Americans and other Quakers. Foremost among them were William Wright and his wife Phebe Wierman Wright, both buried in the Huntington graveyard.

Resources

Debra McCauslin. "Sites Verified by the National UGRR Network to Freedom," in *Freedom Lies Just North: The Underground Railroad in Adams County*. *www.freedomliesnorth.org/index.php?option=com_content&task=b logcategory&id=15&Itemid=28*

"Welcome to Huntington Friends Meeting House." *www.dworley.com/huntington.html*

PEOPLE
· IN THE ·
PLACES

William (1788–1865) and Phebe Wright (1790–1873)

William Still, a free black leader of Underground Railroad activity in the Philadelphia hub, cited William Wright as a "distinguished abolitionist of Adams County" who assisted "nearly one thousand slaves" to freedom beginning in 1819. Wife Phebe Wright partnered with him in the cause. Extended family members engaged in similar activities, particularly Phebe's brother Joel Wierman and his wife Lydia, who also lived in Adams County. From 1820 until 1840 the Wrights lived two miles north of the black community of Yellow Hill, another refuge for freedom seekers *(see p. 43)*. They then moved closer to the Huntington Friends meeting, where they were members. They raised a son and three daughters.

(Adams County Historical Society)

Most notable among the freedom seekers the family aided was twenty-one-year-old Jim Pembroke, escaping slavery in Washington County, Maryland in 1828 *(see profile, p. 93)*. He lived with the Wrights for six months, helping William on the farm. Phebe taught him to read. He adopted the name James W. C. Pennington and settled in New York. There he studied theology, became an ordained Presbyterian minister and pastor, author, international abolitionist, and recipient of an honorary doctorate of divinity from the University of Heidelburg. In his memoir, *The Fugitive Blacksmith*, he expressed his gratitude and continuing affection for the Wrights, calling William his "dear friend." The regard was mutual. He quoted a letter from William and a postscript from Phebe in which she wrote, "James, I hope thee will not attribute my long silence in writing to indifference. No such feeling can ever exist towards thee in our family. Thy name is mentioned almost every day. Each of the children claims the next letter from thee. It will be for thee to decide which shall have it." William and Phebe Wright are buried in the Huntington Burial Ground with their son, the former Union Army General William Wierman Wright, buried beside them.

Resources

James W. C. Pennington. *The Fugitive Blacksmith, or Events in the Life of James W. C. Pennington....* (London, 1849). *docsouth.unc.edu/neh/penning49/menu.html*

William Still. *The Underground Rail Road.* (Philadelphia, 1872). *www.quinnipiac.edu/other/ABL/etext/ugrr/ugrrmain.html*

Albert Cook Myers. "The Wright Family," in *Immigration of the Irish Quakers into Pennsylvania 1682-1750 with Their Early History in Ireland.* (Swarthmore, Penn., 1902), 394-398. *www.altlaw.com/jwright/web79912.htm*

PEOPLE IN THE PLACES Henry Franklin   (1803–1889)

(Courtesy of the Friends Historical Library of Swarthmore College)

Henry Franklin lived a remarkable life. Born as Bill Budd to enslaved parents owned by Adam Good of Carroll County, he was sold at age nine to Abraham Shriner. His parents and sister were sold at the same time to two members of the Church of the Brethren who eventually freed them. Parents Jarrett and Ann Budd bought a house in Gettysburg. Bill managed the Shriner farm and hauled grain and flour to market in Baltimore. He drove Shriner once to the farm of William Wright to purchase fruit trees, and visited other times on his own. William and Phebe Wright gave food and refuge to people escaping slavery. Although Budd had affection for the family and Shriner had promised him his freedom, Budd doubted he would see that day. With permission to visit his parents near Gettysburg in spring of 1837, Bill Budd made his way to the Wrights, then to Daniel Gibbons in Lancaster County, then to Emmor Kimber in Chester County and finally to Richard Moore at Quakertown, Bucks County. The Wrights, Gibbons, Kimbers and Moores were all Quakers.

Abraham Shriner wrote to Emmor Kimber, hoping to regain his slave property. Kimber explained he did not "believe in the right of one man to make 'chattels personal' of another" and he welcomed visitors without questioning their status. *The National Enquirer* published the men's letters.

In Quakertown, Bill Budd took the name Henry Franklin and worked for Richard Moore, a businessman and underground railroad activist. He served as a conductor himself, regularly transporting a wagon of freedom seekers in the evening and returning with coal or other goods in the morning. Franklin married his fiancé from Carroll County, Ann Brooks, but she died a year later, just after they bought a house. Franklin remarried and raised several children. When his second wife died, he married again and moved to Philadelphia in 1864. There he secured work at the Academy of Fine Arts.

After the war and the Thirteenth Amendment abolished slavery, Henry Franklin returned to Carroll County and was warmly welcomed by the Shriners. Alfred Shriner, just a boy when Franklin left, returned the visit and lodged with Franklin in Philadelphia. Later, when Shriner's Kansas farm was ruined by drought and grasshoppers, Franklin sent money. A Quaker friend reported in 1887 that "visitors to the Academy of Fine Arts may almost any day see near the entrance his venerable form, where, in good health, in his eighty-fourth year, with whitened locks and gentlemanly bearing, he may be found polite and attentive to all and wearing his age and honors with a joyful and thankful heart."

Resources

[Hannah Levick]. *Sketch of Henry Franklin and Family. docsouth.unc.edu/neh/franklin/franklin.html*

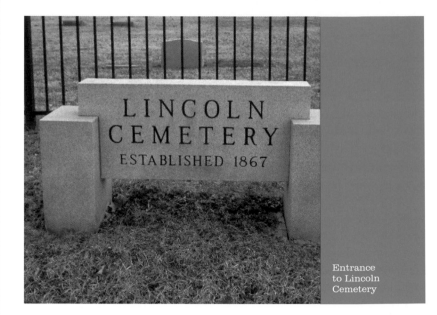

Entrance
to Lincoln
Cemetery

7 Lincoln Cemetery

Lincoln Cemetery is the burial site of Gettysburg's African American citizens and Civil War veterans. In keeping with the customs of the 1860s, African American veterans were mostly denied the honor of being buried in the National Cemetery. The

HISTORIC SITE	Viewable from the road
THINGS TO DO AND SEE	Access by appointment
DESIGNATIONS	National Register of Historic Places
LOCATION	Long Lane and Lincoln Lane, Gettysburg, PA
CONTACT INFORMATION	(717) 334-5533

lone exception was Henry Gooden of Carlisle, Pennsylvania, who served in the 127th USCT, buried in the U.S. Regulars section of the National Cemetery in 1876. For the most part segregated even in death, there are some thirty members of the U.S. Colored Troops buried in Lincoln Cemetery. These men who fought for freedom and the Union were there laid to rest with honor and dignity.

Here you'll find Lloyd Watts *(see profile on p. 36)* who enlisted in the U.S. Colored Troops in 1865 and served in Virginia. You'll also find Isaac Buckmaster who served in the 8th U.S. Colored Troops and both he and his brother were wounded in the battle of Olustee Florida. The 8th U.S. Colored Troops, along with other U.S. Colored Troops, were present at General

Lee's surrender at the Appomattox courthouse.

Not all who are buried here are veterans. Take for example Abraham Brian, a farmer in Gettysburg who left his land during the battle. Union forces occupied Brian's farm during Picketts Charge. After the battle, the government paid Brian $15 for damages. All told, more than 180,000 African Americans enlisted in the U.S. Army during the Civil War and risked all to fight for their rights, their families and the Union.

Many of the town's earliest black residents were re-interred in the Lincoln Cemetery when the town's "Colored Cemetery" was cleared in 1906 to provide space for new houses.

Resources

Betty Dorsey Myers. *Segregation in Death: Gettysburg's Lincoln Cemetery.* Gettysburg, Penn.: Lincoln Cemetery Project Association, 2001.

PEOPLE IN THE PLACES

Catherine "Kitty" Payne   (1816–1850)

Mary Maddox of Rappahannock County, Virginia, inherited her husband Samuel's estate when he died in 1839, with any remainder at her death to go to their nephew Samuel Maddox. In 1843, Mary emancipated all seven of the people she held in slavery. They included 27-year-old "Kitty" and her four children, Eliza (5), and Mary (4), James Arthur (2), George (2 months) along with two men named Ben and James. Virginia's manumission laws required them to leave the state within a year. Mary Maddox accompanied them to Adams County, Pennsylvania, to help them settle there, even filing a deed of manumission with the local court. Her nephew Samuel Maddox, who was deeply in debt, went to Adams County to claim his future inheritance. He and other men kidnapped Catherine "Kitty" Payne and her then three children (infant George had died) and took them back to Rappahannock County. He was about to sell them but Payne somehow charged him with trespass, assault, and battery. The young family was imprisoned for safekeeping.

Meanwhile incensed citizens in Adams County tried and convicted the kidnappers in their absence, with white and black witnesses testifying against them. Back in Rappahannock County, Virginia, however, the Payne family remained in jail in Rappahannock County for almost a year. Quakers in Adams County and Loudoun County, Virginia, devoted themselves to her case, but Maddox was acquitted on a technicality. Eventually, his accomplice was captured and sentenced in Adams County, and Maddox renounced his claim. The family was liberated again. They resided with Loudoun Quakers over the winter before returning to Adams County.

Lincoln Cemetery

Resources

Mary (Goins) Gandy. *Guide My Feet, Hold My Hand.* Mary (Goins) Gandy, 1987.

Debra McCauslin. *Yellow Hill: Reconstructing the Past: Puzzle of a Lost Community.* Gettysburg, Penn.: For the Cause Productions, 2005.

Daphne Hutchison and Theresa Reynolds. *On the Morning Side of the Blue Ridge: A Glimpse of Rappahannock County's Past.* Warrenton, Va.: The Rappahannock News, 1983.

PEOPLE IN THE PLACES   # Lloyd W. Watts   (1835–1918)

(Adams County Historical Society)

Lloyd W. Watts was the fifth son born to Valentine and Violet Watts in Carroll County, Maryland. By 1848, the free black family moved to Adams County, perhaps so that the children could go to school. By 1850, however, Valentine Watts died and the older sons worked as laborers to support the family. Lloyd, however, learned to read and write. Brother John, one year older, enlisted in the U.S. Colored Troops in August 1863, and Lloyd followed in February 1865. He was then 29 years old, 5' 7" tall, with eyes, hair, and skin all described as black. In training at Camp William Penn he was quickly promoted to sergeant. With his unit, Company B of the 24th USCT, he served first at Camp Casey near Alexandria, Virginia (the installation protected Washington, DC), guarded Confederate prisoners at Cape Lookout, Maryland, and distributed supplies in Roanoke, Virginia.

After their respective units mustered out in 1865, the brothers returned to Gettysburg. Lloyd Watts taught in the "Colored School," and served as a deacon and trustee of St. Paul African Methodist Episcopal Zion Church. In 1866 he helped found a civic association, the Sons of Goodwill. The group organized an Emancipation Day celebration and appointed a committee to establish a cemetery. At the time, white cemeteries, including the newly established National Cemetery for veterans who died in the Civil War, excluded people of color from burials. The Sons of Goodwill founded Lincoln Cemetery in 1867. At various times, Lloyd Watts served as president and secretary on the organization's Board of Managers and helped maintain what was then called the "Good Will burying ground." During his lifetime and beyond Watts earned the good will of the people of Gettysburg.

Resources

Betty Dorsey Myers. *Segregation in Death: Gettysburg's Lincoln Cemetery.* Gettysburg, Penn.: Lincoln Cemetery Project Association, 2001.

Menallen
Meeting House
*(Debra Sandoe
McCauslin, Gettysburg,
PA)*

Menallen Friends Quaker Meeting & Burial Ground

8

HISTORIC SITE	Viewable from the road
THINGS TO DO AND SEE	Operating Quaker Meeting House
DESIGNATIONS	The Burial Ground at Menallen Friends Meeting is a National Park Service Underground Railroad Network to Freedom Site.
LOCATION	Village of Flora Dale, PA, Route 34 1107 Carlisle Rd, Biglerville, PA
CONTACT INFORMATION	Debra Sandoe McCauslin historian, author, and meeting member (717) 528-8553 dmccauslin@gettysburghistories.com
ON THE WEB	www.freedomliesnorth.org/ index.php?option=com_content& task=blogcategory&id=15&Itemid=28

Adams County members of the Society of Friends (Quakers) established the Menallen Meeting in 1780, and began worshipping at the present site in 1838. They established the burial ground in 1853 and erected the current meetinghouse in 1883. Menallen Quakers maintained close ties to Friends in Maryland and northern Virginia through kinship and social networks and the institutional umbrella of the Baltimore annual meeting. They visited and corresponded often and the women quilted together, sometimes exchanging signed blocks. They also shared religious values emphasizing freedom, equality, and responsibility. Some of them actively opposed slavery, allied with free blacks, and assisted freedom seekers escaping to the north or west. Members of the Huntington Meeting had a close relationship with residents of Yellow Hill, a black community nearby. Menallen Friends Cyrus Griest and his wife Mary Ann Cook Griest cooperated with Yellow

Hill residents in Underground Railroad activity. Their graves are marked in the burial ground.

Resources

National Park Service Underground Railroad Network to Freedom Nomination. Prepared by Debra Sandoe McCauslin (2007).

Debra Sandoe McCauslin. "Sites Verified by the National UGRR Network to Freedom," in *Freedom Lies Just North: The Underground Railroad in Adams County. www.freedomliesnorth.org/index.php?option=com_content&task=blogcategory&id=15&Itemid=28*

PEOPLE
· IN THE ·
PLACES
Cyrus Griest (1803–1869) and Mary Ann (Cook) Griest (1803–1884)

Farm of Cyrus and Mary Ann Griest.

Cyrus and Mary Ann Griest moved from York County, Pennsylvania, to Menallen Township in 1839. The Griest's son Amos confirmed that his parents' farm was a station on the Underground Railroad, visited about twice a month in warm seasons. Edward Mathews, a property owner and resident of the nearby black community of Yellow Hill, escorted freedom seekers to the Griest barn before dawn *(see p. 43)*. He tapped upon the couple's bedroom window to let them know they had guests. In the morning, Mary Ann prepared a hearty breakfast for them. Freedom seekers usually rested during the day and set off again under cover of dark until they were farther north.

Cyrus Griest spent considerable energy and money helping a free black woman living in Menallen Township named Catherine "Kitty" Payne *(see p. 35)*. Cyrus Griest championed her cause among Quakers in Pennsylvania, Maryland, and Virginia, raised money for her legal defense in Rappahannock, Virginia, and was the only white person to testify against the kidnappers when they were tried and convicted in their absence in Adams County, Pennsylvania.

Resources

National Park Service Underground Railroad Network to Freedom Nomination. Prepared by Debra McCauslin (2007).

Debra McCauslin. "Sites Verified by the National UGRR Network to Freedom," in *Freedom Lies Just North: The Underground Railroad in Adams County. www.freedomliesnorth.org/index.php?option=com_content&task=blogcategory&id=15&Itemid=28*

Russell Tavern

Russell Tavern

9

HISTORIC SITE	Viewable from the road Last site on the Scenic Valley Tour, available at the Gettysburg Convention & Visitors Bureau
THINGS TO DO AND SEE	View exterior of the stone tavern Tavern is privately owned and not open to the public.
LOCATION	Russell Tavern Rd., south of Goldenville Rd., four miles north of Gettysburg.

Russell Tavern sheltered travelers along Black's Gap Road, which ran through the South Mountain and connected York to the east with the Cumberland Valley to the west. Black's Gap was only the second road in Adams County, constructed in spring of 1747. In the early nineteenth century, one Mrs. O'Neill worked at Russell Tavern. She was likely of African and Irish descent. In 1815, she gave birth to a girl she named Lydia. Because Lydia later used the surname Hamilton, some suspect that Enoch Hamilton, who operated the tavern with his wife Jane McClure Russell, fathered the child.

<table>
<tr><td>PEOPLE · IN THE · PLACES</td><td>**Lydia Hamilton Smith**</td><td>(1815–1884)</td></tr>
</table>

A woman of great heart, Lydia Hamilton Smith was born on Valentine's Day at Russell Tavern. She married a free black man named Jacob Smith and bore two sons but they separated before he died in 1852 and she raised the children alone. Thaddeus Stevens of Lancaster, whom Lydia Smith and her mother knew when he was an attorney and abolitionist in Gettysburg, offered her a position as his housekeeper. She moved there with her young sons in 1847. In 1848 Stevens was elected to the U.S. Congress, where he advocated ending slavery. In recent years, archeologists have discovered evidence that the cistern at his Lancaster house was used as a hiding place for freedom seekers and suspect that Stevens and Smith participated in the Underground Railroad. Smith accompanied Stevens on his trips to Washington, D.C. She was a close friend, included in Stevens's social gatherings and addressed as "Madam" or "Mrs. Smith." A noted artist, probably Charles Bird King, painted her portrait. In 1860 Smith purchased her home from Stevens, on a lot adjacent to his.

The 1860s brought hardship and Civil War. Lydia Smith's oldest son William died in 1860 and Isaac, a noted banjo player and barber, enlisted in the 6th U.S. Colored Troops in 1863. He and his regiment served primarily in Virginia. After the Battle of Gettysburg in July, Lydia Smith acted upon her compassion for the tens of thousands of wounded soldiers. Driving a borrowed horse and wagon through Adams County to a field hospital, she collected donations of food and clothing and distributed them among the wounded men, Union and Confederate alike.

Smith and Stevens's partnership lasted twenty-four years, until "the Great Commoner" (as Stevens was known in Congress) died in 1868. He left $5,000 to Smith in his will. She purchased Stevens's home in Lancaster and a large boarding house across from the prestigious Willard Hotel in Washington, DC. She spent most of her time operating the establishment and earned a reputation as an astute businesswoman. Lydia Smith died on Valentine's Day 1884 in Washington, D.C.

Resources

The Stevens and Smith Historic Site. "Who Was Lydia Hamilton Smith?" *www.stevensandsmith.org/index.php/info/lydia_hamilton_smith/*

Fergus Bordewich, "Thaddeus Stevens and James Buchanan: How their Historic Rivalry Shaped America," originally published as "Was James Buchanan Our Worst President? Digging into a Historic Rivalry" in *Smithsonian Magazine* (Feb. 2004). *www.fergusbordewich.com/PAGESjournalism/FBsteve.shtml*

St. Paul AME
Zion Church

St. Paul AME Zion Church

10

HISTORIC SITE	Viewable from the road
THINGS TO DO AND SEE	Operating church
LOCATION	269 South Washington St. Gettysburg, PA
CONTACT INFORMATION	(717) 334-9851

African Americans in Gettysburg established Wesleyan Methodist Episcopal Church in 1838 in a house on Franklin Street. By 1840 they became St. Paul African Methodist Episcopal Church and Thaddeus Stevens offered them the use of a house he owned for worship. The A.M.E. church was very active in opposing slavery and supporting the underground railroad. In December 1840, member Henry O. Chiller organized a Slave Refugee Society at St. Paul's. Henry Butler,

St. Paul AME Zion Church

James Cameron, Henry O. Chiller, James Jones, and John Jones drafted a constitution and the group dedicated themselves to aiding those seeking freedom from "the tyrannical yoke of oppression." In 1843 the growing congregation built a church at the corner of Breckinridge Street and Long Lane. During the Civil War some of its men served in the U.S. Colored Troops. In 1866 St. Paul members established the Sons of Good Will, primarily to provide a suitable burial place for African American soldiers and civilians. In 1867 they purchased land and founded the Good Will Cemetery, which was later renamed Lincoln Cemetery *(See* Lincoln Cemetery, *p. 34)*. St. Paul's congregation continued to grow. In 1917 they built the brick building on South Washington Street that continues to serve its members.

Resources

James M. Paradis. *African Americans and the Gettysburg Campaign,* Scarecrow Press, 2005.
books.google.com/books?id=9IbaTYAFGKIC&printsec=frontcover&source=gbs_summary_r&cad=0

Grave markers
on Yellow Hill
*(Debra Sandoe
McCauslin, Gettysburg,
PA)*

Yellow Hill Community and Burial Ground

11

HISTORIC SITE	Viewable from the road, although site is difficult to locate
THINGS TO DO AND SEE	Graveyard marked by three stone bases that once held headstones
DESIGNATIONS	National Park Service Underground Railroad Network to Freedom Site
LOCATION	Yellow Hill Road near Biglerville, Pennsylvania
CONTACT INFORMATION	Debra Sandoe McCauslin, historian, author, and meeting member (717) 528-8553 dmccauslin@gettysburghistories.com
ON THE WEB	www.freedomliesnorth.org/ index.php?option=com_content& task=blogcategory&id=15&Itemid=28

In 1860 African Americans in Adams County lived mostly in the adjacent townships of Butler, Menallen and Cumberland, which included Gettysburg. Butler township contained Yellow Hill; its residents looked out across Menallen Township's fertile Quaker Valley. In August during the 1840s, hundreds of black and white folks gathered at the breezy site for spirited revival meetings. Free blacks bought land cheaper on the hill than in the valleys. In the antebellum period, community members aided freedom seekers and testified on behalf of Catherine ("Kitty") Payne *(see p. 35)*, who was kidnapped for a return to slavery in Virginia. During the Civil War, men from Yellow Hill served in the Union Army. In 1869 residents erected Yellow Hill Church on land Edward Mathews donated. One person who remembered it described a pretty building with a bell and a white picket fence. On a clear day they could see Gettysburg beyond the orchards and fields. Although Mathews referred to the building as Union church in 1874, indicating use by people of different faiths, Methodists predominated. In 1871 the congregation shared a minister with St. Paul's A.M.E. (African Methodist Episcopal) Church in Gettysburg. It was later christened Fairmount A.M.E. Church. The building burned in the late nineteenth century— by arson, according to local legend. A nearby cemetery served the community and was the burial place for at least two Civil War veterans. In the Adams County Fireman's Association's

View from Yellow Hill. *(Debra Sandoe McCauslin, Gettysburg, PA)*

parade on July 4,1923 the Yellow Hill Fire Company marched at the rear of the procession of fire companies. After that, members of the Yellow Hill community died or moved away. Today, the Mathews house still stands and three headstones bear witness in the graveyard on the hill. Several graves were moved at various times to Lincoln Cemetery in Gettysburg.

Resources

Debra Sandoe McCauslin. *Yellow Hill: Reconstructing the Past: Puzzle of a Lost Community.* Gettysburg, Penn.: For the Cause Productions, 2005.

PEOPLE
· IN THE ·
PLACES
Edward Mathews (1807–1874) **& Annie Mathews** (1820–1893)

Edward and Annie Mathews moved with their first child from Maryland to Adams County, Pennsylvania. They purchased a 16-acre farm on Yellow Hill were they had twelve more children. For a time, two sons lived and worked with Quaker farmers, Samuel with Cyrus Griest and William with Hiram Griest *(see p. 38)*. Samuel, William, a third brother, Nelson, joined the Union Army in late summer 1864. They trained at Camp William Penn and became part of the 127th Regiment Infantry, USCT. The last unit to leave, they traveled to City Point, Virginia, and joined the Army of the James. The 127th participated in the Battle of Deep Bottom, the end of the siege at Petersburg, and Robert E. Lee's surrender at Appomattox. Two sons were wounded: Samuel was shot in the head and William in the knee. After the war, Nelson became active in Asbury M.E. Church and the Sons of Good Will, who established Lincoln Cemetery. Edward and William Mathews were buried in the cemetery at Yellow Hill, then reinterred at Lincoln Cemetery in Gettysburg, where Annie and Nelson are also buried. William's daughter Jessie Ellen Mathews, orphaned in 1891 at age six, married *Pittsburgh Courier* publisher Robert L. Vann and, after his death, published the prominent African American newspaper herself and promoted international civil rights *(see p. 21)*.

Resources

Debra Sandoe McCauslin, *Yellow Hill: Reconstructing the Past: Puzzle of a Lost Community*. Gettysburg, Penn.: For the Cause Productions, 2005.

Harry Bradshaw Matthews. "Revisiting the Battle of Gettysburg: The Presence of African Americans Before and After the Conflict." Manuscript, 1993; revised 2001.

Carroll County
MARYLAND

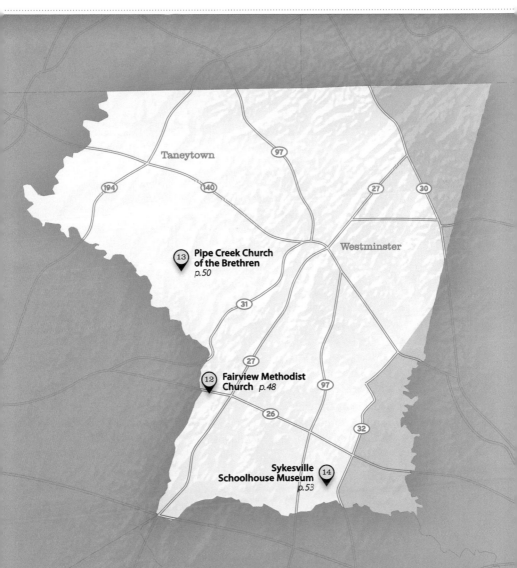

Taneytown

Westminster

13 Pipe Creek Church
of the Brethren
p.50

12 Fairview Methodist
Church *p.48*

14 Sykesville
Schoolhouse Museum
p.53

0   2   4 Miles

Fairview Methodist
Church
*(Catoctin Center for
Regional Studies)*

12

Fairview Methodist Church

African American members of Bethel Methodist Church in New Windsor established their own congregation and built Fairview Methodist Church on Liberty Road around 1851. It is thought to be the oldest African American Church in

HISTORIC SITE	Viewable from the road
THINGS TO DO AND SEE	Operating church
LOCATION	Liberty Rd. & Roop Rd. New Windsor, MD
CONTACT INFORMATION	(410) 875-6555
ON THE WEB	*community.carr.org/ fullrecord.asp?record=471*

Carroll County. Some members lived nearby in the small black community of Newport, established by members of the Cooks, Hills, Toops, and Frances families. Noted stone carver Sebastian "Boss" Hammond and his wife, Marcella, lived in the area and are buried in the church cemetery. To mark their graves, someone re-inscribed two of Hammonds small, older markers. With them are the graves of several men who served the Union Army in the U.S. Colored Troops; their federal markers are inscribed with USCT or USCI (for United States Colored Infantry).

PEOPLE IN THE PLACES | Sebastian "Boss" Hammond (c. 1795–1893)

Boss Hammond carved out a remarkable life as well as artistically excellent tombstones that memorialized the lives of others. He was born in slavery, owned by a member of the prominent Hammond family, probably on a large farm in Frederick County, Maryland. Arianna Hammond owned him in 1824, when she filed a deed of manumission promising him his freedom in twenty years. When Arianna's husband John Walker died, however, Boss Hammond was sold at his estate sale in 1839 and purchased by Colonel Hammond. Boss Hammond likely performed farm work. His first known carved headstone is John Walker's.

Sebastian Hammond carved this stone in a Frederick County cemetery.

Hammond's work is distinguished by deep, even, beautiful script and decorative designs. His obituary stated that he was illiterate, though he never made a spelling mistake on any of the stones that survive. He may have learned from another stone carver in the area who incised his markers with "J.N." Hammond quarried the greenstone himself, likely used a sawmill to slice the slabs, then cut curved corners at the top, sometimes with a semi-circle rising in the center. During his career, Hammond carved more than one hundred headstones that can be found in graveyards along the Carroll/Frederick County border, with the latest found dated 1857.

The stone carving supplemented his farm work and helped Hammond improve his life. Allowed to keep at least some of his earnings, on July 29, 1839 he purchased his freedom and two horses from Colonel Hammond. The following year he bought nine acres of land straddling Buffalo Road on the border of Frederick and Carroll counties; by 1850 he owned seventy acres. Other black families purchased property nearby and established the community of Newport. Although his family appeared to be living with him at the 1840 census, it wasn't until 1856 that Hammond purchased the freedom of his wife Marcella and their several children over thirteen. In 1857 he mortgaged his property—it appears that he may have done so to purchase his younger children before their owner moved to Missouri. He never recovered financially, but he kept his family together. White and black residents of both counties considered him an honorable man and turned out in large numbers at his funeral in 1893.

Resources

Mary Ann Ashcraft. "Sacred to the Memory': The Stonecarving of Sebastian Hammond" in *Catoctin History* 2, no. 1 (Spring 2003): 20-27.

Jay A. Graybeal. "Boss Hammond, African-American Stonecutter," *Carroll County Times* (February 16, 1997). *hscc.carr.org/research/yesteryears/cct1997/970216.htm*

Pipe Creek Church of the Brethren.

Pipe Creek Church of the Brethren

13

The Church of the Brethren began in Germany in 1708, with the first church in North America established in Germantown, Pennsylvania, in 1728. It promoted non-violence and spiritual regeneration. Daniel Saylor, baptized in the

HISTORIC SITE	Viewable from the road
THINGS TO DO AND SEE	Operating church
LOCATION	26 Pipe Creek Rd. Union Bridge, MD
CONTACT INFORMATION	(410) 775-7343 pipecreek1758@wmconnect.com
ON THE WEB	community.carr.org/ fullrecord.asp?record=778

Germantown church in 1750, moved to Maryland and, with Philip Englar, organized Pipe Creek Church of the Brethren in 1758. It is thought to be one of the oldest and a "mother church" of its denomination. Because baptismal candidates were immersed three times in a nearby creek, outsiders called members Dunkers. Congregations usually named their churches after the stream in which they performed baptisms. Throughout its history, the church strongly opposed slavery and barred members from holding slaves, particularly in Maryland, where some African Americans joined the church. In 1835 delegates at the annual meeting debated and affirmed that membership should be the same for people regardless of color.

John T. Lewis, who joined Pipe Creek Church in 1853, later moved to New York where he earned the affection and esteem of Mark Twain and inspired his writing. Lewis kept in touch with the Brethren through church publications. In 1870 the Christian Family Companion published his letter stating, "I am trying by the help of God to live in accordance with the gospel and the order of the Brethren. I hope the brothers and sisters will pray for me that I may be faithful to the end." He was.

Resources

Ronald J. Gordon. *The Little Dunker Church: Who Are the Dunkers?* Church of the Brethren Network, 2002.

PEOPLE · IN THE · PLACES

John T. Lewis   (1835–1906)

Samuel Clemens *(Mark Twain)* and John T. Lewis
(Library of Congress)

John T. Lewis, a free man of color, lived the first twenty-five years of his life in Carroll County, Maryland. At age 18 he joined the Church of the Brethren and was baptized at Meadow Creek Church in Westminster. He became a member of the congregation at the Pipe Creek Church and later transferred to the Beaver Dam Church in Frederick County. In 1860 he moved north to Adams County, Pennsylvania, and the Marsh Creek congregation, then migrated further up the Old Carolina Road (Route 15) and settled in Elmira, New York. There he married Mary Stover, who was born in slavery near the same road south of Leesburg, Virginia. Her uncle was John W. Jones *(see* Loudoun Museum, *p. 124).* There were no Brethren congregations in that part of New York, but he held to his religion.

John Lewis came to know Mark Twain after Twain's marriage to Olivia Langdon and their lengthy stays at her sister's home at Quarry Farm near Elmira. Lewis worked at Quarry Farm in addition to cultivating his own farm and selling its produce. Lewis earned Twain's respect and gratitude when he leaped from his farm wagon to seize the bridle of a horse galloping toward him. He managed to stop the horse before its carriage, containing Twain's sister-in-law, niece, and a nurse, careened over a precipice on an upcoming curve. The extended Langdon family expressed their appreciation by giving Lewis a large sum of money and a watch. Twain reported, "The instant he found himself possessed of money, he forgot himself in a plan to make his old

father comfortable, who is wretchedly poor and lives down in Maryland." In 1903, *Ladies Home Journal* printed a photograph of Twain and Lewis together. The reporter wrote that Twain identified Lewis as "a friend of mine" and added, "I have not known an honester man nor a more respectworthy one." Scholars surmise that Twain based the *Huckleberry Finn* character, Jim, largely on Lewis.

In 1903, John Lewis restored the pulpit Bible to the "Little Dunker Church" at Antietam in

John T. Lewis *(Library of Congress)*

Maryland. A member of a Union regiment in Elmira had removed it from the church after the battle, and eventually gave it to the late sergeant's sister who was widowed and in need. She, however, wanted it returned to the church and told members of the regiment during its 1903 reunion in Elmira. Not knowing how to contact the church or even if it still existed, they sought out the only Brethren member they knew in Elmira—John T. Lewis. Because he read the denomination's periodicals, he was able to tell them that the current pastor was Elder John E. Otto of Sharpsburg. They charged Lewis with returning the Bible, which he did personally. The National Park Service owns it now and displays it in the Antietam visitor center.

Resources

For Mark Twain's description of John T. Lewis and the rescue, see Mark Twain to W.D. Howells and Wife, August 25, 1877. *The Letters of Mark Twain*, Vol. 3. *www.fullbooks.com/The-Letters-Of-Mark-Twain-Vol-31.html*

Ronald J. Gordon. "The Pulpit Bible," in *The Little Dunker Church: Who Are the Dunkers?* Church of the Brethren Network, 2002. *www.cob-net.org/antietam/dunkers.htm*

Antietam National Battlefield. "The Mumma Bible." *www.nps.gov/anti/historyculture/mummabible.htm*

Sykesville
Schoolhouse
Museum

Sykesville Schoolhouse Museum

14

HISTORIC SITE	Open to the public; hours vary (see contact info)
THINGS TO DO AND SEE	Schoolhouse; educational programs available
LOCATION	518 Schoolhouse Rd. Sykesville, MD
CONTACT INFORMATION	Please call Pat Greenwald at 410-795-8959 or email at *SchoolHouse@sykesville.net*
ON THE WEB	*www.sykesville.net/school.html*

In 1903 "two 'colored' men" addressed the Carroll County Board of Education and asked them to build a school for black children. Shortly thereafter, the school board purchased land and paid a builder $530.50 to construct the one-room school. They furnished the school with desks from the "white" school in Detour. Students within a three-mile radius, including some from across the Patapsco River in Howard County, walked to the Sykesville School beginning January 4, 1904. In 1916, when the structure got a new metal roof, thirty-two students attended there. The building served the community until 1938 when area schools were consolidated. Then it was sold and converted to a four-room private residence until 1981, when it was vacated. Threatened several times with demolition since, local citizens fought to preserve it. With their help, the

Sykesville Schoolhouse Museum

Town of Sykesville began a restoration project that was completed in 2006. Educational programs help students today learn about life and learning in the past. Warren Dorsey, a former microbiologist, teacher, and principal who entered the school as a student in 1926, met there in November 2006 with a class from Baltimore. He told them that ten cents an hour was the most he earned from farm work. "Education was the light to the future," he said, "and you had to make the best of every opportunity to learn."

Resources

Historic Town of Sykesville, Maryland. "The Historic Sykesville Colored Schoolhouse." *www.sykesville.net/school.html*

Frederick County
MARYLAND

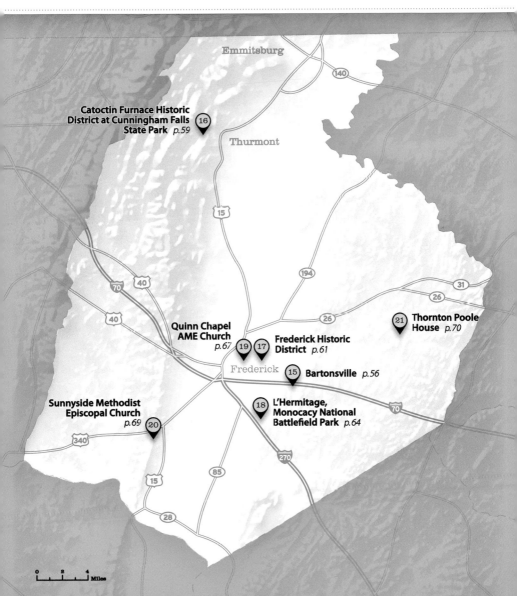

Emmitsburg

Thurmont

Catoctin Furnace Historic
District at Cunningham Falls
State Park *p.59* 16

Frederick

Quinn Chapel
AME Church
p.67

19 17 Frederick Historic
District *p.61*

21 Thornton Poole
House *p.70*

15 Bartonsville *p.56*

Sunnyside Methodist
Episcopal Church
p.69 20

18 L'Hermitage,
Monocacy National
Battlefield Park *p.64*

0 2 4 Miles

Jackson United
Methodist Church

15 | Bartonsville

Not long before the Civil War, Greensberry Barton, a man emancipated from slavery, bought a parcel of land in the New Market district. Others acquired land nearby and the Bartonsville community was born. Other early settlers included William Orange Brooks, also formerly enslaved, and John Thomas, who purchased sev-

HISTORIC SITE	Viewable from the road
THINGS TO DO AND SEE	The churches are still in operation
LOCATION	Three miles southeast of Frederick on Bartonsville Rd.
	St. James A.M.E. Church 6002 Bartonsville Rd. Frederick, MD
	Jackson United Methodist 6027 Bartonsville Rd. Frederick, MD
CONTACT INFORMATION	St. James A.M.E. Church (301) 695-6167
	Jackson United Methodist Chapel (301) 694-7315

eral acres nearby. Little is known about Thomas, but he and his wife Ellen Cromwell have 300-400 descendants today who hold annual reunions. Members of the community formed a Methodist congregation in 1878 and built Jackson Chapel in 1883. They established St. James African Methodist Episcopal Church in 1883. Three small grocery stores and, in 1934, a full-service gas station (the first outside of the city of Frederick) served local residents. The Working Men's Society, later reorganized as a chapter of the fraternal organization, Galilean Fishermen, served one another and the community.

From the 1910s through the 1930s and beyond, Bartonsville was famous for its music. Around 1915, men there formed the Bartonsville Cornet Band and were often invited to perform around the county. The Galilean Fishermen built a meeting hall at the corner of Bartonsville and Tobery Road and held weekly dances there that attracted people countywide. Popular bands included the Nighthawks and the Iantha Orchestra.

One notable resident of Bartonsville, William Lester Bowie, joined the cornet band as a child; he later became a music teacher in St. Louis, Missouri. There, he and his wife, Earxie Willingham, raised three sons. The family periodically visited Bartonsville, and Lester Sr. was a lifelong member of St. James AME Church. The sons earned world recognition for their music: trumpeter Lester Bowie Jr., founder of the Art Ensemble of Chicago; saxophonist and arranger Byron Bowie; and trombonist Joe Bowie of the band Defunkt. Joe Bowie also conducts workshops around the world to teach funk music and promote values of love, compassion, and education that foster world peace.

Lester Bowie Sr. returned to Bartonsville to live in 1983 and remained there until his death in 2000; Byron and Joe Bowie maintain a residence there today.

Resources

Tourism Council of Frederick County. "African American Heritage Sites" Brochure. 2001. Available online at *www.frederickhsc.org/pdf/hsc_aahsbro.pdf*

Joe Bowie. *Joe Bowie, Defunkt, and Kosen Rufu. joebowie.org*

Marie Ann Erickson, "Crossroads: Dance Hall Days," *Frederick Magazine* (Oct. 1993).

PEOPLE
· IN THE ·
PLACES   **Lester Bowie**   **(1941-1999)**

William Lester Bowie Jr. cherished his family's Bartonsville roots even as he pushed jazz into new territory for which he was recognized in the *Down Beat Jazz* Hall of Fame (2000). He began playing the horn at the age of five with the help of his father, and, when he was a teenager, formed a band called the Continentals that played popular music. He became serious about music while in the Air Force stationed in Texas, and devoted himself to it full-time after his discharge. He married soul singer Fontella Bass and produced her hit song, "Rescue Me." They moved to Chicago where there was a larger and richer music scene. There he moved

Bartonsville

beyond blues and Rhythm & Blues and into jazz, with the help of Muhal Richard Abrams's composer's workshop and Experimental Band. Later, Abrams, Bowie, Malachi Favors, and Joseph Jarman formed the Art Ensemble of Chicago. The group introduced unusual whistles and noisemakers into their sound, Favors and Jarman painted their faces and wore African-inspired clothing, while Bowie adopted the white lab coat that would become his trademark. With much enthusiasm but little work, even in Chicago, in 1969 the band moved to France, where there was much interest in new jazz, and became a sensation. When they returned to the U.S. in 1971, Atlantic Records signed them to produce their first album.

Lester Bowie, as he preferred to be called, continued to experiment. He released solo albums and formed other bands, the foremost of which was Brass

(Photo by Barbara Mürdter, CC-BY-SA: Wikipedia))

Fantasy. He was known as "one of the finest trumpeters of his generation" as well as one of the most innovative, yet he believed that music should be accessible to all and retain a sense of humor. Sometimes he was criticized for the unusual squawks and squeals he produced on his horn and compositions such as "Miles Davis Meets Donald Duck." But Bowie explained to Paul A. Harris of the *St. Louis Post-Dispatch*, "Sometime in the '60s, the humor got away from jazz. It got intellectual, and nobody could smile. And it wasn't just the humor that got away—the life was taken out. The whole life was taken out of the music. I think, because of that, we've lost a lot in the music. The music doesn't reach a lot of people for that reason. They think jazz is this very intellectual stuff, and you've got to know all about it to appreciate it."

Perhaps his Bartonsville roots influenced his jazz philosophy. In a nod to his family's hometown, he included the 1915 photograph of the Bartonsville Cornet Band, which included three of his uncles, on the cover of his 1983 album, *All the Magic!*

Resources

Bowie-Thomas Family Tree. *bowiethomasfamilytree.com/12.htm*

"Lester Bowie." *Contemporary Musicians*, Volume 29. Gale Group, 2000.

Standing remains
of Catoctin Furnace
Stack #2
(Kenneth L. Garrett)

Catoctin Furnace Historic District at Cunningham Falls State Park

16

HISTORIC SITE	Open to the public
THINGS TO DO AND SEE	Tours, self-guided
DESIGNATIONS	National Register of Historic Places
	National Underground Railroad Network to Freedom site
LOCATION	14039 Catoctin Hollow Rd. Thurmont, MD
	About 15 miles north of Frederick
CONTACT INFORMATION	(301) 271-7574
ON THE WEB	www.dnr.state.md.us/publiclands/ cunninghamhistory.html
	www.nps.gov/archive/cato/culthist/ furnace.htm

Catoctin Furnace Historic District interprets the American Industrial Revolution. From 1776 to 1903 various enterprises mined the rich ore banks near Catoctin Mountain, smelted it in furnaces, and cast raw pig iron and iron implements of every description. The Johnson furnace was in blast by 1776 and records indicate that the operation produced ammunition for the Continental Army during the Revolutionary War.

The iron industry demanded a huge pool of skilled and unskilled workers to mine the ore, quarry limestone, cut wood for fuel and make charcoal, smelt the ore into pig iron, manufacture cast iron implements, and transport raw and finished products. Enslaved, free black, and white workers often worked side-by-side. Some ironworkers were Africans. In the eighteenth century, Africa had an ancient and sophisticated iron industry that was sorely damaged by colonialism and the slave trade.

Although the process was different in North America, Africans (enslaved and free) were brought across the Atlantic for their particular knowledge and skills. There is some historical and archaeological evidence of "unmixed" Africans at iron furnaces in Pennsylvania and Maryland, including Catoctin. Many of them came to Maryland by way of the Caribbean, from sale or with slaveholders fleeing the Haitian Revolution.

The composition of the work force at Catoctin Furnace varied over time, with historians concluding it was about half enslaved in its early history. By 1830, however, as the slave population declined and foreign immigration increased in western Maryland, a majority of the workers, black and white, were free. At Catoctin that year, 60 out of 80 were free; at Antietam, 222 of 250. Therefore, Maryland's ironworks differed from those in the rest of the South, which utilized mostly enslaved labor.

Catoctin and Antietam Furnaces had the same owner in the 1820s and 1830s, John Brien. He invited Rev. Thomas W. Henry *(see profile on p. 86)* to preach to black workers at both Catoctin and Antietam.

There are documented incidents at Catoctin and Antietam Ironworks of freedom sought and freedom taken away. At Catoctin, an enslaved man named Phil eloped in 1780. Judging from the $100 reward offered (double if captured outside of Maryland), he was a highly skilled worker. A joiner at Antietam Ironworks, who also played the violin and spoke German, escaped from slavery at the Antietam Ironworks in 1807. In 1822 William Humbere, a free laborer at Catoctin Furnace, advertised in the newspaper for information about his son who had recently been kidnapped by a white man. Kidnappings and elopements were both common occurrences in this borderland between slavery and freedom. Freedom seekers often found refuge at furnaces and forges.

Resources

National Park Service, Catoctin Mountain Park. "African American Influence in the Iron Industry." *http://www.nps.gov/cato/historyculture/africanamericans.htm*

_____. National Underground Railroad Network to Freedom Nomination, 2003.

Jean Libby. "African Ironmaking Culture Among African American Ironworkers in Western Maryland, 1760-1850." (Master's thesis, San Francisco State University, 1991).

West All Saints
Street, c. 1900
(I. Blanche Bourne-
Tyree)

Frederick
Historic District

17

HISTORIC SITE	Open to the public
THINGS TO DO AND SEE	Frederick's 50-block historic district offers 18th and 19th century architecture, historic sites, shops, restaurants, and cultural events.
DESIGNATIONS	National Register of Historic Places
LOCATION	Frederick, MD Two blocks E and 3 blocks W of Market St., from South St. to 7th St.
CONTACT INFORMATION	(800) 999-3613 (301) 228-2888 *tourism@fredco-md.net*
ON THE WEB	*www.fredericktourism.org*

The District is significant for its role as the seat of Frederick County and as a regional market and industrial center in Maryland's Piedmont area from the 18th century to the mid 20th century.

During the Civil War, both Union and Confederate armies passed through this city on their way to Antietam in 1862; and parts of the Union army went north through here on the way to Gettysburg in 1863. Confederate Gen. Jubal Early extorted a $200,000 ransom from the city before fighting near the Monocacy River just south. Large numbers of wounded soldiers were brought to the city following the large battles fought nearby.

All Saints Street in the City of Frederick was once the vibrant center of community life for African Americans in Frederick County. Two churches anchored the block, both given over to black members of their congregations during the Civil War: First Missionary Baptist Church and Asbury

United Methodist Church. The current Asbury church dates to 1921, and the Baptist congregation moved to another building. Quinn Chapel African Methodist Episcopal Church, although blocks away, was also important to the community.

During the decades after the Civil War, as the population grew and segregation policies hardened, All Saints Street developed into a black business district. By the early twentieth century, African Americans from the city and surrounding county went there for banking, grocery stores, barbershops and beauty parlors, shoe repair, restaurants, and medical care. They could borrow books from the Free Colored Men's Library or enjoy social events and entertainment such as movies at Pythian Castle or (after 1928) the Mountain City Elks Lodge. On Friday nights and Saturdays the street was especially lively, as people converged downtown for shopping, business, cultural events, and socializing.

The Shab Row neighborhood on North East Street was a center of black residential life. Children played in a small vacant lot with trees and

Shab Row neighborhood on N. East Street

wildflowers, or along East Street, ever mindful of the trolley that periodically rumbled down the center of the road. Although residents were sometimes teased and called "Cross Track People," the neighbors were close; they watched out for one another and minded the children. After integration, residents moved to other neighborhoods. Some houses were torn down; those remaining have been restored and are now part of an upscale shopping district. Former Shab Row residents periodically hold reunions.

Some notable African American residents of Frederick include Alice Palmer Freeman, housekeeper for Eleanor Roosevelt; William H. Grinage, artist; Esther Grinage, educator and kindergarten founder; Lord D. Nickens, decorated World War II veteran and NAACP president; and William O. Lee, educator/administrator, local historian and city alderman.

Resources

Tourism Council of Frederick County. "African American Heritage Sites" Brochure. 2001. Available online at *www.frederickhsc.org/pdf/hsc_aahsbro.pdf*

MARYLAND

FREDERICK COUNTY

Ulysses Grant Bourne (1873-1956)

Ulysses Grant Bourne
(I. Blanche Bourne-Tyree)

Dr. Ulysses G. Bourne uplifted his community. Originally from Calvert County, Maryland, Bourne obtained a medical degree from Leonard Medical College in North Carolina in 1902 and established his practice on All Saints Street in Frederick, Maryland, in 1903. While most patients visited him there, he also used a horse and buggy to make house calls. He delivered 2,600 babies before he retired in 1953. He accepted meat and produce from patients without the money to pay his fees. Initially, black patients were not admitted to the hospital in Frederick, so in 1919, he and another African American physician, Charles Brooks, opened a hospital at 173 All Saints Street. It operated until 1928 when the Frederick City Hospital opened a new wing for black patients, and he became the first black doctor permitted to practice there. A leader in his profession statewide, Dr. Bourne founded the Maryland Negro Medical Society in 1931.

Bourne also led the community in civic affairs. In 1934 he co-founded the Frederick County Branch of the NAACP and served as its president for twenty years. At a time when African Americans were barred from attending the Opera House, he was instrumental in building the stately hall that later became known as

The Bourne Family (left to right): Grace, Mary Frances, Isabella Blanche, Dr. Ulysses G., and Ulysses Jr. *(I. Blanche Bourne-Tyree)*

Pythian Castle. He worked behind-the-scenes for local political candidates and ran himself on the Republican ticket for the Maryland House of Delegates.

Ulysses Bourne and his first wife Grace had two children, Ulysses Jr., and Grace Gladys. After his wife's death, he married Mary Frances Beane of Virginia, with whom he had a third child, Isabella Blanche. The son and youngest daughter followed in their father's footsteps and became doctors. Isabella Blanche Bourne was the first Frederick County woman to earn a medical degree. Dr. I. Blanche Bourne-Tyree, as she is now known, also established a scholarship in her father's name for students wishing to pursue a career in health. Thanks to the research project and initiative of a 10-year-old Frederick County student in 2006, a bust of Dr. Bourne now graces the lobby of Frederick Memorial Hospital.

Resources

Tourism Council of Frederick County. "African American Heritage Sites" Brochure. 2001. Available online at *www.frederickhsc.org/pdf/hsc_aahsbro.pdf*

Secondary house on what was once L'Hermitage. Evidence of slave quarters was found nearby.
(Ken Lund, Wikipedia/CC)

L'Hermitage, Monocacy National Battlefield Park

18

From the late 1790s until 1854, the Best Farm on the Monocacy Battlefield was part of L'Hermitage plantation. The large enslaved community there began with people from Saint Domingue (now Haiti). The wealthy Vincendière family emigrated there in 1793 to escape the violent liberation movement that became known as the Haitian Revolution. They brought with them the maximum of twelve enslaved servants that

HISTORIC SITE	Open to the public
THINGS TO DO AND SEE	Attractions include walks, special programs, an auto tour, and featured events throughout the summer season. Programs are offered by rangers and at special events in coordination with Living History volunteers. Exhibits include an electric map orientation program, interactive computer program, artifacts, and interpretive displays of the battle.
DESIGNATIONS	National Register of Historic Places National Underground Railroad Network to Freedom Site.
LOCATION	4801 Urbana Pike, Frederick, MD South on MD Route 355. The visitor center is .1 mi south of the river
CONTACT INFORMATION	(301) 662-3515
ON THE WEB	www.nps.gov/mono

Maryland law allowed them. They were: Saint-Louis, age about 14; Pierre Louis, age 35; Lambert, age 5; Fillele, age 8; Marianne, age 40, Cecile, daughter of Marianne, age 18, Souris, age 15; Janvier, age 24; Francois Arajou, age 20, Jean Sans-nom, age 16; Veronique, age 16; and Maurice, age 15. In 1797, Pierre Louis successfully petitioned for his freedom in 1797 on the basis that he had been brought to Maryland illegally. By 1800, 90 enslaved people lived at L'Hermitage. Archaeologists have unearthed evidence of their dwellings across the road from the front of manor house, where enslaved people were bought and sold and treated harshly, by some accounts. In 1798 Polish diplomat Julian Niemcewicz passed by in a coach and wrote in his journal:

> *June 15. ... Four miles from the town [of Frederick] we forded the river [Monocacy]. On its banks one can see a row of wooden houses and one stone house with the upper storeys painted white [the secondary house]. ... One can seen on the home farm instruments of torture, stocks, wooden horses, whips, etc. Two or three negroes crippled with torture have brought legal action* ...

In the late 1790s, several enslaved people tried prosecuting their owners for cruelly beating them, while others escaped. Harry, Jerry, Abraham, Stephon, Soll, and George brought suit against Boisneuf Vicendiere, and Jenny brought suit against her mistress, Victoire Vincendière, but were unsuccessful. Shadrack's case against Boisneuf was successful, however. At least two people escaped from slavery at L'Hermitage, according to ads placed in the newspaper in 1795.

Sales of enslaved people from L'Hermitage separated families, for some an even greater hardship than physical violence: John, Ramond, and Black Emmos were sold to a slave dealer in Baltimore in 1819; Indianna was sold in 1822; Daniel in 1824; and seventeen people were sold to a Louisiana slavetrader in 1825.

Some individuals later obtained their freedom from the Vincendières. In 1830 Matilda Murdock and her two-month-old son Robert were emancipated, and Matilda's son John was freed in 1858 under the terms of a will. In 1832 Justice Brown received his freedom with the explanation that he was "uncommonly good." In 1844 Caroline and her daughter Cornelia were freed, although Cornelia was only 5 years old at the time and would not obtain full freedom until age 15. In 1853 Caroline's son Augustus joined his mother in freedom. In 1863, Cornelius obtained his freedom through a will.

Slavery continued at the property under John O'Brien, a large landowner involved in the iron industry in western Maryland, and by David

Monocacy National Battlefield Park, L'Hermitage

Best, his tenant, beginning in 1843. They, too, bought and sold people. In 1860, O'Brien, like the Vincendieres in 1800, was among the largest slaveholders in the Frederick Town District, but he held only six. Agricultural practices in the region had changed and many slaveholders had migrated west. By 1860, a majority of African Americans in Frederick County were free. In 1864, Maryland ended slavery.

Resources

Monocacy National Battlefield. "Slavery at L'Hermitage."
www.nps.gov/mono/historyculture/ei_lhermitage.htm

National Park Service. National Underground Railroad Network to Freedom Site Nomination, 2007.

Quinn Chapel A.M.E. Church

Quinn Chapel African Methodist Episcopal Church

19

HISTORIC SITE	Viewable from the road
THINGS TO DO AND SEE	Operating church
LOCATION	106 E 3rd St., Frederick, MD
CONTACT INFORMATION	(301) 663-1550
ON THE WEB	www.quinnchapelamechurch.org

The congregation of Quinn Chapel AME Church is remarkable because they can trace their origins to the beginning of the denomination. Members of the Free African Society in Philadelphia established Bethel African Methodist Episcopal Church there in 1794 in response to their poor treatment at St. George's Methodist Episcopal Church. An AME congregation formed in Frederick not long after and adopted the same name, Bethel. In 1817, leaders of the growing AME denomination appointed William Paul Quinn among its first itinerant ministers. His charge included Frederick, Maryland, and Carlisle, Chambersburg, and Shippensburg, Pennsylvania. Bethel AME Church in Frederick at that time worshipped in a log cabin shop next to the present day church. They purchased the lot and building that would become the church at 101 East Street in 1819. Although Quinn was not their pastor long, his influence expanded and he became an assistant Bishop in 1822. In 1834 he published a pamphlet denouncing the institution of slavery.

Another notable clergyman, Thomas W. Henry *(see profile, p. 86)*, was ordained Elder in 1838 and assumed his first charge at Bethel. He reported only fifteen members at that time and a church in bad condition; it was a low point for the denomination generally. Thomas remained on the Washington and Frederick Circuit until 1845. Although Henry did not mention it in his autobiography, at some point—perhaps after William Paul Quinn became bishop in 1844—the Bethel congregation honored him by changing its name to Quinn Chapel.

Over the years, the congregation in Frederick grew. In 1855 they built a large structure over the basement of the church that originally served as a machine shop. During the Civil War, the basement sheltered wounded soldiers from the Battle of Monocacy. After the war's end, people of color gathered there to attend school. Benjamin Tucker Tanner was another notable early minister at Quinn Chapel, whose son Henry Ossawa Tanner became a world famous artist. Benjamin Tanner was principal of an AME conference school in Frederick in 1867-68, which was likely held in the church basement as well. The Gothic Revival architecture, including a massive asymmetrical corner bell tower, added in 1923, symbolizes the solid, substantial and beautiful contributions of its congregation to the community it serves.

Resources

Quinn Chapel African Methodist Episcopal Church. *200th Anniversary Souvenir Yearbook* (2000).

Sunnyside
Methodist
Episcopal Church

Sunnyside Methodist Episcopal Church

20

HISTORIC SITE	Viewable from the road
THINGS TO DO AND SEE	Operating church
LOCATION	4521 Mountville Rd., Frederick, MD
CONTACT INFORMATION	(301) 874-1271

In 1887, African American citizens on a south-facing mountain ridge near Buckeystown decided to join together to improve their community, sometimes called Mountville. Jacob and Ellen McKinney, George and Ellen Jones, John and Ellen Weedon, George and Caroline Nicholas, and Joseph Shorter purchased two acres of land and subdivided it into two lots. Upon the first they established a burial ground, on the second they built a schoolhouse and, in 1889, Sunnyside Chapel. They chose the name from a phrase by one of the founders, who called the church "a light on the sunny side of the mountain." The community came to be called Sunnyside as well. The congregation prospered enough that by 1916 they paid off the mortgage. The school continued as a public school until segregation ended in Frederick County in the mid-1960s. The church continues to serve its members and visitors and holds Sunday School classes and other functions in the historic school.

Resources

Sunnyside United Methodist Church brochure (2007).

William Still of Philadelphia assisted some of the Aldridges in their quest for freedom.

21 | Thornton Poole House

HISTORIC SITE	Private residence
THINGS TO DO AND SEE	Not open to the public
DESIGNATIONS	National Underground Railroad Network to Freedom site
LOCATION	Glissans Mill Road near Linganore

A moving story of freedom and family earned the Thornton Poole house a site designation on the National Underground Railroad Network to Freedom. In 1857, twenty-three year old Israel Todd and seventeen-year-old Bazil Aldridge, after a long and dangerous journey from Frederick County, Maryland, arrived in Philadelphia, placing themselves in the care of William Still, a free black man who chaired Philadelphia's Vigilance Committee and aided freedom seekers. Still kept a journal recording the stories of those he met, hoping that the information would help families reunite someday.

Todd was owned by Dr. Greenberry Sappington; he hoped that somehow he could "save his wife ... and her brother from being sold south." His brother-in-law Bazil Aldridge was owned by Thornton Poole, a storekeeper and farmer, who Aldridge claimed was too fond of drink. Two of Aldridge's brothers had escaped the previous spring. A few months later Poole informed the family that he was going to hire out Aldridge's brother and sister "a short distance from home" and took them away, but then sold them to a southern slavetrader. Later in 1857 or early 1858, Bazil's sister Caroline Aldridge met Still and related more of the family saga. The sale of her siblings prompted her mother's elopement to Canada with three other children. Caroline and another brother remaining in Frederick made their escape as well, apparently with the assistance of Israel Todd, Caroline's husband. Although the couple had been married in a slave ceremony in Maryland, Still reported that in the North they had a legal "ceremony performed, and went on their way rejoicing." They hoped to be reunited with the rest of their family in Canada. Eleven of them, all told, successfully found their way to freedom.

Resources

William Still. *The Underground Rail Road.* Philadelphia, 1842. *www.quinnipiac.edu/other/ABL/etext/ugrr/ ugrrmain.html*

Maryland State Archives. *Beneath the Underground Railroad: The Flight to Freedom and Communities in Antebellum Maryland.* *www.msa.md.gov/msa/mdslavery/html/antebellum/fr.html*

National Park Service. "Thornton Poole House, Frederick, Maryland." Underground Railroad Network to Freedom Nomination, 2006.

Washington County
MARYLAND

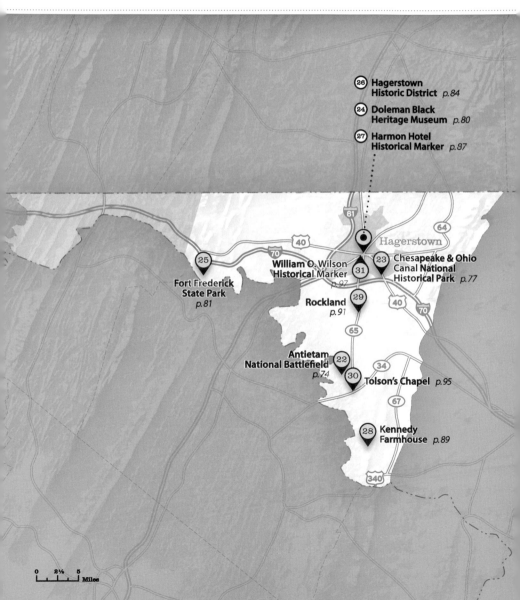

- 26 **Hagerstown Historic District** *p.84*
- 24 **Doleman Black Heritage Museum** *p.80*
- 27 **Harmon Hotel Historical Marker** *p.97*
- 25 **Fort Frederick State Park** *p.81*
- **William O. Wilson Historical Marker** *p.97*
- 23 **Chesapeake & Ohio Canal National Historical Park** *p.77*
- 29 **Rockland** *p.91*
- 22 **Antietam National Battlefield** *p.74*
- 30 **Tolson's Chapel** *p.95*
- 28 **Kennedy Farmhouse** *p.89*

Hagerstown

0   2½   5
Miles

The Preliminary Emancipation Proclamation issued by Abraham Lincoln after the Union victory at Antietam.
(National Archives and Records Administration)

Antietam National Battlefield

22

After twelve hours of savage combat on September 17, 1862, 23,000 soldiers were killed, wounded or missing. The Battle of Antietam ended the Confederate Army of Northern Virginia's first invasion into the North and led to Abraham Lincoln's issuance of the preliminary Emancipation Proclamation.

HISTORIC SITE	Open to the public
THINGS TO DO AND SEE	"Antietam Visit," an award-winning film, recreates the battle as well as President Abraham Lincoln's visit to the Union commander General George B. McClellan. Visitor Center, Guided Tours, Self-Guided Tours, Educational Programs, Kids Activities, Walking Trails, Biking, Fishing, Picnic Area
DESIGNATIONS	National Register of Historic Places
LOCATION	5831 Dunker Church Rd. Sharpsburg, MD
CONTACT INFORMATION	(301) 432-5124 (301) 432-4590
ON THE WEB	www.nps.gov/anti

Freedom at Antietam

As the glowing sun set over the bloody fields of Antietam, the Civil War became a different war. Five days after the battle, armed with pen and paper, Abraham Lincoln issued the Emancipation Proclamation.

The proclamation reflected Lincoln's new way of thinking about the conflict. Until this time, it was seen as a rebellion, a fight to preserve the Union without touching slavery. Now Lincoln was threatening to crush the Confederacy by destroying slavery, the basis of its economy and society. Now the North was waging a moral crusade to free the slaves.

While the Emancipation Proclamation reflected Lincoln's high-minded morality, the President was under great pressure to act. Congress was urging emancipation. Escaped slaves were fleeing to the Union army as it advanced in the South, complicating military operations. And the enlistment of black Americans as soldiers could give the Union's ailing war machine a much-needed boost.

Forever Free, but When?

Lincoln's preliminary proclamation, issued on September 22, 1862, declared that on New Year's Day, 1863, slaves in areas then "in rebellion against the United States shall be then, thenceforward, and forever free." For areas not deemed to be in rebellion, slavery would be unchanged.

The final proclamation, issued January 1, 1863, identified those areas "in rebellion." They included virtually all of the Confederacy, except areas controlled by the Union army. The document notably excluded the so-called border states of Maryland, Kentucky, and Missouri, where slavery existed side-by-side with Unionist sentiment. In areas where the U.S. government had authority, such as Maryland and much of Tennessee, slavery went untouched. In areas where slaves were declared free—most of the South—the federal government had no effective authority.

By the summer of 1862, Congress was pushing hard for emancipation. Now Lincoln's proclamation, a vital step on the gradual path to freedom for American slaves, articulated emancipation as the government's new policy.

Although his famous proclamation did not immediately free a single slave, black Americans saw Lincoln as a savior. Official legal freedom for the slaves came in December 1865 with the ratification of the 13th Amendment to the Constitution abolishing slavery.

Military Necessity

After the proclamation, Union troops became an army of liberation as they advanced in the South. During the war, one out of every seven Confederate slaves (about 500,000) escaped to the Union army. The South was thus deprived of desperately needed labor to till fields, build forts and fix railroads.

Antietam National Battlefield

The Emancipation Proclamation also paved the way for the enlistment of black Americans as soldiers. During the summer of 1862, as Lincoln pondered emancipation, the North was facing a shortage of soldiers. Lincoln even offered volunteers enlistments for only nine months instead of the usual three years, hoping that a shorter enlistment would attract more recruits. One solution: Enlist black Americans, whether free men from the North or freed slaves from the South.

Despite deep and widespread prejudice, the Union began recruiting black Americans in earnest in early 1863. Believed to be physically and spiritually unfit as fighting men, they were initially confined to non-combat jobs. However, African-American soldiers proved their mettle on the battlefield. They distinguished themselves in May 1863 when they bravely attacked across open ground against Port Hudson on the Mississippi River in Louisiana. A month later, black troops made another valiant charge when they stormed Fort Wagner near Charleston, South Carolina. This Famous attack was depicted in the movie *Glory*.

More than 180,000 African-Americans served in the Union army making up about nine percent of Union army forces. The North's advantage in military manpower was a critical factor in its victory in the Civil War. Some northerners supported Lincoln's measure on moral grounds, but many endorsed emancipation because they favored any action that would help defeat the enemy and end the war.

Resources

National Park Service, Antietam National Battlefield. "Freedom at Antietam." *www.nps.gov/anti/historyculture/freedom.htm*

The C&O Canal
(Chesapeake & Ohio
Canal National
Historical Park)

Chesapeake & Ohio Canal National Historical Park

23

HISTORIC SITE	Viewable from the road
THINGS TO DO AND SEE	Visitor Centers, Guided Tours, Self-Guided Tours, Educational Programs, Canal Boat Rides, Kids Activities, Walking Trail, Biking, Backpacking
DESIGNATIONS	National Register of Historic Places
LOCATION	C&O Canal NHP Headquarters 1850 Dual Highway, Suite 100, Hagerstown, MD
CONTACT INFORMATION	Headquarters (301) 739-4200 Visitor Information (301) 739-4200
ON THE WEB	www.nps.gov/choh

Preserving America's colorful Canal era and transportation history, the Chesapeake & Ohio Canal National Historical Park is 184.5 miles of adventure. Originally, the C&O Canal was a lifeline for communities and businesses along the Potomac River as coal, lumber, grain and other agricultural products floated down the canal to market. Today millions of visitors hike or bike the C&O Canal each year to enjoy the natural, cultural and recreational opportunities available.

Although primarily European immigrants dug and built the Chesapeake and Ohio Canal, when it began operating in the 1830s African Americans often worked on the boats, tended the mules that pulled them, and transported cargo at the wharves. African Americans also often worked as watermen on the oceans and the nation's waterways, but the number declined through the early nineteenth century. The Virginia legislature, responding to slave-holder's fears that black boatmen assisted fugitive slaves, passed laws in the early-to-mid nineteenth century that mandated white supervision. Maryland had no such laws, but in 1856 the board of directors of the C&O Canal, in response to complaints by white boatmen and waterway residents, banned African Americans from captaining vessels. Beginning January 1, 1857 they required that all boats have "at least one white person above the age of 18 years, who shall act as master." While the regulation did limit the opportunities for black boat owners and captains—the rule did not stop freedom-seekers from exiting the slave states via the C&O Canal.

The regulation banning black captains was never overturned. Even if it wasn't enforced after the Civil War, it did seem to have a dampening effect. After 1856 there were no black barge captions until 1878, when four men registered. Louis Roberson, Wilson Middleton, Kirk Fields, and J.M. Johnson all captained barges owned by three different coal companies.

Ferry Farm and the Underground Railroad

The Potomac River and accompanying C&O Canal was a major route on the Underground Railroad. Ferry Farm, south of Sharpsburg on the C&O Canal and Potomac River, and now part of the national park, was the site of both escape and capture of freedom seekers. John Blackford purchased the farm in 1813 and a ferry that crossed the Potomac River in 1839. He held eighteen people in bondage. Two of them, Jupe and Ned, operated the ferry. They also kept the records, purchased supplies, and hired free blacks during periods of peak demand. While there is no evidence that they helped freedom seekers, anecdotal evidence suggests that black ferry operators were more likely to render aid than white counterparts.

Aaron and others escaped from slavery at Ferry Farm, at least for a time, and freedom seekers from elsewhere were apprehended there. A woman who escaped from a slavetrader named Malone was apprehended and taken to jail by John Blackford in 1829. Ten years later a group consisting of a man, a pregnant woman and infant, and two girls—probably a family—were taken to the Hagerstown jail by Blackford, who received a $200 reward after their owner collected them.

Civilian Conservation Corps (CCC)

During the Great Depression the Civilian Conservation Corps employed men in public service work around the country. Many units were assigned to develop the nation's national parks, including the C&O Canal National Park acquired in 1938. Companies 325 and 333 assigned there consisted of African American men between the ages of 17 and 25. Most were

Chesapeake & Ohio Canal National Historical Park

originally from Washington, DC, Baltimore, and Pennsylvania, and they lived camps in and near Carderock, Maryland. They received dress and work uniforms, room and board, and a salary of $30 per month, $25 of which was sent home. In return, they repaired breaches in the canal from floods in 1924 and 1936, removed debris from the waterway, cleared and resurfaced the towpath, and restored locks to working order in the first 22 miles of the canal. In dress uniform, they attended classes in trade skills, reading, mathematics, history, and other topics. They

CCC members restoring the C&O Canal in the 1930s.
(Chesapeake & Ohio Canal National Historical Park)

visited the Nation's Capital every other week for recreation. Both in and away from the camps, the men coped with the challenges of segregation and the marked racism of their time, even as they contributed richly to the public good.

Resources

National Park Service, National Underground Railroad Network to Freedom Nomination, "Ferry Hill Plantation," 2002.

Maryland State Archives. *Beneath the Underground: The Flight for Freedom and Communities in Antebellum Maryland.* www.msa.md.gov/msa/mdslavery/html/antebellum/fr.html

National Park Service, Chesapeake and Ohio Canal. "Civilian Conservation Corps." www.nps.gov/choh/historyculture/civilianconservationcorpsccc.htm

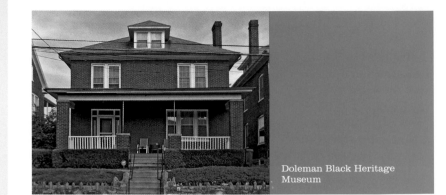

Doleman Black Heritage
Museum

Doleman Black Heritage Museum

24

Charles and Marguerite Doleman began collecting artifacts from Washington County's African American history in 1974. Marguerite spoke about that rich heritage to an Afro-American studies class at North Hagerstown High School, and a student's com-

HISTORIC SITE	Private collection
THINGS TO DO AND SEE	Tours of the museum have been suspended while a major cataloging initiative is underway. Tours are expected to resume in the fall of 2009.
LOCATION	540 N Locust St. Hagerstown, MD
CONTACT INFORMATION	(301) 739-8185
ON THE WEB	www.dolemanbhm.vpweb.com

ment prompted a hobby that became an avocation. Over the years, Marguerite and Charles acquired thousands of documents, autographs, photographs, books, and objects such as furniture, dolls, paintings and sculptures relating to African American history. The collection has a special emphasis on Washington County history, illuminating the black experience there, and saving countless artifacts that might otherwise have been lost.

Marguerite and Charles Doleman passed away in 2000 and 2003, respectively, but their legacy lives on. Their children Charles (Sonny) Doleman and Rosemary Doleman-Lucas head the non-profit board that continues to operate the museum in their parents' former home. The people of Washington County and beyond have come to appreciate its value to the community-at-large. The Hagerstown City Council and Maryland Heritage Area Authority have partnered in a grant to catalog the collections and are working with the board toward establishing a public home for the museum. In the meantime, it continues operation as a private non-profit museum.

Aerial view of
restored stone walls
and barracks at
Fort Frederick
(Kenneth L. Garrett)

Fort Frederick State Park

25

HISTORIC SITE	Open to the public
THINGS TO DO AND SEE	Vistor Center, Orientation Film, Hiking, Camping, Guided Tours, Educational Programs
DESIGNATIONS	National Register of Historic Places
LOCATION	11100 Fort Frederick Rd. Big Pool, MD
CONTACT INFORMATION	(301) 842-2155
ON THE WEB	www.dnr.state.md.us/publiclands/ western/FortFrederick.html

Fort Frederick and the British soldiers stationed at Fort Frederick protected white settlers during the French and Indian War (1754-1763). Maryland Governor Horatio Sharpe had it built in 1756 and named it for Maryland's Lord Proprietor, Frederick Calvert, Sixth Lord Baltimore. Because of its large size and stone construction it was advanced for its time. The State of Maryland sold the fort in 1791, and the area became farmland. During the Civil War, the Union Army stationed troops there to protect the nearby C&O Canal. The State of Maryland purchased the property in 1922. During the Great Depression of the 1930s the Civilian Conservation Corps restored the stone wall and conducted an archaeological survey to find the building foundations. It became Maryland's first state park. The barracks

Fort Frederick State Park

were reconstructed beginning in 1975.

Fort Frederick, known widely as a frontier fort, has another interesting story to tell. A prosperous free black family, that of Nathan and Ammy Williams, owned, expanded, and farmed the property from 1860 to 1911—51 years. Part of their legacy to the community was a school. In 1899, the family sold one-quarter acre to the Washington County School Board for the Fort Frederick "Colored" School. Some of Nathan and Ammy's children taught there. Probably due to low enrollment, it operated sporadically until 1909, when its students were sent to "colored" schools in Clear Spring or Williamsport. The building remains intact and the interior retains the waist-high beaded wainscoting and wooden hat and coat rack from its days as a schoolhouse.

 Nathan and Ammy Williams

Nathan Williams (right) and his family.
(Civil War Trails Historical Marker)

Nathan Williams bought the parcel in 1860 and cultivated a prosperous farm. Born in slavery to Samuel (Big Sam) Williams and his wife, Nathan benefited from his father's industry and good fortune as well as his own. Samuel had managed to earn and save enough money to purchase the freedom of himself, his wife, and his children in 1836. Three years later he bought a farm 3 ½ miles east of Fort Frederick. Son Nathan took after his father. After he fell in love with a young enslaved woman, Ammy, on an adjoining farm, he purchased her freedom in 1847 for $60. In 1860 they purchased the Fort Frederick tract and established their own farm. The Civil War began the following year and arrived at the Williams's farm when the 1st Maryland Infantry garrisoned at the fort over the winter. The unit was assigned there to protect the canal and railroad along with the Potomac River fords and ferries. The Williams turned the situation to their advantage. Nathan sold produce to Union soldiers in Maryland and Confederates across the Potomac, where he also collected information he reported to the Federals. Ammy prepared meals for the officers who occupied their home (which was located near today's gift shop). The family probably witnessed the skirmish on Christmas Day 1861, when Confederate raiders crossed the river, tore out a section of rail line, and tangled with Federal troops.

After the war, Nathan Williams built a large barn near the fort. Inside the fort's remaining stone walls, he planted grapes, vegetables, and an orchard, and tended animals in pens. Outside the walls he planted fields of grain and harvested hay, even adding to his property and extending his fields. Williams died in 1884 and his family maintained the property until 1911. Their stewardship facilitated creation of Fort Frederick State Park. A Civil War Trails Historical Marker tells the family's story at the site.

Resources

Fort Frederick State Park's interpretive signs are available on online at: *freepages.genealogy.rootsweb. ancestry.com/~wvmystica/Fort_Frederick_State_Park.html*

Hagerstown Public Square circa 1900.

Hagerstown Historic District

26

Hagerstown is named for German immigrant Jonathan Hager, who first settled in Pennsylvania and, in 1739, purchased 200 acres of land in Maryland.

Washington County, especially Hagerstown, has a rich concentration of African American history. Even though the county had a lower slave population than Maryland counties to the east, it was the site of fre-

THINGS TO DO AND SEE	See historic sites, buildings, and historical markers
LOCATION	Downtown Hagerstown African American Heritage Sites:
	Asbury United Methodist Episcopal Church, 155 N. Jonathan St., Hagerstown, MD
	Doleman Black Heritage Museum (see p. 80)
	Ebenezer African Methodist Episcopal Church 26 Bethel St., Hagerstown, MD
	Hagerstown Jail Historical Marker 26-28 E. Franklin St., Hagerstown, MD
	Harmon Hotel Historical Marker (see p. 87)
	Slave Auction Block on the Terrace in Hagerstown
	William O. Wilson Historical Marker (see p. 97)

quent slave auctions and underground railroad activity. In 1819 a group of citizens petitioned the Maryland legislature to end the slave trade in their county and complained that their jail was being used to hold enslaved people. In 1825 the county's Grand Jury asked the sheriff to remove the jailer from office, as he was profiting from apprehending freedom seekers. In 1847, a group of free blacks tried to free fugitive slaves being held in the jail, but they were themselves arrested and jailed. After living some years in Pennsylvania, Jacob D. Green, a freedom seeker from the Eastern Shore, was apprehended and sold and kept for a time in the Hagerstown jail. He published his autobiography in 1864 and relates harrowing stories of slavery there and his own three escapes.

Despite the challenges of life in a slave society near a land of freedom, Washington County's African American community was strong enough that by 1818, black members of St. Paul's Methodist Episcopal Church (now John Wesley United Methodist Church) formed their own congregation, Asbury Methodist Episcopal Church. It remained under St. Paul's supervision until after the Civil War. During the war, in 1864, a fire damaged the building to such an extent that they replaced it in 1879.

In 1840 some members of Asbury Church, seeking even more autonomy in their worship and the right to purchase property, founded Ebenezer African Methodist Episcopal (A.M.E.) Church. The A.M.E. Church was a new denomination organized by free African Americans and upheld by the Pennsylvania Supreme Court in 1816. The Hagerstown congregation used a series of different buildings along West Bethel Street. Ebenezer Church was used as a hospital During the Civil War. Its last historic building was demolished in the 1990s. Two other African American congregations founded in the nineteenth century remain: Second Christian and Zion Baptist.

Asbury United Methodist Church, Hagerstown, MD

Resources

Hagerstown Convention Visitors Bureau. *African American Heritage Guide,* Washington County, Maryland. *www.marylandmemories.org/african_american.html#6*

J. [Jacob] D. Green, b. 1813. *Narrative of the Life of J. D. Green, a Runaway Slave, from Kentucky, Containing an Account of His Three Escapes, in 1839, 1846, and 1848.* Huddersfield, [Eng.]: Printed by Henry Fielding, Pack Horse Yard, 1864. *docsouth.unc.edu/neh/greenjd/summary.html*

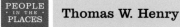

| PEOPLE · IN THE · PLACES | **Thomas W. Henry** | (1794-1877) |

Ebenezer A.M.E. Church, Hagerstown, Maryland, c. 1920 *(Viola Steward)*

A mong the papers found in the Kennedy farmhouse *(see p. 89)* after John Brown's Raid on Harpers Ferry, was a letter recommending "Mr. Thomas Henrie" to Brown as a reliable friend. At that time, the Thomas Henry referenced was a minister in the African Methodist Episcopal Church, a branch of the denomination that was decidedly antislavery and whose ministers and members often aided freedom seekers.

Thomas Henry worked hard and kept religion, family, and community central in his life. Born in slavery in Leonardtown, Maryland, his owner died in 1804 and freed his slaves in his will. The terms varied depending upon the age and sex of the enslaved—Thomas Henry was age 9 and would not become free until he turned 23. He was taken northwest to Washington County and apprenticed to a blacksmith in Hagerstown at about age 15. Raised Roman Catholic, Henry converted to Methodism while he lived with Abraham King, a white member of the Church of the Brethren whose children became Methodists. In 1821 he gained his freedom, became a full member in the Methodist Episcopal Church, and married Catherine Craig, an enslaved woman in Hagerstown. By 1826 Henry raised enough money to purchase his wife and four children, but their owners raised the price and he had to leave two in slavery. They were sold away and lost to him before Henry could raise the additional money. He became a minister in the Methodist Episcopal Church, but grew disillusioned by conflicts and switched to the African Methodist Episcopal denomination in 1835. His first charge was a small congregation at Bethel Church in Frederick, Maryland. Soon after, he established Ebenezer A.M.E. Church in Hagerstown. At times in his career Thomas Henry supplemented his meager wages as a minister with work at the iron furnaces in the area and by selling medicinal linaments he learned to make in his early life. As he grew in his ministerial profession, he was assigned to circuits and churches in Pennsylvania, New York, New Jersey, and Washington, D.C. In 1872 the church published his autobiography. In it he relates his perspective on John Brown and reveals much about life at the Maryland ironworks and the early history of the A.M.E. Church. His life was devoted to service. To many, he was indeed a reliable friend.

Resources

Henry, Thomas W. *Autobiography of Rev. Thomas W. Henry, of the A. M. E. Church.* [Baltimore]: [The Author], [1872]. *docsouth.unc.edu/neh/henry/menu.html.* See also *From Slavery to Salvation: The Autobiography of Rev. Thomas W. Henry, of the A. M. E. Church.* Edited, with an introduction and historical essay, by Jean Libby. Foreword by Edward C. Papenfuse. Jackson: University of Mississippi Press, 1994; ;reprint Palo Alto, California: Allies for Freedom publishers, 2005.

Walter Harmon, 1869-1915

This display courtesy of Each One Teach One
African American Historical Association of Western Maryland

Walter Harmon
and the
Harmon Hotel

Harmon Hotel
Historical Marker

27

HISTORIC SITE	Site and marker only; building no longer exists
THINGS TO DO AND SEE	Read historical marker and view original location of Harmon Hotel
LOCATION	Jonathan Street at intersection with Harmon Ave., Hagerstown, MD
CONTACT INFORMATION	African American Historical Association of Western Maryland
ON THE WEB	www.hmdb.org/ marker.asp?marker=5675

During the era of segregation, the Harmon Hotel provided accommodations for black teachers and travelers, including baseball player Willie Mays. Built by Walter Harmon (1869-1915), an African American businessman originally from McGaheysville, Virginia, who forged a successful career in Washington County, Maryland. He married Florence Keys of Williamsport, Maryland, and together they had ten children and twenty grandchildren. Many of them worked at the hotel before pursuing other careers. By the time of his death, Harmon owned forty properties. Florence then managed them until her death in 1953.

Legendary baseball player and Hall of Fame member Willie Mays was the hotel's most famous guest. He was a nineteen-year-old rookie then, on the New York Giants' minor league farm team, the Trenton Giants.

Harmon Hotel Historical Marker

Mays came to Hagerstown to play his first professional game, at Municipal Stadium in a weekend series against the Boston Braves farm team. Mays was forced to stay at the Harmon Hotel, away from his teammates. During the game, fans yelled racial epithets and slurs at him. During a television interview in 1988, Mays recalled his treatment in Hagerstown as the worst he encountered when he helped integrate professional baseball. He said that, around 2000, he declined an invitation to serve as grand marshal in a Hagerstown parade because he "had a little sadness in his throat." But, upon reflection, he decided, "No, that's not the way to go," and accepted an invitation to speak at a dinner and participate in a pregame ceremony at Municipal Stadium in August 2004. This time, the people of Hagerstown, "treated him like royalty," according to the local paper, and, at Municipal Stadium, the crowd of about 3,000 gave him a standing ovation.

Resources

The Historical Marker Database. "The Harmon Hotel." *www.hmdb.org/marker.asp?marker=5675*

The Kennedy
Farmhouse
(Library of Congress)

Kennedy Farmhouse | 28

HISTORIC SITE	Privately owned; open by appointment.
THINGS TO DO AND SEE	The restored farmhouse is furnished as it might have been when John Brown and his followers lived there. Guided tours by appointment.
DESIGNATIONS	National Register of Historic Places
LOCATION	Samples Manor, South of Sharpsburg, MD 2406 Chestnut Grove Road, Sharpsburg MD
CONTACT INFORMATION	(202) 537-8900 captain@johnbrown.org
ON THE WEB	www.johnbrown.org

In July of 1859, abolitionist John Brown stepped off a train in Sandy Hook, Maryland, across the Potomac River a mile downstream from Harpers Ferry (see p. 104). Already a "wanted man" after his attack on proslavery men in the Kansas Territory, he contemplated his plans to conduct a raid on the armory at Harpers Ferry and spark a liberation movement amongst enslaved people in the South. His sons, Owen and Oliver, and his trusted lieutenant, Jeremiah Anderson, accompanied him. The party introduced themselves as Issac Smith and sons from New York, and looked for a farm to rent. The home of Dr. Kennedy, who had passed away that spring, appeared ideal. Brown's daughter Annie, age 16, and Oliver's wife Martha, age 17, joined them to do cooking and housekeeping and present the appearance of a normal family. Word of the planned raid spread among abolitionist circles and volunteers trickled in. By the end of the summer twenty-two volunteers—18 white and 4 black—for the Provisional Army of the United States lived in the attic of the house awaiting the order to

Kennedy Farmhouse

attack. Just before the raid on Harpers Ferry, Martha and Annie were sent home to North Elba, New York. After the raid, federal authorities searched the Kennedy farmhouse and seized a satchel of papers. Among them were Brown's provisional constitution and three letters from Harriet Newby to her husband Dangerfield Newby. She remained in slavery and longed to be reunited with him. *(See profile of Dangerfield Newby on p. 184, and profile of Harriet Newby on p. 140).*

Resources

The Kennedy Farmhouse. *www.johnbrown.org*

A stylized rendition
of Rockland in 1877
*(Catoctin Center for
Regional Studies)*

Rockland

29

HISTORIC SITE	Privately owned
THINGS TO DO AND SEE	Viewable from the road
DESIGNATIONS	National Register of Historic Places
	National Underground Railroad Network to Freedom Site.
LOCATION	9030 Sharpsburg Pike Fairplay, MD 21733 Six miles south of Hagerstown on Route 65

Built in 1796 for Frisby Tilghman, Rockland is one of Washington County's most significant historic sites. Frisby Tilghman was the eldest son of James Tilghman of Queen Anne's County, Maryland, on the Eastern Shore of the Chesapeake Bay. Like many sons of planters from eastern Maryland, Frisby migrated to the western part of the state in the late eighteenth century, where land was plentiful and comparatively low-priced. Trained as a doctor, he married the wealthy Anna Maria Ringgold and turned his hand to farming instead. He helped found a local agricultural society and an academy and earned a reputation as a progressive farmer. Active in civic life, he served four terms in the Maryland House of Delegates, promoted the C&O Canal project, served on bank boards of directors, and formed and commanded a militia unit (he was known as Colonel Tilghman). Although Tilghman was progressive in agriculture, education, and economic development, he was conservative on issues of slavery and slaveholding. He initiated laws that tightened controls on enslaved people in Washington County, including limiting the number of miles they could travel on Sundays, traditionally their day off when they were often granted passes to visit family members living elsewhere. He instigated the closure of a Sunday School for free blacks operated by local Methodist and Lutheran churches for fear that "slaves should get some benefit of it."

Despite Frisby Tilghman's wealth and prominence in the community, a man that he owned as a slave earned wider and more enduring fame. Jim Pembroke, later known as James W. C. Pennington, earned international renown for his human rights advocacy and an autobiography of his early life in slavery. Pennington's memoir affords a window into slave society on the edge of the South that continues to be acclaimed and widely read. *(See profile, below)*.

The Pembroke family was an important part of the enslaved community at Rockland. Nellie Pembroke and her two oldest children, Robert and James, arrived there around 1810 with their new owner, Frisby Tilghman. Formerly the property of Frisby's father, James Tilghman, who died in 1809, they were forced to leave Bazil Pembroke—

200 Dollars Reward.

RAN AWAY from the subscriber living near Hagers-town, Washington county, Md. on Monday the twenty-ninth of October, a negro man named JAMES PEM-BROOK, about 21 years of age, five feet five inches high, very black, square & clumsily made, has a down look, prominent and reddish eyes, and mumbles or talks with his teeth closed, can read, and I believe write, is an excellent blacksmith, and pretty good rough carpenter ; he received shortly before he absconded, a pretty severe cut from his axe on the inside of his right leg. Any person who will take up and secure him in the jail of Hagers-town shall receive the above reward.

FRISBY TILGHMAN.
November 1.   1—tf.

Nellie's husband and the children's father—behind. Probably at Nellie's behest, Frisby Tilghman purchased Bazil Pembroke from his owner and reunited the family at Rockland. Over time, the couple had eleven additional children. Around 1815, Robert and James were apprenticed to tradesmen in Hagerstown, then James returned and learned blacksmithing at Rockland. By 1820 the enslaved community at Rockland consisted of 29 persons: one man over age 45, 6 males and 5 females between ages 26 and 44, 2 males and 1 female between 14 and 25, and 9 males and 5 females under age 14.

Life at Rockland was often harsh for those in slavery. James Pennington believed that Tilghman was basically kind in nature, yet he brooked no opposition or insubordination from those he held as slaves. He dealt harshly with infractions, punishing swiftly with whippings or sale. In his memoir, Pennington related a pivotal incident that deeply wounded their family and prompted his escape. One Monday morning, as Bazil Pembroke bottle-fed a young orphaned lamb, Tilghman railed against three enslaved field hands who had yet to return from their Sunday furlough. He vented his fury on Pembroke and whipped him severely while James was nearby. The incident traumatized the family and proved transformative for James. "In my mind and heart," he wrote, "I never was a Slave after it." He escaped in 1827. The rest of the family was sold after Tilghman intercepted a letter from their son. Some years later, Tilghman repurchased the parents. Pennington reported that he helped his father and two brothers find freedom in Canada. He purchased his own freedom as well as that of a younger brother after the brother's unsuccessful escape attempt.

James W. C. Pennington (1807-1870)

REV. J. W. PENNINGTON

Born Jim Pembroke, James W. C. Pennington escaped from slavery at Rockland, the home of Frisby Tilghman, in Washington County, Maryland, in 1827. From this modest beginning he eventually won world renown. After staying six months with Quakers William and Phebe Wright in Adams County, Pennsylvania, Pennington settled in New York. (*See a profile of the Wrights on p. 31*). Working first as a coachman, he found spiritual guidance from Presbyterian minister Dr. S. H. Cox and experienced a religious awakening in 1829. At the same time he became involved in abolitionist activities and found them compatible with his study of religion. For a while he taught black children at a school in Long Island. In 1834 he moved to Connecticut where he audited classes in Theology at Yale University and pastored Temple Street Congregational Church, a black congregation. Under his leadership, his church championed abolition and civil rights, and Pennington spoke widely on those issues. He also supported temperance and African missions, but denounced the colonization movement to send free blacks from the United States to settle in Liberia. In 1841 he wrote and published one of the first histories of Africans in America. The same year he became founding president of the Union Missionary Society and raised money for the kidnapped Africans on the slave ship Amistad to

Rockland

return home. As the Connecticut delegate to the World Anti-Slavery Convention in London in 1843, Pennington developed an international reputation as a human rights advocate.

Pennington kept his enslaved status secret for decades for fear of discovery and capture, but ultimately found power in it. In 1844 he enlisted an intermediary to contact Frisby Tilghman and negotiate the purchase of his freedom, but the $1,000 price Tilghman set was too high. Pennington publicly told the story of his early life in *The Fugitive Blacksmith,* first published in 1849. It sold briskly and remains one of the most acclaimed of all slave narratives. That same year the University of Heidelburg recognized his international achievements by awarding him an honorary Doctor of Divinity degree. He attended world peace and abolition conferences in Great Britain and spoke publicly to raise consciousness and funds for the cause. Meanwhile, the United States passed the Fugitive Slave Law of 1850. Abolitionists in Scotland, fearing for Pennington's safety, helped him raise money and successfully purchase his freedom from Tilghman's estate administrators in 1851. He returned to the United States the same year. He pastored Shiloh Baptist Church in New York City but experienced difficulties in the position and resigned in 1855. His involvement in the Underground Railroad included his own escape, his book, and his assistance to freedom seekers including several family members. In 1848 he raised $50 at Shiloh to help Paul Edmonson purchase his two daughters after their thwarted escape from Washington, DC, on the Pearl. Until his death in 1870 he continued teaching, ministering, and advocating human rights.

Resources

Dean Herrin. *Forging Freedom: The Fugitive Blacksmith James W. C. Pennington. Catoctin History* 1 (Fall 2002), 24-28.

James W. C. Pennington. *The Fugitive Blacksmith,* 1849. *docsouth.unc.edu/neh/penning49/menu.html*

Tolson's Chapel
(Historic American
Buildings Survey,
Library of Congress)

Tolson's Chapel

HISTORIC SITE	Owned by Save Historic Antietam Foundation
THINGS TO DO AND SEE	Under restoration
DESIGNATIONS	National Register of Historic Places
LOCATION	111 East High St. Sharpsburg, MD
CONTACT INFORMATION	Friends of Tolson's Chapel P.O. Box 162 Sharpsburg, MD 21782

In October 1866, when black residents of Sharpsburg laid the cornerstone of this chapel, they were making a commitment to the future of the community. Just four years after the Civil War battle at Antietam and Abraham Lincoln issued the Emancipation Proclamation, and two years after Maryland abolished slavery in a new constitution, they pooled their meager resources and built an institution. In October of 1867 the Methodist congregation dedicated their church and, in choosing the name, honored their first minister, John Tolson. By 1868, with the help of the Freedmen's Bureau, they established a school in the building. Teacher

Tolson's Chapel

Ezra Johnson taught eighteen students on weekdays and additional adults at night in the American Union School held in the chapel. He also started a Sabbath School and a temperance organization. Between 1870 and 1871, operation of the school shifted from the Freedmen's Bureau, which Congress dismantled, to the state of Maryland. The building continued its dual purpose until 1899, when students and teacher moved to a new building on High Street. David Simons, and then his son, James F. Simons taught at the county-operated school and are buried in the Tolson's Chapel cemetery.

Over time, the congregation dwindled and died out as its members aged or moved away for job opportunities. Recognizing the historic and cultural value of the chapel, local Methodists, the Town of Sharpsburg, the Save Historic Antietam Foundation, and others banded together to preserve the structure. Volunteers formed the Friends of Tolson's Chapel and are continuing to raise funds for additional restoration and maintenance.

Resources

Friends of Tolson's Chapel brochure, 2007.

William O. Wilson

William O. Wilson Historical Marker

31

HISTORIC SITE	Home privately owned
THINGS TO DO AND SEE	Viewable from the road
LOCATION	Home: 108 West North St., Hagerstown, MD
	Burial Place: Rose Hill Cemetery, 600 South Potomac St., Hagerstown, MD
	Historical Marker: On Jonathan St. at the intersection of Pennsylvania Ave.
ON THE WEB	www.hmdb.org/ marker.asp?marker=5755

William Othello Wilson left Hagerstown as a young man and returned a hero—the recipient of the Nation's highest military award, the Medal of Honor. When Wilson enlisted in 1889 he was assigned to the Ninth Cavalry, popularly known, along with the Tenth Cavalry, as Buffalo soldiers. In

William O. Wilson Historical Marker

1890 Corporal Wilson's unit was sent in search of a Sioux band led by Big Foot. They were about fifty miles from the Pine Ridge Reservation when a courier arrived with news of the battle at Wounded Knee the previous day and orders for them to return to Pine Ridge as soon as possible. To expedite their return, the Lt. Colonel and the main part of the unit left immediately ahead of the slow supply wagons and a small detachment under Captain Loud that included Wilson. When the supply train was about two miles from Pine Ridge, Indians attacked and cut off the wagons. The Captain wrote a message to send to Major Henry for help but scouts refused to carry it. Wilson volunteered and successfully delivered the message, despite Indian pursuit. For his "gallantry in action" he was awarded the Medal of Honor on September 17, 1891.

William Wilson returned to Hagerstown in 1898, after his military service. There he married Margaret Virginia Brown and together they had seven children. He worked at carpentry, upholstering, cooking and calligraphy; he was adept at many skills. His family knew of his distinguished military service, and he is the only Washington County person to have received the Medal of Honor, but he received little recognition until recently. In 1988 a traffic triangle was named for him and a marker placed there. In 1997, his grave was located at Rose Hill Cemetery and the Veterans Administration placed a military marker there.

All told, eighteen black soldiers serving in the frontier Indian Campaigns were awarded the Medal of Honor for heroism. *(See Clinton Greaves on p. 216).* William O. Wilson was the last African American soldier to receive the Medal of Honor during the Indian Campaigns and on American soil.

Resources

National Park Service, Fort Davis National Historic Site. "Black Recipients of the Medal of Honor." *www.nps.gov/archive/foda/Fort_Davis_WEB_PAGE/About_the_Fort/BLACK_RECIPIENTS_Con_Medal_of_Honor.htm*

Frank N. Schubert. *Black Valor: Buffalo Soldiers and the Medal of Honor, 1870-1898.* Rowman & Littlefield, 1997.

Harpers Ferry
WEST VIRGINIA

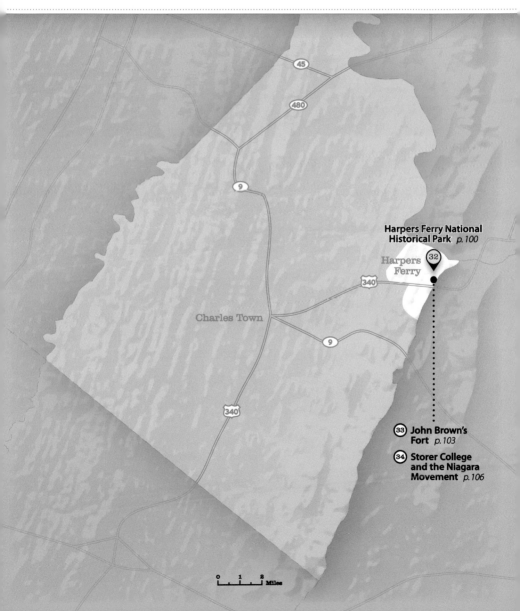

Harpers Ferry National
Historical Park *p. 100*

Harpers
Ferry (32)

Charles Town

(33) **John Brown's
Fort** *p. 103*

(34) **Storer College
and the Niagara
Movement** *p. 106*

0   1   2
Miles

1859 view of Lower Town Harpers Ferry and the covered Baltimore and Ohio Railroad Viaduct. The Point was a bustling commercial district at the time. This is one of the earliest known photographs of Harpers Ferry

(Historic Photo Collection, Harpers Ferry NHP)

Harpers Ferry National Historical Park

32

The history of Harpers Ferry has few parallels in the American drama. It is more than one event, one date, or one individual. It is multi-layered—involving a diverse number of people and events that influenced the course of our nation's history. Harpers

THINGS TO DO AND SEE	The park is open daily from 8 AM – 5 PM and closed Thanksgiving Day, Christmas Day, and New Year's Day.
DESIGNATIONS	National Register of Historic Places Underground Railroad Network to Freedom Site
LOCATION	Harpers Ferry, WV
CONTACT INFORMATION	(304) 535-6029 www.nps.gov/hafe/contacts.htm
ON THE WEB	www.nps.gov/hafe

Ferry witnessed the first successful application of interchangeable manufacture, the arrival of the first successful American railroad, John Brown's attack on slavery, the largest surrender of Federal troops during the Civil War, the education of former slaves in one of the earliest integrated schools in the United States, and the first public meeting in America of the Niagara Movement.

John Brown's Raid

John Brown believed he could free the slaves, and he selected Harpers Ferry as his starting point. Determined to seize the 100,000 weapons at the Arsenal and to use the Blue Ridge Mountains for guerrilla warfare, abolitionist Brown launched his raid on Sunday evening, October 16, 1859. His 21-man "army of liberation" seized the Armory and several other strategic points. Thirty-six hours after the raid begun, with most of his men killed or wounded, Brown was captured in the Armory fire enginehouse (now known as "John Brown's Fort") when U.S. Marines stormed the building.

Brought to trial at nearby Charles Town, Brown was found guilty of treason, of conspiring with slaves to rebel, and murder. He was hanged on December 2, 1859. John Brown's short-lived raid failed, but his trial and execution focused the nation's attention on the moral issue of slavery and headed the country toward civil war.

Today John Brown's Fort and the Arsenal ruins are part of the legacy of our nation's struggle with slavery.

African American History

African Americans have been a part of the Harpers Ferry story since before the American Revolution. The first black arrived here in the mid-1700s as a slave to Robert Harper. By the time of John Brown's Raid in 1859, about ten percent of the town's residents were black. The town's 150 slaves, considered property, could be rented out, sold, used as collateral for business transactions, or given away. Another 150 "free" blacks often worked as laborers or teamsters, but some prospered as skilled masons, plasterers, butchers, and blacksmiths.

Enslaved people seeking freedom, most of them undocumented in the historical record, eloped from or traversed Harpers Ferry on their way to the North or West. Two stories are known better than most. In 1844, Joseph Blanhum, a free black man who operated a ferry at the town, was convicted, fined $100, and sentenced to three years in prison for helping seven Fauquier County men escape from bondage to a Mr. Diggers. Another man, Wesley Harris, had been born in slavery in Martinsburg but hired to Margaret Carroll, a white widow who operated a tavern in town. She treated him kindly, but her overseer did not. When, in 1853, he attempted to beat Harris, Harris instead beat the overseer. Learning that he would be sold for the offense, Harris decided to leave Harpers Ferry for the North. Three brothers with the surname of Matterson joined him. Heading for Gettysburg, Pennsylvania, they stopped in Taneytown, Maryland, where they were captured. Shot in the arm and near death, Harris was left in Taneytown, while the three brothers were taken to Westminster, then Baltimore, and sold. Harris recovered and escaped again, passing through Gettysburg and Philadelphia, where William Still recorded his story, then settled in Canada, where he found work on the Great Western Railroad.

During the Civil War, when the Union Army held Harpers Ferry, refugees from slavery traveled there in search of freedom. By March of 1862 Federal forces established a "contraband" camp (the refugees were officially known as contraband) at Harpers Ferry to accommodate them.

Following the Civil War, New England Freewill Baptist missionaries acquired several vacant Armory buildings on Camp Hill and, in 1867, started Storer College, an integrated school designed primarily to educate former slaves but open to students of all races and both genders.

By the end of the 19th century, the promise of freedom and equality for blacks had been buried by Jim Crow laws and legal segregation. To combat these injustices, Dr. W.E.B. Du Bois and other leading African-Americans created the Niagara Movement, which held its first conference in America on the campus of Storer College in 1906. The Niagara Movement was a forerunner to the NAACP *(see p. 106)*.

In 1954, legal segregation was finally ended by the landmark school desegregation decision handed down by the Supreme Court in *Brown v. Board of Education*. A year later Storer College closed its doors. Today the National Park Service continues the college's educational mission by using part of the old campus as a training facility.

Resources

National Park Service. Harpers Ferry. *www.nps.gov/archive/hafe/history.htm*

Underground Railroad Network to Freedom Nomination for Harpers Ferry (2001).

1882-1886 photo of John Brown's Fort. The building to the right of the fort was the former Armory superintendent's office. Advertisements painted on buildings and walls were aimed at rail travelers passing through Harpers Ferry

(Historic Photo Collection, Harpers Ferry NHP)

John Brown's Fort

33

THINGS TO DO AND SEE	The park is open daily from 8 AM – 5 PM and closed Thanksgiving Day, Christmas Day, and New Year's Day.
DESIGNATIONS	National Register of Historic Places
LOCATION	Harpers Ferry, WV
CONTACT INFORMATION	(304) 535-6029 www.nps.gov/hafe/contacts.htm
ON THE WEB	www.nps.gov/hafe

The structure we now call John Brown's Fort was erected in 1848 as the Armory's fire engine and guard house. The building was described in a June 30, 1848, Armory report: "An engine and guard-house, 35½ × 24 feet, one story brick, covered with slate, and having copper gutters and down spouts, has been constructed, and is now occupied." It was in this building that John Brown and several of his followers barricaded themselves during the final hours of their ill-fated raid of October 16, 17, and 18, 1859.

John Brown's Fort, as the structure became known, was the only Armory building to escape destruction during the Civil War. In 1891, the fort was sold, dismantled, and transported to Chicago where it was displayed a short distance from The World's Columbian Exposition. The building, attracting only 11 visitors in ten days, was closed, dismantled again and left on a vacant lot.

John Brown's Fort

In 1894, Washington, D.C. journalist Kate Field, who had a keen interest in preserving memorabilia of John Brown, spearheaded a campaign to return the fort to Harpers Ferry. Local resident Alexander Murphy made five acres available to Miss Field, and the Baltimore & Ohio Railroad offered to ship the disassembled fort to Harpers Ferry free of charge. In 1895, John Brown's Fort was rebuilt on the Murphy Farm about three miles outside of town on a bluff overlooking the Shenandoah River.

In 1903, Storer College began their own fundraising drive to acquire the structure. In 1909, on occasion of the 50th Anniversary of John Brown's Raid, the building was purchased and moved to the Storer College campus on Camp Hill in Harpers Ferry.

Acquired by the National Park Service in 1960, the building was moved back to the Lower Town in 1968. Because the fort's original site was covered with a railroad embankment in 1894, the building now sits about 150 feet east of its original location.

Resources

Harpers Ferry National Historical Park. "John Brown's Fort."
www.nps.gov/hafe/historyculture/john-brown-fort.htm

PEOPLE · IN THE · PLACES **John Brown** (1800–1859)

On October 16, 17, and 18, 1859, John Brown and his "Provisional Army of the United States" took possession of the United States Armory and Arsenal at Harpers Ferry. Brown had come to arm an uprising of slaves. Instead, the raid drew militia companies and federal troops from Maryland, Virginia, and the District of Columbia. On the morning of October 18, a storming party of 12 Marines broke down the door of the Armory's fire enginehouse, taking Brown and the remaining raiders captive.

Brown, charged for "conspiring with slaves to commit treason and murder," was tried, convicted, and hanged in Charles Town on December 2, 1859. Before the sentence was carried out, however, Brown issued a prophetic warning:

John Brown in 1859
(Black and Batchelder, Library of Congress)

I wish to say furthermore, that you had better—all you people at the South—prepare yourselves for a settlement of that question that must come up for settlement sooner than you are prepared for it. The sooner you are prepared the better. You may dispose of me very easily; I am nearly disposed of now; but this question is still to be settled—this negro question I mean—the end of that is not yet.

John Brown's Raid remains part of the legacy of our nation's struggle with slavery.

Resources

Harpers Ferry National Historical Park. "John Brown." *www.nps.gov/hafe/historyculture/john-brown.htm*

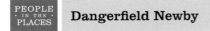

PEOPLE
· IN THE ·
PLACES   **Dangerfield Newby**   (1820–1859)

See Culpeper Historic District, *p. 184.*

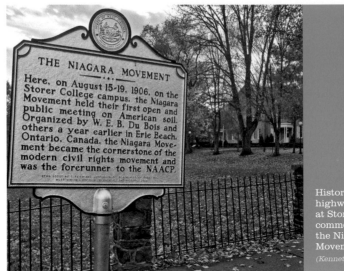

THE NIAGARA MOVEMENT

Here, on August 15-19, 1906, on the Storer College campus, the Niagara Movement held their first open and public meeting on American soil. Organized by W. E. B. Du Bois and others a year earlier in Erie Beach, Ontario, Canada, the Niagara Movement became the cornerstone of the modern civil rights movement and was the forerunner to the NAACP.

Historical highway marker at Storer College commemorating the Niagara Movement
(Kenneth L. Garrett)

Storer College and the Niagara Movement

34

C amp Hill, upon which several armory residences had been erected during the first half of the 19th century, served host to both Union and Confederate forces during much of the Civil War. Here could be found officer's quarters, encampments, drill and parade grounds.

THINGS TO DO AND SEE	The school is within the Harpers Ferry National Park. The park is open daily from 8 AM – 5 PM and closed Thanksgiving Day, Christmas Day, and New Year's Day.
DESIGNATIONS	National Register of Historic Places
LOCATION	Fillmore St. Harpers Ferry, WV
CONTACT INFORMATION	(304) 535-6029
ON THE WEB	www.nps.gov/hafe

During the Civil War, Harpers Ferry also became one of many Union garrison towns where runaway slaves, or "contraband," sought refuge. Following the Civil War, the Reverend Dr. Nathan Cook Brackett established a Freewill Baptist primary school in the Lockwood House on Camp Hill. Brackett's tireless efforts to establish freedmen's schools in the area inspired a generous contribution from philanthropist John Storer of Sanford, Maine, who offered $10,000 for the establishment of a school in the South. The donation was offered on the condition that the school be open to all regardless of sex, race or religion.

Storer College and the Niagara Movement

On October 2, 1867, "Storer Normal School" was opened, and two years later, in December 1869, the federal government formally conveyed the Lockwood House and three other former Armory residences on Camp Hill to the school's trustees. Frederick Douglass served as a trustee of Storer College, and delivered a memorable oration on the subject of John Brown here in 1881.

Resources

Harpers Ferry National Historical Park. "Camp Hill and Storer College." *www.nps.gov/archive/hafe/storer.htm*

The Niagara Movement

The Niagara Movement at Harpers Ferry was the Cornerstone of the Modern Civil Rights Era. At the dawn of the twentieth century, the outlook for full civil rights for African Americans was at a precarious crossroads. Failed Reconstruction, the Supreme Court's separate-but-equal doctrine *(Plessy v. Ferguson)*, coupled with Booker T. Washington's accommodationist policies threatened to compromise any hope for full and equal rights under the law.

Niagara Movement leaders W.E.B. Du Bois *(seated)*, and *(left to right)* J.R. Clifford, L.M. Hershaw, and F.H.M. Murray at Harpers Ferry. *(Historic Photo Collection, Harpers Ferry NHP)*

Harvard-educated William Edward Burghardt Du Bois committed himself to a bolder course, moving well beyond the calculated appeal for limited civil rights. He acted in 1905 by drafting a "Call" to a few select people. The Call had two purposes; "organized determination and aggressive action on the part of men who believed in Negro freedom and growth," and opposition to "present methods of strangling honest criticism."

Du Bois gathered a group of men representing every region of the country except the West. They hoped to meet in Buffalo, New York. When refused accommodation, the members migrated across the border to Canada. Twenty-nine men met at the Erie Beach Hotel in Ontario. The Niagarites adopted a constitution and by-laws, established committees and wrote the "Declaration of Principles" outlining the future for African Americans. After three days, they returned across the border with a renewed sense of resolve in the struggle for freedom and equality.

Thirteen months later, from August 15 – 19, 1906, the Niagara Movement held its first public meeting in the United States on the campus of Storer College in Harpers Ferry, West Virginia. Harpers Ferry was symbolic for a number of reasons. First and foremost was the connection to John Brown. It was at Harpers Ferry in 1859 that Brown's raid against slavery struck a blow for freedom. Many felt it was John Brown who fired the first shot of the Civil War. By the latter part of the nineteenth century, John Brown's Fort had become a shrine and a symbol of freedom to African Americans, Union soldiers and the nation's Abolitionists. Harpers Ferry was also the home of Storer College, the only school in West Virginia that offered African Americans an education beyond the primary level.

The Niagarites arrived in Harpers Ferry with passion in their hearts and high hopes that their voices would be heard and action would result. They were now more than fifty strong. Women also attended this historic gathering where, on August 17, 1906, they were granted full and equal membership to the organization.

The week was filled with many inspirational speeches, meetings, special addresses and commemorative ceremonies. Max Barber, editor of *The Voice of the Negro* said, "A more suitable place for the meeting of the Niagara Movement than Harpers Ferry would have been hard to find. I must confess that I had never yet felt as I felt in Harpers Ferry."

A highlight for those gathered was John Brown's Day. It was a day devoted to honoring the memory of John Brown. At 6:00 a.m. a silent pilgrimage began to John Brown's Fort. The members removed their shoes and socks as they tread upon the "hallowed ground" where the fort stood. The assemblage then marched single-file around the fort singing "The Battle Hymn of the Republic" and "John Brown's Body."

The inspirational morning was followed by an equally stirring afternoon. The Niagarites listened to Henrietta Leary Evans whose brother and nephew fought along side Brown at Harpers Ferry, then Lewis Douglass, son of Frederick Douglass, and finally Reverdy C. Ransom, pastor of the Charles Street African Methodist Episcopal Church in Boston. Ransom's speech on John Brown was described as a "masterpiece." The late black scholar, Dr. Benjamin Quarles, called the address, "...the most stirring single episode in the life of the Niagara Movement."

The conference concluded on Sunday, August 19th, with the reading of "An Address to the Country," penned by W.E.B. Du Bois. "We will not be satisfied to take one jot or title less than our full manhood rights. We claim for ourselves every single right that belongs to a freeborn American, political, civil and social; and until we get these rights we will never cease to protest and assail the ears of America. The battle we wage is not for ourselves alone but for all true Americans."

Storer College and the Niagara Movement

The Niagara Movement laid the cornerstone of the modern civil rights era. A new movement found a voice. The organization continued until 1911, when almost all of its members became the backbone of the newly formed National Association for the Advancement of Colored People (NAACP). There, the men and women of the Niagara Movement recommitted themselves to the ongoing call for justice and the struggle for equality.

With thunderous applause, the Harpers Ferry conference drew to a close. Years later recalling this conference, Du Bois referred to it as "...one of the greatest meetings that American Negroes ever held."

Resources

Harpers Ferry National Historical Park. "The Niagara Movement."
www.nps.gov/hafe/historyculture/the-niagara-movement.htm

PEOPLE IN THE PLACES   **Frederick Douglass**   (1818–1895)

Frederick Douglass was born in slavery in eastern Maryland but escaped to freedom in the North in 1831. There he read William Lloyd Garrison's antislavery newspaper *The Liberator* and joined the abolition movement. Through his speeches and his autobiography, *Narrative of the Life of Frederick Douglass,* he became the movement's most powerful witness against slavery and the most famous black abolitionist. Unlike many of them who denounced the Constitution as a proslavery document, however, Douglass thought that it, together with the Declaration of Independence, supported freedom, justice, and equality. During the Civil War, he helped persuade

Frederick Douglass, c. 1879. *(National Archives and Records Administration)*

President Abraham Lincoln to issue the Emancipation Proclamation and allow black men to fight in the Union Army. Lincoln called Douglass "the most meritorious man of the 19th century." After the War, Douglass continued to advocate for civil rights for all men and women and continued his role as the leading spokesman for his race. He was the clear and eloquent voice of the national conscience in his era and helped the United States grow into its early promise.

Storer College and the Niagara Movement

Frederick Douglass addressed audiences in parts of all four states now in the Journey Through Hallowed Ground National Heritage Area. In 1869, he delivered a speech on moral leadership entitled "William the Silent" in Gettysburg, Pennsylvania. In 1870, he spoke at the old Opera House in Westminster, Maryland. In 1879, he addressed an estimated two thousand people in a wooded grove near Purcellville, Virginia. He delivered one of his most famous speeches, "A Lecture on John Brown," at the fourteenth anniversary of Storer College in Harpers Ferry, West Virginia, in 1881. In it he explored the question, "Did John Brown fail?" In 1894 he spoke at the dedication of the Manassas Industrial School in Prince William County, Virginia.

Resources

PBS. Africans in America. "Frederick Douglass." *www.pbs.org/wgbh/aia/part4/4p1539.html*

Frederick Douglass. "A Lecture on John Brown ", "Speech at the Dedication of the Manassas (VA.) Industrial School", and "William the Silent." Frederick Douglass Papers, Library of Congress. *memory.loc.gov/ammem/doughtml/doughome.html*

PEOPLE IN THE PLACES

W.E.B. (William Edward Burghart) Du Bois (1868–1963)

William Edward Burghardt Du Bois broke new ground on many frontiers in his remarkable and controversial life. Du Bois earned the first Harvard doctorate awarded to an African American. During a prolific career of writing and publication, including sixteen thought-provoking books on sociology, history, politics, and race relations, Du Bois became the principal architect of the civil rights movement in the United States. He perceptively said, "The problem of the Twentieth Century is the problem of the color-line."

W. E. B. Du Bois in 1904. *(Library of Congress)*

Du Bois' connection to Harpers Ferry began in Canada in 1905, when he became the leader of an elite group of African Americans known as the Niagara Movement. The formation of this group marked the beginning of Du Bois' public assault on racial discrimination. The next year the Niagara Movement met on the campus of Storer College in Harpers Ferry. Du Bois returned to Harpers Ferry 44 years later as the commencement speaker for the 1950 graduating class of Storer College.

Resources

Harpers Ferry National Historical Park. "W E B DuBois." *www.nps.gov/hafe/historyculture/w-e-b-dubois.htm*

National League of Colored Women

From 1895-1909, John Brown's Fort stood on the Alexander Murphy Farm on a bluff overlooking the Shenandoah River. In this photograph taken on July 14, 1896, members of a pilgrim party from the National League of Colored Women pose in front of the fort. *(Historic Photo Collection, Harpers Ferry NHP)*

During the Progressive Era, from the 1890s through the 1920s, many Americans formed and joined organizations. African American women did so with enthusiasm, but since it was also the era of Jim Crow segregation, they created what is known as the black women's club movement. Many of these women had been active in their churches, but in the 1890s they banded together to discuss issues and to work for the betterment of people of color, especially women of color, and society. In 1892 in Washington, D.C., a group of female educators and community activists organized the Colored Women's League.

Founders included Helen Appo Cook (the first president), Josephine Wilson Bruce, Anna J. Cooper, Anna Evans Murray, Mary Church Terrell, and Fannie Barrier Williams. The members affirmed the value of education and of their responsibility, as educated women, to help others and lead reform efforts. They started chapters across the country and became the National League of Colored Women, but they operated in competition with similar institutions. In 1895, after considerable public slander against black women in the media, black women organized the National Federation of Afro-American Women to promote a more accurate and positive image. Helen Appo Clark served as vice-president. In 1896 the National Federation of Afro-American Women and the National League of Colored Women merged to form the National Association of Colored Women.

Also in 1896, before the consolidation, the National League of Colored Women convened at Storer College in Harpers Ferry. It seemed fitting, as these women carried the torch passed on by earlier abolitionist leaders such as Frederick Douglass, Sojourner Truth, Harriet Tubman, and Mary Ann Shadd Cary. While the earlier generation of leaders had come from modest means, sometimes no means at all, the new generation was more likely to possess enough material wealth and formal education to place them in the black elite. In their lives and their work together, they embodied the motto adopted by the National Association of Colored Women, "Lifting as We Climb."

Resources

Jacqueline M. Moore. *Leading the Race: The Transformation of the Black Elite in the Nation's Capital, 1880-1920.* Charlottesville: University of Virginia Press, 1999.

Loudoun County
VIRGINIA

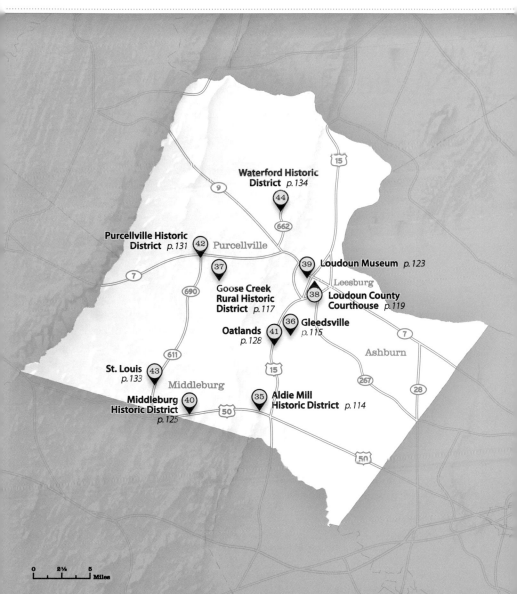

Waterford Historic District *p.134*

44

662

Purcellville Historic District *p.131*

42 Purcellville

9

37

7

690

Goose Creek Rural Historic District *p.117*

39 Loudoun Museum *p.123*

Leesburg

38 Loudoun County Courthouse *p.119*

15

611

36 Gleedsville *p.115*

Oatlands *p.128*

41

7

Ashburn

267

28

St. Louis *p.133*

43 Middleburg

Middleburg Historic District *p.125*

40

35 Aldie Mill Historic District *p.114*

15

50

50

0 2½ 5
Miles

Mount Pleasant Baptist Church, on New Mountain Road south of Aldie, served African Americans in the area.

35 | Aldie Mill Historic District

Charles Fenton Mercer, a congressman whose home overlooks Aldie Mill, owned slaves, yet called the institution of slavery "the blackest of blots, and foulest of all deformities." With others in 1816, he founded the American Colonization Society, to establish a colony

HISTORIC SITE	Viewable from the road
THINGS TO DO AND SEE	Aldie Mill open to the public seasonally on weekends with guided tours and demonstration grinding
DESIGNATIONS	National Register of Historic Places
LOCATION	39401 John Mosby Highway, Aldie, VA
CONTACT INFORMATION	(703) 327-9777 aldiemill@nvrpa.org
ON THE WEB	www.nvrpa.org/parks/aldiemill

for free blacks and newly emancipated slaves on the west coast of Africa. Many proponents hoped it would encourage a gradual end to slavery.

In the antebellum period enslaved and free people of color worked at Aldie Mill and in the vicinity. Wavin Corum, a free black entrepreneur, hauled goods and cut cordwood for mill operators. Daniel Dangerfield was an enslaved "mill boy," hired to the owner of a mill near Aldie, before he escaped to Pennsylvania where his capture, fugitive slave hearing, and release in 1859 fanned sectional animosity in both states.

After the Civil War, African Americans established communities near Aldie such as Bowmantown, Stewartown, Dover, and Back-in-the-Hollow. Near Bowmantown, they built Mount Pleasant Baptist Church (1875) and a school. Women founded the Housekeepers' Club in 1914 for fellowship and learning, and it still meets today.

Resources

Deborah A. Lee. *Loudoun County's African American Communities: A Tour Map & Guide*. Leesburg, Va.: Black History Committee, Friends of the Thomas Balch Library, 2004.

Mount Olive Methodist Episcopal Church, now Unitarian-Universalist Church of Loudoun.

Gleedsville

36

HISTORIC SITE	Viewable from the road
THINGS TO DO AND SEE	Properties are privately owned
DESIGNATIONS	Mount Olive Methodist Episcopal Church is on the National Register of Historic Places
LOCATION	Mount Olive Methodist Church, now Unitarian-Universalist Church of Loudoun: 20460 Gleedsville Rd., Leesburg, VA
CONTACT INFORMATION	Unitarian-Universalist Church of Loudoun, (703) 737-7644

In the years after general emancipation, on a nearby ridge known as Negro Mountain freed people from Oatlands Plantation established a small settlement. The community was called Gleedsville, for a leader among them, John "Jack" Gleed. In 1880, after building homes and cultivating their farms, the men founded the Mountain Gap Odd Fellows Lodge and built a meeting hall. Ten years later, the women organized a Household of Ruth auxiliary. In 1889 the school board established Mountain Gap (Colored) School, which looked much like the red-painted school of the same name built on Route 15 for white students. Grace Murray and Elizabeth Johnson taught for the first few years, then Bushrod "Bush" W. Murray assumed the role until he retired around 1933. In 1890, community members built a church in Gothic Revival style, with German siding, French Gothic windows, and stained wood tongue-and-groove paneling inside. The congregation took the name Mount Olive Baptist Church for a similar mountain ridge near Biblical Jerusalem. Gleedsville cemetery, about one-half mile away, is one of the largest African American cemeteries in Loudoun County. Alonzo "Bud" Daniel operated a store in the community, and his son Thomas took over later. Robert Connor had a thriving shoe shop for about twenty-five years, beginning in the early 1890s. The church and cemetery are about all that remain.

Resources

www.balchfriends.org/bhmap.htm

National Register of Historic Places Registration Form. "Mount Olive Methodist Episcopal Church, Loudoun County, Virginia. "VDHR File No. 053-0994, prepared by Leslie Wright, 2004. Available online in PDF format.

Eugene M. Scheel. *Loudoun Discovered: Communities, Corners and Crossroads, vol. 2, Leesburg and the Old Carolina Road.* Leesburg, Va.: Friends of the Thomas Balch Library, 2002.

PEOPLE IN THE PLACES   Martin VanBuren Buchanan   (1844–1924)

Mahala Jackson, a free woman of color, welcomed her child Martin into the world in 1844. His father Robert Buchanan was enslaved, owned by George and Elizabeth Carter at Oatlands. When Martin was older, he worked there for wages. The Civil War stirred him, however, and when black men were allowed to enlist, he struck out on his own. Between June 20 and November 1863, he joined the Union Army and began training at Camp Casey in Arlington. He joined the 2nd Regiment, composed primarily of men from Virginia, Maryland, and the District of Columbia, and was assigned to Company G. In December they shipped out, by train to New York and by steamer to New Orleans. The regiment served in Mississippi and Florida, and Buchanan remained with them until the end of the war.

Martin Buchanan returned home to Loudoun County and joined the newly freed people of the Oatlands area in establishing a community they named Gleedsville. He and his father Robert worked as gardeners at Oatlands for the Carters and, later, the Eustises. In 1890, Martin Buchanan and John Gleed collected fieldstones from their farms for the foundation of a new church. With others in the community they built Mount Olive Methodist Episcopal Church. A few years later Buchanan married John Gleed's sister Amelia. The couple raised a family that today counts more than 350 descendants.

Resources

Lee, Deborah A. *African American Heritage Trail, Leesburg, Virginia.* Leesburg, Va.: The Loudoun Museum and the Friends of the Thomas Balch Library, 2002. Text available at *www.balchfriends.org/bhmap.htm*

Catrice R. Montgomery. "The Robert Buchanan Family Home Page." *familytreemaker.genealogy.com/users/m/o/n/Catrice--R-Montgomery/index.html*

John Lamb. "2nd U.S. Colored Troops." In*The Second Maryland Infantry, U.S.A. & Maryland in the Civil War. www.2ndmdinfantryus.org/USCT2.html*

Mount Olive Baptist Church. Grace Methodist Church and the shared cemetery appear above the sign.

Goose Creek Rural Historic District

③⑦

THINGS TO DO AND SEE	Viewable from the road
DESIGNATIONS	National Register of Historic Places
LOCATION	Routes 611, 728, 622, 704, 709 and the village of Lincoln, VA
	Mount Olive Baptist Church is located on Cooksville Road in Lincoln

Quakers from Pennsylvania and nearby Waterford, Virginia, settled here beginning in 1745 and formed a community that was hospitable to free African Americans. Quakers hired men for farm labor and women for domestic work. A few black students attended the Oakdale School, established in 1815. In 1824, antislavery Quakers met in the building and founded the Loudoun Manumission and Emigration Society. In 1827 they hosted the First Virginia Convention for the Abolition of Slavery. In the antebellum period, Goose Creek was a center of Underground Railroad activity. During the Civil War, most residents of the area remained loyal to the Union. During Reconstruction, with the help of the Freedmen's Bureau, they built a stone school for black children. African Americans established two religious congregations in the village of Lincoln; Methodists in 1872 and Baptists in 1879. Using local fieldstone, they constructed Grace Methodist Church in 1884/85 and Mount Olive Baptist in 1884. Their cemeteries adjoin. Mount Olive still has an active congregation, but Grace's moved to Purcellville—Grace Annex—in 1951, since most of their members lived there.

PEOPLE IN THE PLACES — James R. Hicks (1845–1933)

The home of James R. Hicks in nearby North Fork. *(Virginia Department of Historic Resources)*

James Hicks fashioned his world with care, as he did the shoes he crafted to compensate for his shorter leg. Born to Letitia Hicks in Philomont, Virginia, enslaved until 1865 in the household of a Methodist minister, James managed six years of formal schooling besides learning the shoemaking trade. In 1878 he married Laurinda Murray. They never had children, but they showed special affection for nephew J. Walter Brown, who became a teacher in Hamilton. James Hicks tended his community as well; in 1883 he represented it in a "Colored Mass Meeting" held at the courthouse in Leesburg. Delegates petitioned for rights regularly denied, such as serving as jurors and election officials, though they didn't accomplish their goal. In 1890 Hicks led in founding the Loudoun County Emancipation Association, established to commemorate Emancipation Day and work for racial uplift. In addition to civic leader, Hicks was an astute farmer, tradesman, and businessman. By 1900 he had clear title to a house and farm on Lincoln Road and a cobbler's shop and orchard in nearby North Fork. In 1911 he also owned a house in Lincoln. Beginning in 1905, Hicks combined his civic and business interests as he shepherded the Emancipation Association into becoming a shareholding corporation and purchasing land in Purcellville. In 1925 he lobbied for the organization to offer the site to the Loudoun County School Board for a high school. The board did not approve, but his efforts demonstrate his vision and commitment to education and equality.

Resources

Elaine E. Thompson. "James Hicks." In *The Essence of a People II: African Americans Who Made Their World Anew in Loudoun County, Virginia, and Beyond.* Edited by Kendra Y. Hamilton. Leesburg, Va.: Black History Committee of the Friends of the Thomas Balch Library, 2002.

Loudoun County Courthouse

Loudoun County Courthouse

38

HISTORIC SITE	Viewable from the street
THINGS TO DO AND SEE	Working courthouse
DESIGNATIONS	National Register of Historic Places
	National Park Service, National Underground Railroad Network to Freedom Site
LOCATION	Corner of King and Market Streets, Leesburg, VA
CONTACT INFORMATION	(703) 777-0270
ON THE WEB	www.loudown.gov

Three brick courthouses—dating from 1761, 1811, and 1895—have served Loudoun County on this same site. Slave auctions were once held on the steps. Today the building is recognized for its role in the struggle for freedom and equality. The National Park Service designated the Loudoun County Courthouse as an Underground Railroad Network to Freedom site because two free black men were tried here for helping women and children escape from slavery. In 1883, African Americans petitioned for their rights and, fifty years later, Charles Hamilton Houston became the first African American attorney to argue a major case in a southern courtroom.

Resources

Friends of the Thomas Balch Library. "The National Underground Railroad Network to Freedom: The Loudoun County Courthouse." *www.balchfriends.org/Glimpse/URNCourt.htm*

Leonard A. Grimes   (1815–1874)

Leonard A. Grimes

Leonard Grimes, a free black man, operated a successful hackney carriage business—similar to today's taxi service—in Washington, D.C. in the 1830s. Grimes also helped people escape from slavery, and became an early organizer of the Underground Railroad. In 1839 authorities arrested Grimes and charged him with aiding a woman named Patty and her six children flee from slavery in Loudoun County. Prosecutors tried Grimes at the courthouse in Leesburg in early 1840. Noted attorneys argued his case and prominent white patrons from Washington testified to his good character. Grimes was found guilty but given the lightest sentence possible: two years in prison in Richmond.

After his release Leonard Grimes became a minister, moved with his family to Massachusetts, and became pastor of Twelfth Baptist Church in Boston. It became known as "the Fugitive's Church," since it helped people fleeing slavery. One member, Anthony Burns, attracted national attention when authorities captured and re-enslaved him. When Grimes and members of his congregation could not free him from jail or secure his release through the courts, they raised money to purchase him from his owner in Virginia.

During the Civil War, Grimes led a delegation of ministers who met with President Abraham Lincoln. They asked for and received Lincoln's promise of official protection as they went South and ministered to refugees from slavery in the Union lines. Grimes also lobbied the government to allow black soldiers to fight for the Union and, when successful, recruited for the Army. After general emancipation he helped freed people improve their lives. Even though he lived most of his life in the North, Grimes dedicated himself to people of the South in various ways. Through his work, he became a widely-know and highly respected statesman as well as clergyman. At Boston's day-long memorial for Abraham Lincoln, he rode in the carriage of dignitaries during the procession and delivered the closing benediction at the service.

Resources

Lee, Deborah A. "Leonard Andrew Grimes" in *The Essence of A People II: African Americans Who Made Their World Anew in Loudoun County, Virginia, and Beyond.* Kendra Y. Hamilton, ed. Leesburg: Black History Committee of the Friends of the Thomas Balch Library, 2002.

Friends of the Thomas Balch Library. *A Glimpse into the History of African Americans in Loudoun County.* www.balchfriends.org/Glimpse/lgrimes.htm

PEOPLE
· IN THE ·
PLACES

Nelson T. Gant

(1822–1905)

N elson Gant was liberated in 1845 when John Nixon emancipated him in his will and provided money for the resettlement of Gant and other freed people in Ohio. But Gant was reluctant to leave Loudoun County, as his wife Maria remained enslaved in Leesburg. Gant worked hard for the year he was allowed to stay in Virginia and tried to purchase his wife, but her owner Jane Russell refused. He joined his family and friends in Zanesville, Ohio, and became acquainted with abolitionists there. He raised more money and returned to Virginia, staying for a time with Underground Railroad activist Dr. Julius LeMoyne in Washington, Pennsylvania, where he met Martin Delany. Russell still refused Gant's

Nelson T. Gant.
(Zanesville Times-Recorder)

offer, and the couple disappeared. They were betrayed by a black man and arrested in Washington, D.C., then transported to Leesburg for trial. Prominent attorneys, including John Janney (later president of Virginia's secession convention), argued that, because Maria's mistress allowed the couple to be married by a minister, she could not testify against her husband. This decision, that the holy law of matrimony trumped the customs of slaveholding, marked the height of antislavery sentiment in Loudoun County. Nelson and Maria Gant were released and local Quakers helped finance her purchase. The couple worked off the debt on a farm near Goose Creek and then moved to Zanesville, Ohio. There, Nelson Gant served as a conductor on the Underground Railroad, became an innovative farmer, successful businessman, and a lay leader in the African Methodist Episcopal Church.

Resources

Friends of the Thomas Balch Library. *A Glimpse into the History of African Americans in Loudoun County.* "The National Underground Railroad Network to Freedom: The Loudoun County Courthouse." *www.balchfriends.org/Glimpse/URNCourt.htm*

Ohio Cultural Facilities Commission. Nelson T. Gant Homestead. *culture.ohio.gov/project.asp?proj=nelson*

Loudoun County Courthouse

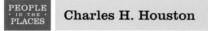

| PEOPLE • IN THE • PLACES | **Charles H. Houston** | (1895-1950) |

Charles Houston *(second from left)* with NAACP executive secretary Walter White *(far left)* and other NAACP attorneys in 1933. *(NAACP Records, Library of Congress)*

In 1933 at the Loudoun County Courthouse, Charles Houston became the first African American attorney to argue a major case in a southern courtroom. The case reveals the deep roots of the civil rights movement of the 1960s. A black man, George Crawford, was arrested for the murder in 1932 of Middleburg socialite Agnes Illsley and her maid Mina Buckner. The NAACP had engaged Charles Hamilton Houston, the vice dean of the Howard University Law School, to head its legal defense team and it was looking for a case that would highlight inequities in the legal system. Although Crawford was convicted—by the time of his trial almost everyone thought he was guilty—the case was considered an important legal victory for Houston and the NAACP. Houston proved that black citizens were barred from serving on juries and Crawford was given life in prison instead of the expected death penalty. Additionally, the defense team was all black; another civil rights milestone in the South.

Charles Houston became known as "the man who killed Jim Crow." His legal strategy led to *Brown v. Board of Education* and the Supreme Court decision that segregated schools were not equal.

Resources

McNeil, Genna Rae. *Groundwork: Charles Hamilton Houston and the Struggle for Civil Rights.* Philadelphia: University of Pennsylvania Press, 1983.

Kluger, Richard. *Simple Justice: The History of* Brown v. Board of Education *and Black America's Struggle for Equality.* 1975. New York: Vintage Books, 2004.

Friends of the Thomas Balch Library. *A Glimpse into the History of African Americans in Loudoun County.* "Essential Understandings and Their Supporting Documents," Section 6. *www.balchfriends.org/Glimpse/EssUnderstanding.htm*

Howard University School of Law. Brown @ *50: Fulfilling the Promise.* *www.brownat50.org/brownBios/BioCharlesHHouston.html*

Library of Congress. *With an Even Hand:* Brown v. Board *at Fifty. www.loc.gov/exhibits/brown*

Letter from Mars Lucas, who was emancipated from slavery and emigrated to Liberia. *(Loudoun Museum)*

Loudoun Museum

HISTORIC SITE	Open to the public
THINGS TO DO AND SEE	Offers changing exhibits of Loudoun County history. Also provides maps and walking tours.
DESIGNATIONS	National Historic District
LOCATION	16 Loudoun St., Leesburg, VA
CONTACT INFORMATION	(703) 777-7427 info@loudounmuseum.org
ON THE WEB	www.loudounmuseum.org

Black-owned businesses once flourished in the building now occupied by the Loudoun Museum. In the 1920s Nathan Johnson operated a butcher shop; it later became a restaurant called the Dew Drop Inn. Patrons climbed the stairs inside to visit a beauty shop and a doctor. Other buildings that stood along the block were black-owned. One large house was moved to Church Street for the construction of the parking garage. It was subsequently named for John W. Tolbert, who became the first black member of the Leesburg Town Council in 1976 and served for fourteen years. Further down the block, Robinson's Barber Shop remains in business.

Loudoun Museum collections feature letters exchanged in the 1830s between brothers Mars and Jesse Lucas in Liberia and their emancipators in Purcellville, brothers Albert and Townsend Heaton. Exhibitions include

Loudoun Museum

African American history, such as information on John W. Jones, who escaped from slavery in Loudoun County and became a prominent Underground Railroad stationmaster in Elmira, New York.

Resources

Deborah A. Lee. *African American Heritage Trail, Leesburg, Virginia.* Leesburg, Va.: Loudoun Museum and Black History Committee, Friends of Thomas Balch Library, 2002.

Loudoun Museum. "The Lucas-Heaton Letters." *www.loudounmuseum.org/collectn.html*

| PEOPLE IN THE PLACES | John W. Jones | (1817–1900) |

In 1844, at the age of twenty-seven, Jones, his two younger brothers, and two other men escaped from slavery in Loudoun County. They traveled north almost 300 miles along the Old Carolina Road and settled in Elmira, New York. Jones found work as a sexton there, maintaining the Baptist church and burying the dead in the cemetery. He also married and had children. Additionally, with funding from prominent whites such as Jervis Langdon, Jones ushered around 800 other refugees from slavery onto the train bound for St. Catherine's, Canada. He kept in touch with friends in the South and received communication about freedom seekers.

During the Civil War, the federal government established a Confederate prison camp in Elmira. John Jones buried the dead in neat rows and kept careful records. One casualty he recognized as his former overseer's son, and Jones notified the family. After Lincoln's Emancipation Proclamation, Jones invited his sister in Loudoun to live with him, and she moved to Elmira with her children. After the war, Jones visited his old home place where he was received as a guest. Families of the prisoners he had buried traveled to Elmira, but most chose to leave their loved ones interred at Woodlawn Cemetery. Jones saved enough money to purchase first a house near the church and later a farm on the edge of town. His house, moved to a spot near Woodlawn Cemetery, has been preserved as a museum.

Resources

Black History Committee of the Friends of the Thomas Balch Library. "John W. Jones." *In The Essence of a People: Portraits of African Americans Who Made a Difference in Loudoun County, Virginia.* Friends of the Thomas Balch Library, 2001.

The opening of the
Marshall Street
Community Center
in 1950
(Courtesy Howard Allen)

Middleburg
Historic District

40

HISTORIC SITE	Open to the public
THINGS TO DO AND SEE	Middleburg's visitor center, the Pink Box, is located at 12 Madison St. Open Monday to Friday from 11 AM to 3 PM, Saturday and Sunday from 11 AM to 4 PM. Stop by to pick up a self-guided book tour
DESIGNATIONS	National Register of Historic Places
	National Historic District
LOCATION	10 West Marshall St., Middleburg, VA
CONTACT INFORMATION	(540) 687-5152 • (540) 687-8888
ON THE WEB	www.middleburg.org

African Americans were among Middleburg's earliest inhabitants; as enslaved or free laborers and skilled craftsmen they built many of its structures, tilled the soil on surrounding farms, and tended its livestock. When freedom came to all after the Civil War, many continued their occupations and passed their knowledge on to succeeding generations. In the twentieth century, some men continued trades as stonemasons, general contractors, blacksmiths, and horsemen, while women worked as cooks, caterers, domestic workers, midwives, and seamstresses. Community life centered around the town's two churches, Asbury Methodist, built in 1829 and assumed by African Americans in 1864, and Shiloh Baptist, whose congregation organized in 1867 and built the present structure in 1913. A Freedmen's Bureau office was located on the corner of Marshall and North Jay streets, which became known as Bureau Corner, anchored by the Grant School.

By the 1930s and 1940s, the town was largely African American. For the town's bicentennial in 1987, resident Johnnie T. Smith recalled a score of black-owned businesses from that era, including a barbershop, two beauty shops, restaurants, a pool hall, three taxicabs, three general contractors, a tailor, chair caner, and a blacksmith shop. Maurice Edmead Sr., M.D., treated some white as well as black patients. Chauncey Brown, who grew up just east of Middleburg, was a popular musician at society events. William Nathaniel Hall, the largest general contractor in Loudoun County and the only one licensed and bonded, built the original Middleburg Bank, a new wing on the Leesburg hospital, and reconstructed George Washington's Gristmill. He owned property east of town, known as Hall's Park, where the community gathered for picnics, ballgames, horse shows and celebrations. On Memorial Day and July 4th, events at the park followed a parade through town. After Banneker Elementary School was opened in 1948, the Grant School location became the Marshall Street Community Center for recreation, entertainment, and education.

Resources

Johnnie T. Smith. "Why Did We Lose So Much in 44 Years?." In *Middleburg Mystique,* edited by Vicky Moon. Sterling, Va. Capital Books, Inc., 2001.

Maral S. Kalbian and Leila O. W. Boyer. *Destination Middleburg: A Walking Tour Into the Past: Middleburg, Virginia.* Middleburg, Va.: Middleburg Beautification and Preservation, Inc., 2001.

Deborah A. Lee. *Loudoun County's African American Communities: A Tour Map & Guide.* Leesburg, Va.: Black History Committee, Friends of the Thomas Balch Library, 2004.

PEOPLE IN THE PLACES | **Frank Wanzer** (c. 1830–?)

The Wanzer party, from William Still's book, *The Underground Rail Road.*

Loudoun County's most dramatic escape from slavery began near Middleburg on Christmas Eve in 1855. Elizabeth Grigsby, her husband Barnaby Grigsby, her sister Emily Foster, and Emily's fiancé Frank Wanzer procured a horse and wagon and drove north. Since it was the holiday season, and enslaved people were often granted leave to visit relatives, they thought their chances of successfully escaping were better then. Two men on horseback from neighboring Fauquier County accompanied them. Probably traveling the Carolina Road, they were near Frederick, Maryland, when a group of white men tried to accost them.

The freedom seekers drew guns and demanded that the men allow them to continue on their journey. At first they did, but then the white men opened fire, killing one of the men on horseback and capturing the other. The two couples continued on to Philadelphia, where they met William Still, the son of slaves and acknowledged "president of the Underground Railroad." Frank and Emily were married and the two couples continued on to Canada. The next year, however, Frank Wanzer risked his freedom and his life to return to Middleburg for other members of his family.

Resources

William Still. *The Underground Rail Road*. Philadelphia: Porter and Coates, 1872. Available online at *www.quinnipiac.edu/other/ABL/etext/ugrr/ugrrmain.html*

PEOPLE
· IN THE ·
PLACES
John Wesley Wanzer   (1888–1957)

John Wanzer in his blacksmith shop, with Charles Fisher. *(Courtesy Howard Allen)*

John Wanzer, the fifth child of fourteen in his family, grew up in Middleburg, attended Grant School, and worked hard from an early age. He apprenticed to blacksmith and wheelwright Will Mitchell and bought the business after a few years. When the building burned he built a new one of stone and opened a hardware store besides. Although John Wanzer and his wife Frances Hall did not have children, he valued education and deplored the substandard conditions of the black schools in Loudoun County during segregation. When an initiative began to press for a full and accredited high school for black youth, Wanzer signed on as president of the County-Wide League of parents, teachers, and others. Activists then risked losing their jobs. Wanzer was a self-employed, successful businessman with little competition, but some white clients boycotted his business. The County-Wide League enlisted the help of civil rights attorney Charles Hamilton Houston and the initiative was successful in 1941. In 1948 Wanzer was among citizens demanding that a new consolidated school for black children be named for an African American, inventor Benjamin Banneker. Wanzer was a member of the Loudoun branch of the NAACP and a trustee of Aberdeen Lodge of the Grand United Order of Odd Fellows.

Resources

Black History Committee of the Friends of the Thomas Balch Library. "John Wesley Wanzer." In *The Essence of a People: Portraits of African Americans Who Made a Difference in Loudoun County, Virginia*. Friends of the Thomas Balch Library, 2001.

The dependencies at Oatlands likely held kitchen and laundry facilities. Some enslaved workers may have lived there as well.

41

Oatlands

George Carter, the owner of Oatlands, was one of Loudoun County's wealthiest men and largest slaveholders. He insisted that white tradesmen and laborers build his house and operate his mill, but he relied heavily on enslaved labor to operate his estate. Carter supported the institution of slavery despite his father Robert Carter's opposition and manumission of

HISTORIC SITE	Open to the public
THINGS TO DO AND SEE	Tour the 22-room Greek Revival house that was once the center of a thriving 3,400-acre plantation. Meander through four acres of formal gardens and connecting terraces. Marvel at the 1810 greenhouse, the second oldest of its type in America.
DESIGNATIONS	National Register of Historic Places
National Historic Landmark
National Historic District
LOCATION	20850 Oatlands Plantation Lane Leesburg, VA
CONTACT INFORMATION	(703) 777-3174
ON THE WEB	www.oatlands.org

more than five hundred slaves. Some of George Carter's bondmen and women eloped to the North in search of freedom. By 1818, Carter complained of "struggling with the most enthusiastic and invincible opposition in the recovery of my property, from the Quakers and others … The sneers, the contempt, and scorn of the whole mass of aiders, advisors, and accomplices of runaway slaves, who are now triumphing at my shame." In recognition of the freedom seekers, Oatlands is a site in the National Park Service's Underground Railroad Network to Freedom Program.

After the Civil War and general emancipation, some African Americans in Loudoun County migrated north and west, but many of those who worked at Oatlands chose to remain and established the community of Gleedsville nearby.

Throughout its history under private ownership, enslaved and free African American workers shaped and cultivated the gardens, tilled fields, and cared for livestock. They also tended the house and furnishings, cooked and served meals to the estate owners and their numerous guests, drove carriages and automobiles, and supported the socially-prominent owners from the Carters to the Eustises.

Resources

National Park Service. National Underground Railroad Network to Freedom nomination. Available online at *www.balchfriends.org/Glimpse/URNOatlands.htm*

Claudia Jellet. "The Rise and Fall of the Carter Family at Oatlands, Loudoun County, Va." M.A. Thesis, Dalhousie University, Nova Scotia, 1993. [Copy available at Thomas Balch Library, Leesburg, Va.]

PEOPLE IN THE PLACES

William Jordan Augustus (c. 1779–?)

Ten Dollars Reward.

RAN AWAY from the subscriber, on the first instant, a Mulatto Man, a slave, named BILLY, sometimes calls himself *William Jordan Augustus*—his color nearly as light and approaches that of a whiteman—his hair is straight and he generally wears it platted and turned up behind with a comb—his visage is remarkably thin, and his cheek bones high—he has been brought up in the house and is a very good dining room servant—is about 5 feet 10 or 11 inches high, very straight built—his constitution is not strong and he is subject to indisposition—is about 30 years of age. I cannot describe any part of his cloathing, except that he wore a blue coat and a silver watch.—As Billy is related to some mulattos emancipated by *R. B. Lee*, Esq. who live in the neighborhood of Alexandria and George-Town, the probability is that he is to be found in that neighborhood. I will give the above reward and reasonable charges if brought home.

George Carter.

Oatlands, near Leesburg,
February 4—[8]   3t

Alexandria Gazette, February 8, 1809.

William Jordan Augustus—whom George Carter knew as his slave "Billy"—was a man of refinement and ambition, and was about thirty years old when he left Oatlands on February 1, 1809 to obtain his freedom. Raised in the manor house, Carter valued him as "a very good dining-room servant." Tall, straight, and fair, with a thin face and high cheekbones, Augustus usually wore his hair "plaited and turned up behind with a comb." He escaped with a forty-five year old woman called Nelly. Carter felt humiliated and injured by Augustus's elopement, and in another ad in May, offered $100 (the equivalent of more than $1,000 today) for his capture north of the Potomac River. Augustus was successful in his bid for freedom, although he was captured in Philadelphia in 1817 and jailed in Baltimore. Before Carter could retrieve him and sell him to a Georgia slave trader, Dr. John Arnest, the husband of Carter's niece Anna Arnest, arranged for his release, claiming that Carter had given "Billy" to Anna. George Carter was incensed and denied any such gift, but Augustus remained free.

Resources

(Leesburg, Va.) *Genius of Liberty,* February 8 and May 13, 1809.

George Carter to Edmund McGinnis, May 11, 1814; to Thomas Maund, Sept. 25, 1817; and to John Arnest, Nov. 20[?], 1817. *George Carter Letterbook.* Virginia Historical Society, Richmond, Va.

PEOPLE IN THE PLACES | **Basil Turner**   (c. 1843–early 1930s)

Basil Turner. *(Courtesy Oatlands)*

Basil Turner first worked at Oatlands as a slave under George Carter's widow Elizabeth Carter, but chose to remain and work for wages after general emancipation in 1865. He helped shepherd the estate through the tenures of Elizabeth Carter; her son George and his wife Kate during and after the Civil War, when it was a summer boarding house; absentee owner Stilson Hutchins; and finally, William Corcoran and Edith Morton Eustis beginning in 1903.

It is a testament to his regard for Oatlands that Basil Turner married 21-year-old Frances Day there on April 27, 1871. A minister from First Mount Olive Baptist Church in Leesburg performed the ceremony. The couple lived nearby in the vicinity of Gleedsville, and they raised two sons and four daughters. In the years before his death in the early 1930s, Basil Turner lived with his son Oden.

Resources

Friends of the Thomas Balch Library. "Basil Turner." In *A Glimpse into the History of African Americans in Loudoun County.* Available online at *www.balchfriends.org/Glimpse/bturnerIM.htm.*

Carver School, once the heart of Purcellville's black community, is now a community/senior center.

Purcellville Historic District

42

HISTORIC SITE	Open to the public
THINGS TO DO AND SEE	The historic downtown has at its center a restored train station, the site of the local Farmers Market. View the charming turn-of-the-century homes or visit nearby farms where you can pick-your-own fruits, vegetables, herbs, and flowers.
DESIGNATIONS	National Register of Historic Places
LOCATION	130 East Main St., Purcellville, VA
ON THE WEB	www.purcellvilleva.com

Purcellville's black community developed on the south side of the town along G Street, known to most residents as "the Color Line." After the Civil War, a Quaker family named Birdsall sold small lots of land there to Freedmen from Loudoun County and beyond. Early black family names included Brown, Cook, Dade, Furr, Lee, Johnson, Simms, and Stewart. After someone bought a lot, the community helped them build their house, usually on weekends. Many members had construction expertise—some were engaged in building suburban Washington, D.C. The community included an active Elks Lodge. In 1910, the Loudoun County Emancipation Association (founded in Hamilton) bought ten acres on the corner of A and 20th Streets and established Lincoln Park. They built a tabernacle, organized Emancipation Day Celebrations, and hosted baseball games, Horse and Colt Shows, Field Day, ministers' conventions, and a host of other events. At first, black Purcellville residents walked two miles to the Quaker village of Lincoln for school and church. In 1919 residents formed a Willing Workers Club that borrowed money, purchased land, and built a school. They established a library there, too, since they were banned from the "public" library founded in town by Clarence Robey. In 1942, residents constructed Grace Annex Methodist Church. In 1948, Loudoun County built the larger brick Carver Elementary School that educated black students in the area through the seventh grade. Long used only for storage after the public schools were fully integrated in 1968, the beloved school reopened as a senior center in early 2007.

Resources

Deborah A. Lee. Loudoun County's African American Communities: A Tour Map & Guide. Leesburg, Va.: Black History Committee, Friends of the Thomas Balch Library, 2004.

Interview with Basham Simms by Deborah A. Lee, November 3, 2004. Thomas Balch Library.

PEOPLE
· IN THE ·
PLACES

Billy Pierce (1890–1933)

Sheet music for a dance Billy Pierce introduced on Broadway.
(StreetSwing.com Dance Archives)

In the early twentieth century there was little opportunity in Virginia for a man of color as talented and ambitious as Billy Pierce. Born in Purcellville, and educated at Storer College in Harpers Ferry, West Virginia, and Howard University in Washington, D.C., he also served in the Army during World War I. Pierce then worked as a newspaper editor in Washington and Chicago, but his real love was the arts. He performed for a time, dancing and playing the trombone or banjo, then opened the Broadway Dance Studio in New York City. He started small but soon attracted noted white clients such as Fred and Adele Astaire, and choreographed dances for Broadway shows. Trade magazines credited him with dances such as the Charleston and Black Bottom that became popular worldwide. They were part of the African American cultural flowering known as the Harlem Renaissance. In the early 1930s Pierce took a show of African American dance to European cities including London, Paris, and Rome. Despite his fame he held fondly to his roots. On the wall of his New York dance studio, he kept a large tinted photograph of his parents standing in front of their Purcellville home. He and his young family returned for an extended visit each summer. In 1929, a newspaperman reported that Pierce "comes back to Virginia annually to see his aged mother, and never fails to write down the steps observable in the breakdowns and barn dances of the Old Dominion." He died suddenly at the age of forty-three and returned home one last time to a large funeral service with memorials and visitors from afar. He was buried in his church's cemetery in Lincoln.

Resources

Elaine E. Thompson. "William Pierce." In The Essence of a People: African Americans Who Made Their World Anew in Loudoun County, Virginia and Beyond. Leesburg, Va.: Black History Committee, Friends of the Thomas Balch Library, 2002.

St. Louis

HISTORIC SITE	Viewable from the road
THINGS TO DO AND SEE	Properties are privately owned
LOCATION	Route 611, one mile north of Route 50 west of Middleburg

Former slaveholder Thomas Glascock sparked this settlement in 1881 when he subdivided land and offered one-acre lots for twenty dollars each. African Americans in the area, many of them freedmen from Glascock's and other local estates, seized the opportunity to become property owners. Perhaps the offer attracted Charles McQuay home from St. Louis, Missouri—it is said that his return inspired the settlement's name. Wormley Hughes, grandson of Thomas Jefferson's enslaved gardener at Monticello, helped residents establish St. Louis New School Baptist Church. They built a school in 1887 and worshipped there until they constructed a church in 1893, and adopted the name Mt. Zion Baptist Church. The congregation returned to the school when the church burned down around 1918, then rebuilt a church in 1929 that is still in use today. Around 1900, Charles McQuay and Shirley Smith organized the St. Louis Horse Show and established the village's reputation as a horse center. Many men in the community worked in the horse industry and some traveled on the national flat-racing and steeplechase circuits. Another fixture in St. Louis was Phil McQuay's store, which he operated for almost a half-century beginning around 1916. The Middleburg Training track gave the community a boost in the 1920s, as did the consolidated school for children of color, Banneker Elementary School, built in 1948. The old and new school both still stand, an enlarged training track is still in use. It is the largest African American village in Loudoun County; signs relating its history and significance welcome visitors at each end.

Resources

Deborah A. Lee, Loudoun County's *African American Communities: A Tour Map & Guide*. Leesburg, Va.: Black History Committee, Friends of the Thomas Balch Library, 2004.

John Wesley
Methodist Episcopal
Church
(Waterford Foundation)

Waterford Historic District

44

Slavery and freedom rubbed shoulders in Waterford. The settlement was founded by Quakers who witnessed against slavery, but slaveholders also lived in the vicinity and traded in the village. In the early nineteenth century, free blacks migrated to Waterford for work in the mill or tannery, to ply other trades such as blacksmithing and cooper-

HISTORIC SITE	Open to the public
THINGS TO DO AND SEE	Stop by the Waterford Foundation at the Corner Store on Main Street to get a walking tour booklet before exploring the village. Call ahead to schedule a guided tour.
DESIGNATIONS	National Register of Historic Places National Historic Landmark National Historic District
LOCATION	Clarke's Gap Rd., Waterford, VA
CONTACT INFORMATION	(540) 882-3018
ON THE WEB	*www.waterfordfoundation.org* *www.waterfordva.org*

ing, or to work on Quaker farms. Black women performed domestic work and practiced as midwives, delivering babies black and white. Some free blacks bought homes themselves in the village. At the same time, slaveholders bought and sold enslaved people at auctions on Main Street. During the Civil War, Waterford sympathized with the Union and organized a federal cavalry unit, the Loudoun Rangers. At least one free black man of Waterford, Daniel Webster Minor, joined as an auxiliary, and several other Waterford men of color fought in other Union regiments. In 1866, just after the war, African Americans, with the help of Quakers, bought a lot and erected a building they used as a church and school. The Freedmen's Bureau assisted in its early operation. From the 1870s until 1957, it was a Loudoun County Public School. In 1885, black men organized an Odd Fellows Lodge and built a hall on Big Hill. In 1891, after years of meeting in the school, black Methodists built John Wesley Church on Main Street overlooking the mill. In the first half of the twentieth century, African Americans made up a large part of the village's population, but gradually they moved away, as did most of the white residents from the same era.

The Waterford Foundation has extensively researched the village's African American history. It shares the information through publications, including a walking tour, and a living history program at the Second Street School for fourth-grade students.

Resources

Souders, Bronwen C. and John M. A Rock in *A Weary Land, A Shelter in a Time of Storm: African-American Experience in Waterford, Virginia.* Waterford, Va.: Waterford Foundation, 2003.

_____. "Waterford's African American Experience." In the History of Waterford. *www.waterfordhistory.org/history/waterford-african-american.htm*

Waterford Foundation. *Share With Us: Waterford, Virginia's African-American Heritage: An Interpretive Guide to Your National Historic Landmark.* Waterford Foundation, 2002.

_____. "The School on Second Street." *www.waterfordva.org/education/sss.shtml*

PEOPLE · IN THE · PLACES   ## Joseph R. Winters   (1830–1907)

THE AUTOGRAPHICAL WRITINGS
—OF—
JOSEPH R. WINTER.
Written ten days after the Battle of Gettysburg.
Now in my 90th year, having been born in Leesburg, Virginia, on the 29th of August 1810. Came to this town on the 14th of November 1830 when the town was known as Chamberstown. I am the oldest man in town today.
INDIAN DICK or JOSEPH WINTER.

Advertising card. *(Franklin County Historical Society-Kittochtinny, Chambersburg, PA)*

Joseph R. Winters invented and patented an improved fire escape ladder in 1878, and for that he is still known today. But his early life is also noteworthy. According to family tradition, Winters was the great-great-grandson (on his father's side) of Powhatan chief Opechancanough. Joseph began his life in Leesburg, but in 1834 his free parents left Joseph with his maternal grandmother, Betsy Cross, in Waterford, where she had been born in 1767. Of Shawnee ancestry, Cross was known as the "Indian Doctor woman" and she passed on some of her knowledge to her grandson. Joseph's father James made bricks at Harpers Ferry for the expansion of the

Waterford Historic District

federal gun factory and arsenal there, which began in 1845. He went to visit his parents, but they would not allow his return and put him to work sanding brick molds. The family later moved to Chambersburg, Pennsylvania, and grandmother Cross joined them there. In 1859, Joseph Winters arranged the meeting between Frederick Douglass and John Brown at the quarry in Chambersburg. A machinist for the Cumberland Valley Railroad, Winters also wrote poetry and an autobiography. Black and white residents long remembered him for his great knowledge of nature and his skills in fishing and fly making. He received much praise but little money from his innovative fire escape design.

Resources

Edna Christian Knapper. "Outstanding Colored Citizens of Chambersburg—Past and Present: Joe Winters." In *John Brown Mysteries: Allies for Freedom,* ed. Jean Libby. Missoula, Mont.: Pictorial Histories, 1999. First published in [Chambersburg, Penn.] Public Opinion, 1954.

About: Inventors. "Joseph R. Winters." *inventors.about.com/library/inventors/bl_Joseph_Winters.htm*

Prince William County
VIRGINIA

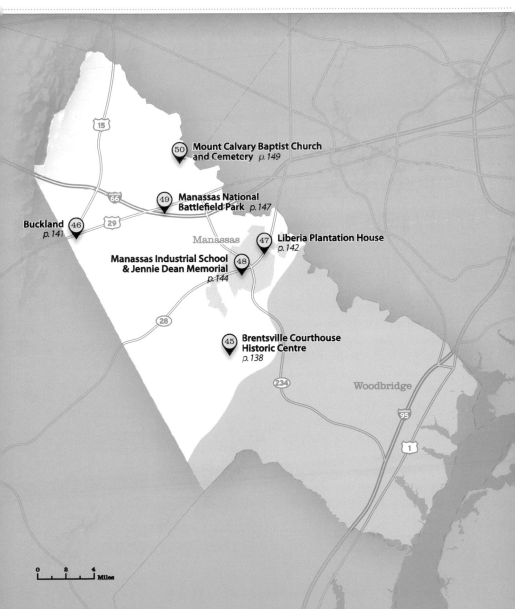

PA

WV

MD

VA

15

50 **Mount Calvary Baptist Church and Cemetery** *p. 149*

66

49 **Manassas National Battlefield Park** *p. 147*

Buckland 46
p. 141

29

Manassas

47 **Liberia Plantation House** *p. 142*

Manassas Industrial School & Jennie Dean Memorial *p. 144* 48

28

45 **Brentsville Courthouse Historic Centre** *p. 138*

234

Woodbridge

95

1

0   2   4
Miles

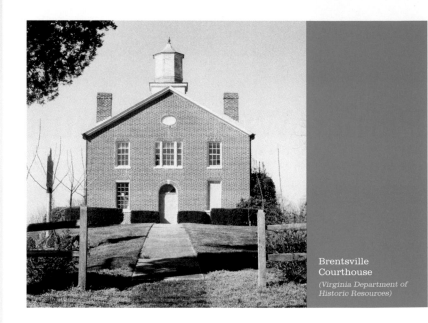

Brentsville
Courthouse

*(Virginia Department of
Historic Resources)*

Brentsville Courthouse Historic Centre

45

During the 1700s, the population of Prince William County expanded westward, cultivated new farmland, and built new towns. In 1820 the Virginia General Assembly decided to move the county seat from Dumfries to the west along the busy Bristow toll road. They divided six acres of land confiscated from British loyalists after the Revolutionary War into lots and built a brick courthouse and jail. By 1835, according to the Virginia Gazetteer, the village contained "19 dwelling

HISTORIC SITE	Historic properties owned and administered by Prince William County Department of Public Works, Historic Preservation Division
THINGS TO DO AND SEE	The Brentsville Courthouse and jail, both built in 1822 Brentsville Union Church, c. 1874 John Hall Cabin, c. 1825 A one-room schoolhouse c. 1928 Surrounding homes are privately owned. Currently the site is open every day, from sunrise to sunset with self-guided history and nature trails available. Site is open for tours May-October, Saturday – Sunday, 11 AM – 4 PM. Other tours can be scheduled by request.
DESIGNATIONS	Brentsville Courthouse and jail: National Register of Historic Places, Virginia Historic Landmark.
LOCATION	12229 Bristow Rd., Bristow, VA
CONTACT INFORMATION	(703) 365-7895
ON THE WEB	www.co.prince-william.va.us

houses, 3 miscellaneous stores, 2 handsome taverns built of brick and stock, 1 house of entertainment, 1 house of public worship, free for all denominations, a bible society, a Sunday school, a temperance and a tract society...population 130 persons, of whom 3 are attorneys and 3 are regular physicians." Brentsville remained the county seat until 1893 when it was moved to Manassas, by then a larger town with better railroad access. The historic centre also contains Brentsville Union Church, built around 1874, and a one-room schoolhouse from about 1928.

In 1810, African Americans comprised about half of Prince William County's population. Enslaved and free people of color lived and worked in the small courthouse town of Brentsville from its inception. During the 1820s, for example, at Hampton's hotel and tavern, freeborn James Robinson waited tables. He saved as much as he could and invested in property in Brentsville and near Manassas. His farm became part of the battlefield in 1862.

African Americans suspected of escaping slavery were confined in the jail. In 1833 a local physician treated an inmate named Billy on three successive days. That same year William Hayden, a free black man from New York, was arrested and sold into slavery. The buyer could not pay, so Hayden remained in the jail for almost a year, when he managed to escape. In 1839, Landon from Fauquier County attempted to burn down the jail during his tenure; he was convicted of arson and sentenced to death by hanging.

As sectional tensions over slavery increased, white people were sometimes prosecuted for challenging the right to own slaves. In 1857, "Crawford," who declared himself an Abolitionist, and John Underwood, a justice of the peace who spoke out against slavery, were both convicted and fined. Black abolitionist Dangerfield Newby tried unsuccessfully to purchase his wife from slavery after her owner, Dr. Louis A. Jennings, moved her and the Newby children, along with his own family, to Brentsville. In his frustration, Newby joined John Brown in the raid on Harpers Ferry in 1859. He was the first of Brown's men to die.

Resources

Underground Railroad Network to Freedom Nomination, 2007.

Prince William County, Virginia. *Brentsville Courthouse Historic Centre Trust Project.* www.co.prince-william.va.us/default.aspx?topic=040110001690000792

Brentsville Courthouse Historic Centre

PEOPLE · IN THE · PLACES   Harriet Newby

"**O**h, Dear Dangerfield," Harriet Newby wrote her husband, "com this fall without fail, monny or no monny. I want to see you so much." Dangerfield Newby, newly freed himself, was working in Ohio to obtain money to purchase his wife from slavery in Prince William County, Virginia. Unfortunately, he could not raise enough or Harriet's owner refused to sell. Desperate, Dangerfield Newby joined John Brown for the raid on Harpers Ferry. In papers found at the Maryland farmhouse where Brown and his men had stayed, officials found three poignant letters from Harriet Newby to her husband. They carried news of their children, including the baby, "who commenced to crall today" and pleas for their reunion. Dangerfield Newby was the first of Brown's men killed at Harpers Ferry. Harriet Newby and their three youngest children were sold and taken to Louisiana. After General Emancipation she married William Robinson, a freedman born in Berkeley County, (West) Virginia. The couple moved to Fairfax County, Virginia, and had additional children together.

Resources

Sherrie Carter. "Who We Are: A Story of Strong and Lasting Roots of Black Fauquier County Families." Manuscript in possession of the author, 2007.

Schwarz, Philip. "The Newby Families in Virginia and Ohio." Chapter 7 in *Migrants Against Slavery: Virginians and the Nation*. Carter G. Woodson Institute Series in Black Studies. University of Virginia Press, 2001.

Ned Distiller's house

Buckland

HISTORIC SITE	Open to the public
THINGS TO DO AND SEE	Historic Marker
DESIGNATIONS	National Register of Historic Places
LOCATION	Buckland Mill Rd. and Route 29, Buckland, VA
ON THE WEB	www.nps.gov/history/nr/travel/ journey/buc.htm

Free and enslaved African Americans worked in the industries, homes, and on the farms of this prosperous stagecoach and industrial community. Samuel King, a free man of color purchased his wife and manumitted her in 1811. She operated the tollhouse on the turnpike in Buckland. Ned Distiller, a free man of color, operated the distillery in town and owned a home in Buckland in 1820. By 1835, according to the Virginia Gazetteer, the population numbered 185 people, 50 of them black.

Resources

David William Blake. "Buckland: A Virginia Time Capsule." *Prince William Reliquary 3*, no. 1 (Jan. 2004): 1-7. www.pwcgov.org/docLibrary/PDF/002613.pdf

Liberia
Plantation House

Liberia Plantation House

With slave labor, William J. and Harriet Weir built a federal style brick mansion and operated a farm near Manassas that they named Liberia. The name highlights Weir's ambivalence about slavery—he supported general emancipation with resettlement of former slaves in Liberia, Africa. He also vot-

HISTORIC SITE	Historic property owned and administered by the Manassas Museum
THINGS TO DO AND SEE	The historic home is undergoing restoration but is open to the public for special events and group tours
DESIGNATIONS	National Register of Historic Places
LOCATION	8601 Portner Ave. Manassas, VA
CONTACT INFORMATION	(703) 368-1873
ON THE WEB	www.manassascity.org/ index.aspx?NID=221

ed against secession in 1861, but two of his sons fought in the Confederate Army. In 1860, eighty enslaved people lived at Liberia. Among them were Nellie Naylor and her seven children. Her husband Samuel had purchased his freedom and worked for the Weirs. Their son Cornelius "Neil" operated a gristmill nearby that Weir also owned.

During the Civil War, William and Harriet Weir moved to Fluvanna County for safety. Twenty-two enslaved people accompanied them, including the Naylor's daughter Sallie. Other slaves were sent farther South, some seized the opportunity for freedom behind Union lines, while some black workers—likely including Samuel, Nellie, and Neil Naylor—stayed on at Liberia and managed the property during the owners' absence. At different times the house served as headquarters for Union and Confederate armies; presidents Abraham Lincoln and Jefferson Davis both visited there. Unlike most of the homes and farms in the area, Liberia passed through the war in good condition. In November 1865, after the Weirs returned, Samuel Naylor bought over fifty acres of land from them in exchange for $500 he managed to save. The Weirs gave Nellie another twelve acres in recognition of "the love and affection they have for their faithful servant." The Naylor children eventually inherited the property, though most moved away. Sallie Naylor Randolph inherited the family house on Centreville Road and lived there in 1920.

Resources

Charlotte Cain, "Divided Loyalties: An Account of the Family of William J. Weir During the Civil War." *Prince William Reliquary 3*, no. 3 (July 2004): 55-61. *www.pwcgov.org/library/relic/PDF/PWR_7-2004_Liberia.pdf*

_____ . "The Descendants of Samuel and Nellie Naylor, an African American Family of Prince William County." *Prince William Reliquary 1*, no. 4 (Oct. 2002): 73-80. *www.pwcgov.org/library/relic/PDF/PWR_10-2002.pdf*

_____ . Milford Mill: The Lost Landmark. *Prince William Reliquary 1*, no. 4 (July 2005): *www.pwcgov.org/library/relic/PDF/PWR_7-2005.pdf*

Hackley Hall,
c. 1920, Manassas
Industrial School
*(Courtesy of the
Manassas Museum
System, Manassas,
Virginia)*

Manassas Industrial School & Jennie Dean Memorial

48

After general Emancipation, when the law allowed them an education, African Americans struggled to obtain it. One-room schoolhouses and then larger consolidated schools typically provided education only through the seventh grade. Those who wanted a secondary education hired private tutors or moved to cities such as Washington, D.C. Jennie Dean, a Christian evangelist born in slavery in Prince William County, instigated churches and Sunday

HISTORIC SITE	Archeological park; open to the public sunrise to sunset.
THINGS TO DO AND SEE	Landscaped four-acre park with outlines of building foundations, bronze model of the original school campus, and exhibit kiosk with audio program and interpretive panels. The Manassas Museum is located nearby and features exhibits that include African American History, artifacts and photographs from the Manassas Industrial School. The museum store carries two books and a teachers' guide about Jennie Dean. The museum archives hold records and original photographs of the Manassas Industrial School.
LOCATION	9601 Wellington Rd., Manassas, VA The Manassas Museum is located at 9101 Prince William St., Manassas, VA
CONTACT INFORMATION	(703) 368-1873
ON THE WEB	*www.manassasmuseum.org*

Schools in the Manassas area. In the 1880s, she and other black citizens saw the need for higher education and vocational training for their youth. With them, Dean worked out a plan to establish a school and discussed the matter with a young white woman, Jennie E. Thompson, who lived in Thoroughfare Gap among many black people her parents had once owned. Thompson supported the idea and facilitated a fundraising campaign among wealthy whites, including former abolitionists in Boston and other northern cities. Local black families contributed money, labor, and goods. Former Confederate Captain Robert H. Tyler was among the founding trustees — he gave advice and helped them raise funds. The organizers found suitable land in Manassas near the railroad depot. On September 3, 1894, Frederick Douglass delivered the address for the dedication ceremony in front of the newly completed Howland Hall, named for Emily Howland, a northern philanthropist and friend of Dean's. Douglass observed that "No spot on the soil of Virginia could be more fitly chosen for planting this school." Once the scene of the opening battle in a fratricidal war over the issue of slavery, it had become a "place where the children of a once enslaved people may realize the blessings of liberty and education."

Students at the school studied academic subjects and learned vocational skills. Boys chose from trades such as blacksmithing, carpentry, or shoemaking while girls learned domestic skills. Parents, sometimes with the help of relatives and friends, paid tuition and provided transportation. Donors helped support the school as well, but it always struggled financially. In 1896, the United States Supreme Court ruled that public schools should be separate but equal. Nonetheless, public high schools for black children remained decades behind those for white children. The private Manassas Industrial School continued despite constant financial challenges. Finally, in 1937, the counties of Fairfax, Fauquier, and Prince William purchased the 100-acre school campus and jointly operated a regional public high school for African Americans. Black citizens in all three counties continued to agitate for their own public high schools, mostly through the NAACP. In 1954 the Supreme Court ruled in *Brown v. Board of Education* that "separate but equal" was inherently unequal and mandated integration, but it was not until the mid-1960s that schools in the three counties were fully integrated. The buildings no longer stand but the site is now a memorial park.

Resources

Jennie Dean. *The Beginning of the Manassas Industrial School for Colored Youth and Its Growth.* Manassas, Va.: Manassas Industrial School, 1900.

Frederick Douglass, "Speech at the Dedication of the Manassas (VA.) Industrial School." Frederick Douglass Papers, Library of Congress. *memory.loc.gov/cgi-bin/ampage?collId=mfd&fileName=49/49002/49002page.db&recNum=0&itemLink=%2Fammem%2Fdoughtml%2FdougFolder9.html&linkText=7*

Stephen Johnson Lewis. *Undaunted Faith: The Story of Jennie Dean.* 1942. Memorial Edition. Manassas, Va.: Manassas Museum, 1994.

William A. Link. *Jackson Davis and the Lost World of Jim Crow Education.* Library of Virginia. Includes some rarely seen photographs of the Manassas Industrial School. *www.lib.virginia.edu/small/collections/jdavis/linkarticle.html*

Geraldine Lee Susi. *For My People: The Jennie Dean Story.* Manassas Museum, 2002. (This biography for grades 4 and up comes with a teachers' guide upon request).

Manassas Industrial School & Jennie Dean Memorial

 PEOPLE IN THE PLACES — **Jane Serepta "Jennie" Dean**   (c. 1852–1913)

At the age of fourteen, Jane Serepta "Jennie" Dean of Prince William County set out for Washington, D.C. to find a job and save her family's farm. Formerly enslaved, she and her father Charles both strove to improve their lives. Charles had learned to read and write, and so had Jennie, even though she had just two years of formal education in the new Freedmen's Bureau school. Charles was trying to buy a small farm when he died suddenly. Jennie, determined to help her family hold onto it, found domestic work for prosperous whites in Washington, D.C., and a supportive black community there in 19th Street Baptist Church. Not only did

Jane Serepta "Jennie" Dean. *(Courtesy of the Manassas Museum System, Manassas, Virginia)*

she secure the farm, she financed her sisters' educations. On visits home, she evangelized and organized Baptist missions that became full churches. Some survive today. Troubled by the lack of educational opportunities for black children, she encouraged schools in the churches. In the 1880s she conceived and campaigned for the Manassas Industrial School for Colored Youth. She raised money among local black and white people as well as northern white philanthropists. The school opened in 1894 and eventually educated over 6,500 students on a 100-acre campus. Jennie Dean remained active on the managing board, fundraising, and supervising the women's dorm until her death in 1913. One who knew her observed, "She taught that life is a privilege as well as a responsibility and that birth or origin have but little bearing on success or failure if the will to help one's self is cultivated and encouraged." Today, besides a memorial at the original campus, an elementary school there bears her name.

Resources

Rita G. Koman. "Legacy for Learning: Jennie Dean and the Manassas Industrial School" in *OAH Magazine of History* 7, No 4 (Summer 1993). *www.oah.org/pubs/magazine/africanamerican/koman.html*

Stephen Johnson Lewis. *Undaunted Faith: The Story of Jennie Dean.* 1942. Memorial Edition. Manassas Museum, 1994.

Geraldine Lee Susi. *For My People: The Jennie Dean Story.* Manassas Museum. 2002. (This biography for grades 4 and up comes with a teachers' guide upon request).

The Robinson house
in 1862
*(Library of Congress.
photo by George N.
Barnard)*

Manassas National Battlefield Park

49

HISTORIC SITE	Open to the public
THINGS TO DO AND SEE	The Visitor Center provides a good beginning point for park visitors. Visit the museum, see the film "Manassas End of Innocence," or join a ranger on an interpretive tour about the First Battle of Manassas. A one-mile, self-guided walking tour for the First Battle of Manassas is available. A park brochure also provides information on the thirteen-mile, self-guided driving tour of the Second Battle of Manassas.
DESIGNATIONS	National Register of Historic Places
LOCATION	12521 Lee Highway Manassas, VA NW of Manassas off VA 215
CONTACT INFORMATION	(703) 361-1339 • (703) 754-1107
ON THE WEB	www.nps.gov/mana

Generations of enslaved people trod and tilled the soil now preserved in Manassas National Battlefield Park, and a free black man owned a farm there during the Civil War. Parts of six slaveholding plantations— Brownsville, Hazel Plain, Peach Grove, Pittsylvania, Portici, and Rosefield—once occupied the parkland. By 1860, however, eighteen percent of African Americans in Prince William County were free. James Robinson, freeborn in 1799 and relatively prosperous, bought a 170-acre parcel of land along

Manassas National Battlefield Park

Warrenton Turnpike by 1840. He and his family lived there in July 1861 as troops gathered for the First Battle of Manassas. James's grown son Tasco escorted his mother, wife, and children to the neighboring Van Pelt house where they hoped to find shelter in its cellar. Tasco Robinson later recalled, "Our house was between the lines and the shells were falling all around it." James Robinson, separated from his family, took cover under the bridge spanning Young's Branch.

During Second Manassas, in August 1862, the Robinson's home became a Union Army field hospital, with about 100 soldiers "packed in the room and yard as thick as sardines," according to a Confederate reporter. Robinson and other local farmers saw their crops ruined, their fences destroyed, their livestock and household goods gone. The battle lingered in the soil and air; Oswald Robinson's great-aunts smoked long-stemmed clay pipes to "smother the stench of bodies." In his application for reimbursement from the federal government, James Robinson detailed $2,608 of loss. By the 1880s the family added substantially to their home. They removed the original 1840s portion during a major renovation in 1926. An arson fire in 1993 severely damaged the remaining structure. The foundation remains. Another African American family, that of Philip Nash, lived nearby during the 1870s and 1880s. Archaeologists have studied both sites.

Resources

Manassas National Battlefield Park. *African-American Households from Manassas National Battlefield Park.* *www.nps.gov/rap/exhibit/mana/text/rhouse01.html*

Matthew B. Reeves. "Reinterpreting Manassas: The Nineteenth-Century African American Community at Manassas National Battlefield Park." *Historical Archaeology* 37, no. 3 (2003): 124-137.

Linda Sargent Wood. "Coming to Manassas: Peace, War, and the Making of a Virginia Community." Historic resource study of Manassas National Battlefield Park, Manassas, Virginia. National Park Service, 2005. Quotations on p. 91 and 108.

Burial site of
Jane Serepta "Jennie" Dean

Mount Calvary Baptist Church and Cemetery

50

HISTORIC SITE	Viewable from the road
THINGS TO DO AND SEE	Mount Calvary Baptist Church and the burial place of Jane Serepta "Jennie" Dean
LOCATION	4949 Sudley Rd., Catharpin, VA
ON THE WEB	www.gmccc.org

Members of Mount Calvary long remembered founder Jennie Dean riding out in her light sulky pulled by her bay horse Chaney. Although she worked during the week in Washington, DC, the young woman returned to western Prince William on the weekends to organize and teach in Sunday schools. Through her participation in Nineteenth Street Baptist Church in DC she embraced the independent church movement among African Americans and became an evangelist. In 1880, with local black citizens, she founded Mount Calvary Baptist Church in Catharpin. Others followed, including Ebenezer Baptist Church in 1883, Prosperity Baptist Church in 1899 (Loudoun County), Dean Divers Church in 1909, and Pilgrim's Rest in 1908 (Fauquier). The churches supported

Mount Calvary Baptist Church and Cemetery

education and personal and community development.

At Mount Calvary in 1880, Reverend D.G. Henderson served as the first pastor, and led the congregation in purchasing a half-acre of land, building a church, and expanding to 123 members before he moved to another church in 1903. In the ensuing years, under seventeen pastors, the church continued its growth. A new sanctuary replaced the first structure, and the congregation now has a second church—a large modern one in Manassas, known as Greater Mount Calvary Christian Church. Jennie Dean also founded Prosperity Baptist Church in nearby Loudoun County, Dean Divers Baptist Church in Manassas, and the Manassas Industrial School. Jennie Dean is buried in the adjacent Mount Calvary Cemetery beneath a stone memorial.

Mount Calvary Baptist Church

Resources

Greater Mount Calvary Christian Church. "The History." *www.gmccc.org/History.htm*

Fauquier County

VIRGINIA

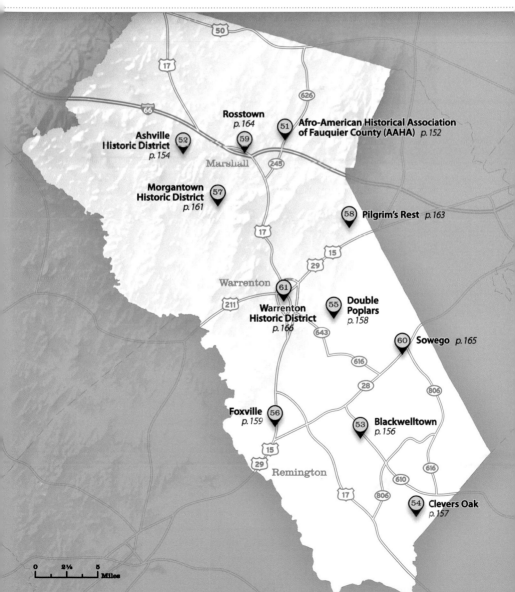

0   2½   5
Miles

Afro-American
Historical
Association of
Fauquier County

51

Afro-American Historical Association of Fauquier County (AAHA)

K aren Hughes White, co-founder and director of AAHA, traces her family back eight generations in Fauquier County. She and Karen King Lavore started the resource center in 1992 as an outgrowth of their own genealogical research.

HISTORIC SITE	Open to the public
THINGS TO DO AND SEE	Exhibitions on local history, a resource center, reference and genealogical library, and auditorium
LOCATION	4243 Loudoun Ave., The Plains, VA
CONTACT INFORMATION	P.O. Box 340, The Plains, VA 20198 (540) 253-7488 info@aahafauquier.org
ON THE WEB	www.aahafauquier.org

African American genealogy usually requires oral history supported with painstaking work in primary sources such as wills, deeds, and court records. Hughes and Lavore realized the remarkable stories they had pieced together were not just about individuals, but of communities, of Fauquier County, and beyond. By sharing their extensive research, they could help others get a boost in their own projects. In the same spirit, researchers share their work and findings with AAHA. Thus, the tremendous resources and expertise assembled prove invaluable to anyone wanting to know more about African Americans, especially those from Fauquier and surrounding counties.

The collections include works of art, historical photographs, clothing, ceremonial items, rare books, everyday objects, documents, oral histories, and memorabilia. The sharing of information and the many gifts of family photographs and artifacts from local residents give the museum and resource center a personal feel. The museum exhibitions are focused on local African American history within a national and global context. AAHA hosts many programs and special events throughout the year.

First Ashville
Baptist Church
*(Afro-American Historical
Association of Fauquier
County)*

52

Ashville Historic District

A shville is a particu-
larly well-preserved
post-Emancipation
African American settlement.
It began when Catherine and
Harriet Ash, sisters and former slaveholders, drew up
identical wills in 1869 and

HISTORIC SITE	Viewable from the road
THINGS TO DO AND SEE	Properties are privately owned
DESIGNATIONS	National Register of Historic Places National Historic District
LOCATION	First Ashville Baptist Church 4218 Ashville Rd., Marshall, VA

left land to people who had served them in slavery. They willed fifty-five
acres each to Frances Settle and Jacob Douglas. Other families, including
Brooks, Ford, Gant, Henderson, O'Neill, and Sanford settled there as well.
The new community organized a Baptist congregation in 1874. They built
a church in 1883, then, according to the cornerstone of the church still
standing, rebuilt it in 1899. The church managed the community cemetery,
located on land once owned by William Sanford and referred to even in
1869 as "Sanford's Cemetery." Residents also valued education. In 1876
Jacob Douglas sold a lot to the Trustees for the Public Free Schools for the

nominal sum of $25. The school that still stands today next to Ashville Baptist Church on land belonging to the church is evidence of the once-close ties between the two institutions in African American culture. Residents Dave Jackson and Jacob Douglas, with others, built this school in 1910. In 1942 a monthly African American monthly newspaper in Fauquier County, *The Circuit*, carried this message from Ashville: "Patrons and Parents of our school are much pleased with the splendid progress being made by our children in school." The schoolhouse remained in use until 1963. In 1911, William O'Neill purchased property from Franklin Settle and established a store, later operated by Skinny Sanford.

Ashville School. *(Afro-American Historical Association of Fauquier County)*

Resources

Afro-American Historical Association of Fauquier County. *www.aahafauquier.org*

National Register of Historic Places Registration Form. "Ashville Historic District, Fauquier County, Virginia." VDHR File No. 030-5323, prepared by Maral S. Kalbian and Margaret T. Peters, 2003. Available online in PDF format.

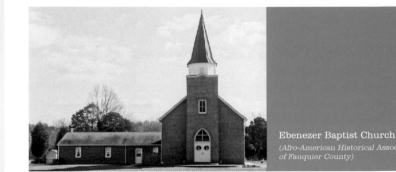

Ebenezer Baptist Church
(Afro-American Historical Association of Fauquier County)

53 Blackwelltown

As a widow, Elizabeth Fox Blackwell controlled an estate of 830 acres. When she died in 1859, she emancipated 87 people from slavery. She also stipulated that the land be sold to help them settle in a new state. Since 1806,

HISTORIC SITE	Viewable from the road
THINGS TO DO AND SEE	Properties are privately owned
LOCATION	Ebenezer Baptist Church 4487 Ebenezer Church Rd., Midland, VA
CONTACT INFORMATION	Afro-American Historical Association of Fauquier County (540) 253-7488
ON THE WEB	www.aahafauquier.org

Virginia law required that manumitted individuals had to leave the state within one year. Ohio was a popular destination for freed Virginians, but friends of the family were investigating various alternatives until the Civil War started. Afterward, in 1866, the Freedmen initiated and won a chancery suit, and the land was divided among the families listed in Elizabeth Blackwell's will.

Blackwelltown School. *(Afro-American Historical Association of Fauquier County)*

As soon as the Freedmen gained title to their property, Henley Chapman initiated a meeting in the home of former owner Millie Blackwell and established Ebenezer Baptist Church. The community built Blackwelltown School the following year and probably held religious services there. In 1876 they erected a church, which continues to serve an active congregation. Ebenezer Community Cemetery and the Blackwelltown Community Cemetery lie nearby.

Resources

Afro-American Historical Association of Fauquier County. *www.aahafauquier.org*

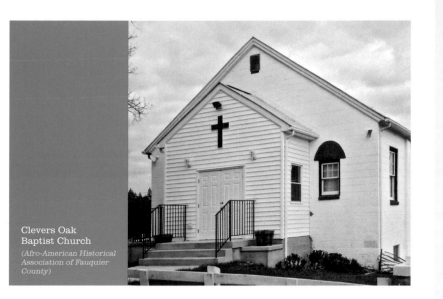

Clevers Oak
Baptist Church
*(Afro-American Historical
Association of Fauquier
County)*

Clevers Oak

54

HISTORIC SITE	Viewable from the road
THINGS TO DO AND SEE	Properties are privately owned
LOCATION	Clevers Oak Baptist Church 752 Sillamon Rd., Goldvein, VA
CONTACT INFORMATION	Afro-American Historical Association of Fauquier County (540) 253-7488
ON THE WEB	www.aahafauquier.org

Probably named for an old oak tree with generous shade, enslaved people worshipped at this site even before the American Revolution. By the antebellum period they had such claim to the property that the white landowners gave it to them even before the Civil War. In the closing months of the war, Rev. George Taylor preached in the open arbor. In the place of an altar, two cut cedar trees were joined together and the Bible was laid upon them. The Cedar tree had great significance to African American Christians. Mentioned many times in the Bible, it was a symbol of strength, tenacity and resurrection. The congregation built a log slab church in 1865 and replaced it with a larger weatherboard structure in 1906. It is still active.

Resources

Afro-American Historical Association of Fauquier County. *www.aahafauquier.org*

Eugene Scheel. *The Guide to Fauquier: A Survey of The Architecture and History of a Virginia County.* Fauquier County Bicentennial Commission. (Warrenton, Va.: Warrenton Printing and Publishing, 1976).

Poplar Fork Church
*(Afro-American Historical
Association of Fauquier
County)*

Double Poplars

55

Before the Civil War, Virginia law did not allow people of color to congregate without a white minister present, so they sometimes gathered in secret in the woods. They often chose sites of particular beauty or striking natural

HISTORIC SITE	Viewable from the road
THINGS TO DO AND SEE	Properties are privately owned
LOCATION	Poplar Fork Church 5366 Old Auburn Rd., near Warrenton
CONTACT INFORMATION	Afro-American Historical Association of Fauquier County (540) 253-7488
ON THE WEB	www.aahafauquier.org

occurrences that were safe from disapproving whites. In this case, it was double poplar trees in a community of free blacks. After the Civil War, worshippers often chose those special sites to establish a church. In Double Poplars, Elder John Clark led the community in founding a Baptist Church with the same name on June 20, 1870. They purchased land from Philip and Susan Hughes in 1874 and erected a sanctuary. As in many black communities, it doubled as a school in the early years. Later, they erected a schoolhouse on land formerly owned by Minor Grayson. The name of the church was later changed to Poplar Fork. The cornerstone of the existing building indicates it was rebuilt in 1960. It still shelters an active congregation.

Resources

Afro-American Historical Association of Fauquier County. *www.aahafauquier.org*

National Center for Cultural Resources, National Park Service. *African Reflections on the American Landscape: Identifying and Interpreting Africanisms.* U.S. Department of the Interior, 2003.

Saint James
Baptist Church

*(Afro-American Historical
Association of Fauquier
County)*

Foxville

56

HISTORIC SITE	Viewable from the road
THINGS TO DO AND SEE	Properties are privately owned
LOCATION	Saint James Baptist Church 7353 Botha Rd., Bealeton, VA
CONTACT INFORMATION	Afro-American Historical Association of Fauquier County: (540) 253-7488 Saint James Baptist Church: (540) 439-8700
ON THE WEB	www.aahafauquier.org

The story of Foxville extends beyond Virginia and includes a cast of hundreds. John Fox inherited many slaves and grew wealthy from their labor and rental. Upon his death in January 1859, his will directed they be freed and his land sold to purchase property for them in Ohio, since Virginia law required emancipated persons to leave the state. The case moved slowly in the courts and many of the almost two hundred African Americans seized the opportunity for freedom and migrated North in the ensuing years. Eli Tackett, a miller, remained and sought legal counsel beginning in 1860. He was appointed to manage the property until the case was settled.

In 1866, after the Civil War and general Emancipation, the Freedmen initiated and won a chancery suit to retain ownership of the Fox lands in Fauquier County, which were then divided among the families. It was a complex case because so many people had left for Ohio and Pennsylvania before and during the war. Among them were Elsey Pollard, the common law wife of a white man named Henry Newby, and their children, including Dangerfield who died at Harpers Ferry in support of John Brown.

Once the land was theirs, the Freedmen established Foxville Baptist

Church in 1866, making it the first official African American church in Fauquier County. Rev. Leland Warring, an energetic and visionary leader, helped them reorganize as St. James Baptist Church. He also founded Fox Hill School, later known as Routts Hill School. The church continues. One member described it as "a small rural church with a loving heart for the Word of God."

Resources

Afro-American Historical Association of Fauquier County. *www.aahafauquier.org*

Sherrie Carter. "Who We Are: A Story of Strong and Lasting Roots of Black Fauquier County Families." Manuscript in possession of the author, 2007.

PEOPLE · IN THE · PLACES

Leland Warring (c. 1823–1891)

Rev. Leland Warring. *(Afro-American Historical Association of Fauquier County)*

When the Civil War broke out, Leland Warring escaped slavery in Spotsylvania County and found refuge behind Union lines in Alexandria. There Rev. Doctor E. Turney helped him improve his literacy skills. In 1862 Warring started a "pay evening" school where he taught fifty other newly free "contrabands." Feeling a strong call to religious service, Warring also became a minister and the founding pastor of Shiloh Baptist Church in Alexandria in 1863, serving that congregation until 1889. With his first wife, Mary, he raised three sons, Frederick, Henry, and Carter. Henry became a teacher and followed his father as pastor of Shiloh in Alexandria.

Leland Warring's desire to aid the Freedmen and spread the Gospel also took him to the Virginia Piedmont where he is remembered as a wise man, "a powerful preacher, and a very capable leader." In Fauquier County in 1866, he founded Foxville Baptist Church (later Saint James), and Fox Hill School (later Routts Hill). In 1867, he established three additional churches: First Baptist in Warrenton (Fauquier), Shiloh at Brandy Station (Culpeper), and Shiloh in Middleburg (Loudoun). Warring served as pastor of Shiloh in Culpeper until 1891. All five of the churches he founded remain active. Warring married his second wife, Sarah Johnson from Culpeper, in 1883.

Resources

Afro-American Historical Association of Fauquier County files.

Alexandria Black History Museum. Self-Guided Walking Tour of Black Historic Sites, Alexandria, Virginia. *oha.alexandriava.gov/bhrc/bh-walking_tour.html*

Mount Nebo
Baptist Church,
built in 1902
*(Afro-American Historical
Association of Fauquier
County)*

Morgantown
Historic District

57

HISTORIC SITE	Viewable from the road
THINGS TO DO AND SEE	Properties are privately owned
DESIGNATIONS	National Register of Historic Places National Historic District
LOCATION	Two miles south of Marshall at the intersection of Freestate Rd. and Mount Nebo Church Rd.
CONTACT INFORMATION	Afro-American Historical Association of Fauquier County (540) 253-7488
ON THE WEB	www.aahafauquier.org

In the 1870s, at this hilly crossroads, Ann R. Morgan, widow of white landowner William J. Morgan deeded land to people he once held in slavery; it became known as Morgantown with the recording of these deeds. The landowners soon organized Morgantown Baptist Church. Trustees George Brent, James Lee, Henry Welch, and William Williams purchased land from Joseph and Letha Lawson in 1875 and built a church. A cemetery surrounded the church, now known as Morgantown Community Cemetery. Enclosed by a wooden fence, the cemetery contains around 100 marked and unmarked graves, including veterans from the Civil War, World War I and World War II, and the Korean War.

Morgantown Historic District

Morgantown children initially attended school in the church, with sisters Georgette Hughes and Lula Welch teaching. As the community flourished, adults built a separate school building in 1891. The church congregation bought additional land near the road and built a larger church with a steeple in 1902. They christened it Mount Nebo Baptist Church and moved their old building behind the new one around 1910 to serve as a meeting hall. Two two-story houses built nearby in the same decade had large front porches over two front doors, indicating they served as two-family dwellings or a business/

Original Mount Nebo Baptist Church *(Afro-American Historical Association of Fauquier County)*

residential combination. Peter Grigsby operated a store in another building nearby. Community members valued education and supported their school. In 1957, when 38 students crowded the one-room school, the community held fundraising dinners, donated time and materials, and constructed a 42 by 18-foot multi-purpose addition. The school closed when Fauquier County School Board consolidated colored one-room schools into Northwestern Elementary, now Claude Thompson Elementary, in 1964.

Resources

Afro-American Historical Association of Fauquier County. *www.aahafauquier.org*

National Register of Historic Places Registration Form. "Morgantown Historic District, Fauquier County, Virginia." VDHR File No. 030-5322, 2003. Available online in PDF format.

Pilgrim's Rest School
(Afro-American Historical Association of Fauquier County)

Pilgrim's Rest

58

HISTORIC SITE	Viewable from the road
THINGS TO DO AND SEE	Properties are privately owned
LOCATION	Beulah Baptist Church 6049 Pilgrim's Rest Rd. Broad Run, VA
CONTACT INFORMATION	Afro-American Historical Association of Fauquier County, (540) 253-7488
ON THE WEB	www.aahafauquier.org

The settlers of this post-emancipation community called it Pilgrim's Rest from a passage from the Bible: "All these died according to faith, not having received the promises but beholding them afar off and saluting them and confessing that they are pilgrims and strangers on the earth. For they that say these things do signify that they seek a country... But now they desire a better, that is to say, a heavenly country." (Hebrews 11:13-16) Residents wanted a spiritual as well as an earthly place of rest. Consequently, Richard Horner, Arthur Butler Sr., William H. Lewis and Reuben Clark, with the help of evangelist Jennie Dean *(see profile, p. 146)*, founded Beulah Baptist Church. Other members included Thomas Gaskins, William Stewart, John Fountain, Bristoe Cheeks, Patsy Barry, Lucelia Wells, and Arthur Butler. They purchased land from Anderson and Susan Smith on July 14, 1899 and built a sanctuary that a fire destroyed in the mid-1960s, but the congregation rebuilt and still worships there today. Pilgrim's Rest School still stands.

Resources

Afro-American Historical Association of Fauquier County. *www.aahafauquier.org*

Eugene Scheel. *The Guide to Fauquier: A Survey of The Architecture and History of a Virginia County.* Fauquier County Bicentennial Commission. (Warrenton, Va.: Warrenton Printing and Publishing, 1976), 3.

Robert Ross
(Afro-American Historical Association of Fauquier County)

59 | # Rosstown

Blacksmith Robert "Bob" Ross and his wife Ellen, both emancipated from slavery, established this community with Joe Black, Samuel Boyd, Henry Braxton, Lewis Craig, Mary King, Robert Lacey, and their families. They organized Salem Baptist Church in 1872. To build the first church building, the men dragged logs from Morgantown, another African American settlement nearby. The growing congregation erected the present building in 1929. The cemetery is across the road.

HISTORIC SITE	Viewable from the road
THINGS TO DO AND SEE	Properties are privately owned
LOCATION	Salem Baptist Church 4172 Rosstown Rd., Marshall, VA
ON THE WEB	*www.aahafauquier.org*

Salem Marshall Baptist Church.
(Afro-American Historical Association of Fauquier County)

Resources

Afro-American Historical Association of Fauquier County. *www.aahafauquier.org*

Heart's Delight
Baptist Church
*(Afro-American Historical
Association of Fauquier
County)*

Sowego

60

HISTORIC SITE	Viewable from the road
THINGS TO DO AND SEE	Properties are privately owned
DESIGNATIONS	National Register of Historic Places National Historic District
LOCATION	Heart's Delight Church 11229 Brent Hill Rd., Catlett, VA Bristersburg School 2045 Courthouse Rd., Catlett, VA
ON THE WEB	www.aahafauquier.org

In 1868, at Zoar Baptist Church in Bristersburg, Jesse D. Howe and Noah Bumbray led black members in a meeting to establish their own church. In 1869, they asked for letters of dismission and, with white members of Zoar Baptist, built a log house of worship on church property. They called their church Heart's Delight. In 1894, trustees Jesse D. Howe, Hamilton Toles, Marshall Hedgman, Hiram Edwards, and Marshall Gordon bought one acre of land from trustee Gordon and the congregation erected a larger brick edifice that continues to serve its members. Children in Sowego attended school at Bristersburg School #16, sometimes known as Good Hope School.

Bristersburg School. *(Afro-American Historical Association of Fauquier County)*

Resources

Afro-American Historical Association of Fauquier County. *www.aahafauquier.org*

Fauquier County
Courthouse

Warrenton Historic District

In the years following the Civil War and Reconstruction, African Americans built institutions, neighborhoods, and businesses. In 1865 local freedmen persistently lobbied the Freedmen's Bureau for a school for seventy-five children eager to attend. In mid-February of 1865 a school opened at the corner of Lee and Fourth Streets with a teacher from

THINGS TO DO AND SEE	Stop by the visitors center for a Civil War Trail map and information about the many facets of Old Town Warrenton.
DESIGNATIONS	National Register of Historic Places National Historic District
LOCATION	33 North Calhoun St. Warrenton, VA The Warrenton Historic District is roughly bounded by Main, Waterloo, and Alexa Streets
CONTACT INFORMATION	(540) 341-0988 • (800) 820-1021 visitorcenter@warrentonva.gov
ON THE WEB	www.fauquierchamber.org/ visitors_guide

Massachusetts. In 1867, black Christians in Warrenton established First Baptist Church. Rev. Leland Warring, a gifted minister and leader from Spotsylvania County, helped them organize and purchase property on Lee Street for $400. They accomplished this amidst reports by a Freedmen's Bureau agent of Ku Klux Klan activity in Warrenton. At midnight groups of mostly young men were "disturbing the colored people, and committing outrages upon them." The congregation purchased and worshipped in a former Presbyterian church on Alexandria Pike. They built the current church from 1887 to 1890. Mount Zion Baptist Church in Warrenton also traces its origins to Lee Street.

Warrenton contained several African American neighborhoods, including Frytown, Haiti, Madison Town, Oliver City, and Shipmadilly.

While many African Americans worked in agriculture, with some buying or leasing farms, others continued in trades such as masonry. Beverly Howard and Minor Grayson, "colored men and good mechanics" according to the local newspaper, purchased and operated two blacksmith shops in town. Maury Mason Dade opened a store in Frytown.

Resources

Afro-American Historical Association of Fauquier County. www.aahafauquier.org

Eugene M. Scheel. *The Civil War in Fauquier County, Virginia.* Warrenton: The Fauquier Bank, 1985.

Linda Sargent Wood. "Coming to Manassas: Peace, War, and the Making of a Virginia Community." Historic resource study of Manassas National Battlefield Park, Manassas, Virginia. National Park Service, 2005. Quotation on p. 156.

PEOPLE · IN THE · PLACES

Samuel Johnson (c. 1775–1842)

Samuel Johnson worked diligently to overcome legal obstacles to financial success and freedom. In 1802 he arranged for owner Edward Digges to transfer him to Richard Brent with the agreement that he would be freed when he paid $500. By 1812 he had raised the money "by great exertion himself and through the aid of benevolent friends." In 1806, however, Virginia passed a law requiring that manumitted slaves leave the state within a year. Johnson did not want to risk being separated from his wife and two children still in bondage. So, he found 38 white men who agreed he was a "meritorious man" and signed his legislative petition for permission to remain in the state. The legislature approved, in part because the emancipation agreement was made prior to the law.

Johnson continued to work at Norris's Tavern and in three years he purchased his wife and children. Before he manumitted them, however, he petitioned the legislators again for permission for them to remain in Virginia. His petition was ignored, so he tried again in 1820, this time documenting his considerable financial worth to prove he could afford to free them. He tried again in 1822, after which his son must have died. Thereafter, he focused on his daughter, Lucy, petitioning again in 1823, '24, '26, '28, '35, and '37.

In 1826, 229 white people signed Johnson's petition, likely because the family situation increased in urgency. In 1827, Lucy married a free man of mixed ancestry. Caught in a legal dilemma, Johnson officially manumitted her so the marriage would be legal, but continued to claim her as his property so she would not be forced out of the state. In 1837, he manumitted his wife and his daughter a second time, stating in his petition that he was "getting old" and wished to "liberate his said daughter and her children before his death." Samuel Johnson died in 1842 and left a will that again manumitted his wife and children, but if they could not remain in the state, left his other property to a trusted white doctor, Thomas Thornton Withers, to be sold for their settlement elsewhere. They remained, in part because they enjoyed the support of many of Warrenton's white as well as black citizens, but their story shows how legally tenuous a free black person's status was.

Resources

Eva Sheppard Wolf. *Race and Liberty in the New Nation: Emancipation in Virginia from the Revolution to Nat Turner's Rebellion.* Baton Rouge: Louisiana State University Press, 2006.

PA
WV   MD
VA

Rappahannock County
VIRGINIA

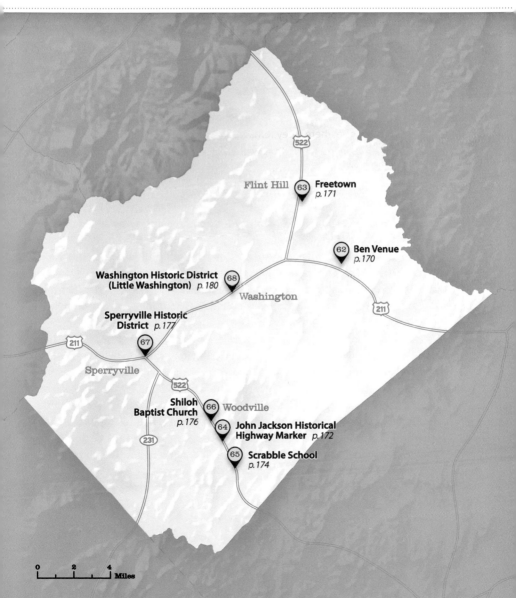

522

Flint Hill 63 **Freetown**
p. 171

62 **Ben Venue**
p. 170

**Washington Historic District
(Little Washington)** *p. 180* 68
Washington

**Sperryville Historic
District** *p. 177*

211 67

Sperryville

522

**Shiloh
Baptist Church** 66 Woodville
p. 176 64 **John Jackson Historical
Highway Marker** *p. 172*

231 65 **Scrabble School**
p. 174

211

211

0   2   4
Miles

Slave quarters at
Ben Venue
*(Virginia Department of
Historic Resources)*

62

Ben Venue

Few slave quarters survive in Virginia, especially those built before 1800. Crudely constructed of wood—often

HISTORIC SITE	Viewable from the road
THINGS TO DO AND SEE	Properties are privately owned.
LOCATION	Route 729, just off U.S. 211

including the chimney—and hidden away from the main house they provided poor shelter and didn't last. By 1810, however, slaveholders became more conscious of their responsibilities, the increasing value of their slave property, and outward appearances. They began building quarters that were more substantial and that coordinated with the architecture of the main house. James Leake Powers, a master mason in Rappahannock County, probably built the dependencies and these three slave quarters. The Virginia Department of Historic Resources calls them "the most architecturally sophisticated grouping of slave quarters surviving in Virginia."

A descendant of enslaved people at Ben Venue researched her Rappahannock County heritage. Emma Fletcher was born there in 1860 and continued to work for Ben Venue's owners after emancipation. She had three children with Arthur Harris, the white son of a prominent slaveholder. Virginia law at the time did not permit interracial marriages. So the family moved to Pennsylvania but the children returned to Rappahannock when their mother became fatally ill, where they lived with their mother's youngest sister. The oldest daughter, Harriet, remained in the county and was a member of First Baptist Church of Washington.

Resources

Calder Loth, ed. *Virginia Landmarks of Black History: Sites on the Virginia Landmarks Register and the National Register of Historic Places.* Carter G. Woodson Institute. University Press of Virginia, 1995.

The Broadest Branches: The History of the Richardson Family in Rappahannock County Virginia.
back2past.com/Broadbranch.htm

Macedonia Baptist
Church in Flint Hill

Freetown

63

HISTORIC SITE	Viewable from the road
THINGS TO DO AND SEE	Operating church
LOCATION	Macedonia Baptist Church 574 Zachary Taylor Highway (Rt. 522) Flint Hill, VA
CONTACT INFORMATION	Macedonia Baptist Church (504) 675-3284

Freetown was an African American community on Fodderstack Road a mile west of Flint Hill. In 1865, just after the Civil War and general Emancipation, black residents established Macedonia Baptist Church. With a grant from the Rosenwald fund, established by the founder of Sears, Roebuck, local citizens built Flint Hill Graded School in 1925. The single room served students through the fifth grade; then they traveled to Washington for sixth and seventh. In 1958 the community renamed the school to honor Warner A. Russell, who taught there and at Hume, Virginia, for forty-one years.

Resources

Rappahannock Historical Society church and school files, Washington, Va.

John Jackson
Historical Highway
Marker

John Jackson Historical Highway Marker

64

This tribute to Piedmont blues musician John Jackson was dedicated in August 2005. He was born

HISTORIC SITE	Viewable from the road
LOCATION	Route 522/Zachary Taylor Highway, 0.4 mile southeast of Woodville, VA

and raised in Woodville, an area with a significant African American presence. *See also* Scrabble School *(p. 174)*, Shiloh Baptist Church *(p. 176), and the profile of* Isaiah Wallace *(p. 175).*

Resources

Anita L. Sherman. "Remembering John Jackson." *Times Community Newspapers* (August 24, 2005). *www.timescommunity.com/site/tab4.cfm?newsid=15092917&BRD=2553&PAG=461&dept_id=506086&rfi=6*

PEOPLE · IN THE · PLACES

John Jackson   (1924–2002)

(Alligator Records)

Born in 1924 in the foothills of the Blue Ridge Mountains, the seventh of fourteen children, John Jackson grew up steeped in Piedmont agricultural and musical traditions. Instead of attending school, he performed farm labor with his family, and learned the guitar from his father at age four. His parents played often at house parties and, when John was six, bought a phonograph and 78 RPM blues and country records. John played along and learned open tunings and slide guitar from "Happy," a water boy on a chain gang constructing Route 29. In the tough economic times following World War II, however, house parties sometimes became violent, and he gave up playing.

In 1949, John Jackson moved to Fairfax County with his wife and young children to find work. He took up the guitar again in the 1960s when a cash-strapped friend pawned him an old Gibson. Folklorist Chuck Perdue heard him and convinced him there was an audience eager to hear his style of music. In the decades that followed John Jackson released nine albums, played in more than sixty countries, and became widely known as "King of the Piedmont Blues." Jackson was also a strong proponent of civil rights and an active member of the Falls Church Branch of the National Association for the Advancement of Colored People (NAACP). One fan wrote in 1970 that he "sings music that cuts across centuries, racial lines and regional differences." In 1986 the National Endowment for the Humanities awarded him the Lifetime Honor of National Heritage Fellow. Shortly before his death in 2002, he helped establish the John Jackson Center for Piedmont Blues at the Tinner Hill Heritage Foundation in Falls Church, Virginia.

Resources

Wikipedia. "John Jackson." *en.wikipedia.org/wiki/John_Jackson_(blues_musician)*

Drawing of
Scrabble School
(Scrabble School
Preservation Foundation)

65 | # Scrabble School

African Americans in the Woodville area, led by Isaiah Wallace, wanted a better school for their children. They raised money and learned about the Rosenwald Foundation. Sears magnate Julius Rosenwald, at the behest of Booker T. Washington, established a fund to help build schools for black children in the South. It required matching funds from black and white citizens. In Rappahannock County, white residents contributed, but African Americans donated ten times more, plus they donated the land and built the school themselves in 1921. The structure was light and airy, a good example of Rosenwald school design, with a central sliding partition that divided the interior space in half.

HISTORIC SITE	Viewable from the road; fenced and under renovation
THINGS TO DO AND SEE	Rappahannock Senior Citizen Center and Scrabble School Heritage Center.
LOCATION	174 Scrabble Rd., Scrabble, VA
CONTACT INFORMATION	Scrabble School Preservation Foundation 174 Scrabble Rd. Scrabble, VA 22716 President Bob Lander kplander@aol.com
ON THE WEB	www.rappahannock.gov

African American community members supported the school throughout its history, raising money, contributing time, even making homemade soup for students and the two teachers every Friday—"Soup Day." Students in grades one through seven sat in rows according to their grade. Some also hauled wood or coal, and water before indoor plumbing was added in the 1960s. The building served until 1967 when Rappahannock County integrated its public schools. In 2005, the community rallied again around the school, this time to preserve it and advocate its use as a senior citizens' center and heritage center.

Resources

Scrabble School Foundation. *www.scrabbleschool.org*

PEOPLE
IN THE
PLACES
Isaiah Wallace
(1876–19--)

E ducation was hard-won for Isaiah Wallace. One of eleven children born to parents who had known slavery, Isaiah grew up on Red Oak Mountain where the family lived off the land. For a year and a half, he attended school in a 14 x 20-foot log building. There, eighty-eight pupils, including four adults, sat on slab benches. Wallace then worked full-time for various employers who helped or allowed him to continue his education on the side. Around the age of fifteen, he fled to Pittsburgh, where he stayed first with relatives, then worked at various jobs in Pennsylvania, West Virginia, and Rhode Island. He returned to Virginia, married Malinda Payton from Culpeper, and took up the stone masonry and plastering trades. After soldiers returned from World War I he organized a league to work for a better school. With money from black and white citizens and a grant from the Rosenwald Foundation (which required interracial cooperation), they built Scrabble School in 1921. By then a widower, Wallace married Lila Dangerfield, a college-educated teacher who helped him continue his own education. She taught in a crude and overcrowded schoolhouse at Eldorado in Culpeper County, so he organized a similar initiative for another Rosenwald School there. He tried forming other leagues but, he regretted, "the people would not work together." Wallace expressed deep satisfaction that, through the model schools at Scrabble and Eldorado, he helped children of color gain access to the quality education they needed and deserved.

Resources

Nancy J. Martin-Perdue & Charles L. Perdue Jr., eds. "Isaiah Wallace," in *Talk about Trouble: A New Deal Portrait of Virginians in the Great Depression.* Chapel Hill: University of North Carolina Press, 1996.

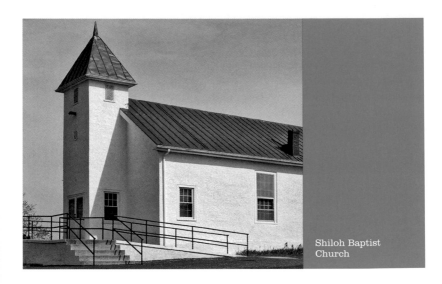

Shiloh Baptist Church

66

Shiloh Baptist Church

On July 27, 1873, ministers from four Culpeper County Baptist churches—Antioch, Beulah, Jeffersonton, and Salem—met as a council and established Shiloh Baptist Church. The initial members—Lewis Johnson, Lewis Dickson, Ellen Dean, Frances Lewis, and Lydia Lawson came from the biracial Mount Lebanon Church, founded in 1873 and located on Route 522 in Scrabble. The fledgling congregation grew and in 1874 the trustees bought a lot. Members immediately built a church that served the thriving community of Woodville, which included about 200 African American families around 1900. When the church was rebuilt in 1905, the original founders laid the cornerstone. Shiloh was the only one of four churches in Woodville to survive a tornado in 1929. Unlike many black churches, Shiloh never did double duty as a school. Woodville's African American children attended school in Scrabble; first in a one-room log cabin behind Mount Lebanon Baptist Church, then at Scrabble School built with Rosenwald funds.

HISTORIC SITE	Viewable from the road
THINGS TO DO AND SEE	Operating church
LOCATION	15 Red Oak Rd., Woodville, VA
CONTACT INFORMATION	(540) 987-8515

Resources

Shiloh Baptist Church 130th Anniversary booklet, October 17, 2003.

Former Home of James Arthur and Florence Engham on Main Street in Sperryville.

Sperryville Historic District

67

HISTORIC SITE	Open to the public
THINGS TO DO AND SEE	View old wood residences and enjoy the many specialty shops, antique stores, galleries, and several restaurants
LOCATION	Sperryville, VA, at the intersection of U.S. 211 and Route 522

In the century after emancipation many black families in the Virginia Piedmont worked as tenant farmers. Farm owners allowed them to live in a house on the property and gave them some meat and produce in addition to a small daily wage. Sometimes owners charged tenants room and board when they couldn't work. Blues musician John Jackson, for example, earned $3.00 a day as a tenant farmer in Rappahannock County. When he became ill with measles, the landowner charged him $3.75 for each day he couldn't work. Tenant farmers thus easily sank into debt and found it hard to leave.

In the crossroads town of Sperryville, there were other opportunities for work, such as in the mills or tannery, and for social life. A group of twelve African Americans, formerly members of the primarily white Sperryville (Reynolds Memorial) Baptist Church, organized Hopewell Baptist Church in 1873. They soon after built their first church on Route 600, and replaced it with a larger structure in 1922. Members of the Grand United Order of Odd Fellows, a fraternal organization, laid the cornerstone. The congregation established a cemetery on Route 211 on land they purchased from Arthur

Sperryville Historic District

Engham. By 1960 they built a larger church on a bigger lot. They remain active today. The Sperryville colored school still stands in a new location on Woodward Road above the town.

Resources

Elisabeth B. Johnson and C. E. Johnson Jr. *Rappahannock County, Virginia: A History*. Orange, Va.: Green Publishers, 1981.

PEOPLE IN THE PLACES   ## Caroline Terry   (1833–1941)

As the southern states seceded from the Union, Caroline's owner sold his most valuable slaves. A Rappahannock slaveholder purchased Caroline, a young woman, and put her in a cabin near his home. As the Civil War began, she bore a son she described as "a gift from the Big House." The master's two children, both girls, coddled the fair skinned infant and named him Theodore. They taught him to read and he became a house servant.

Caroline vividly remembered a wartime encounter with Yankees at the farm, when one soldier, cavorting on rocks that edged the pond, fell in and drenched himself.

Caroline Terry
(Courtesy John Tole)

Fellow soldiers and the master's daughters all laughed, but when the young man saw Caroline laughing as well, he drew his gun and threatened to shoot her. Later, working with a burial detail after a battle—probably a cavalry engagement near Sperryville in July 1862—she recognized him among the fallen. She picked up his pistol and, heavy again with child, she hid it beneath her loose dress. The artifact remains in the family. During slavery, Caroline and her fellows dreamed of freely going "beyond the rim" of the plantation. When freedom came in Spring1865, they rejoiced together. With her children, she walked the rim.

During and after the war, Caroline chose to stay in the area with people she knew and the sure source of sustenance. After emancipation, her former owner gave each farmhand a house to live in, a garden plot, flour, firewood, and some weekly wages. Caroline married Jeffrey Terry and bore three more children. Eventually, with the help of her grown youngest daughter, she moved into her own home in Sperryville. There, she and friends organized Hopewell Baptist Church. In her later years, her great-grandson James Russell helped to care for her, and one day published the reminiscences of his beloved and spunky ancestor.

Resources

Russell, James D. *Beyond the Rim: From Slavery to Redemption in Rappahannock County, Virginia*. [Sperryville, Va.: James D. Russell], 2003.

PEOPLE
· IN THE ·
PLACES

James Arthur Engham   (1858–1935)

James Arthur Engham
(Courtesy James D. Russell)

Toiling long hours in the fields in post-emancipation Rappahannock County, James Arthur Engham declared, "There must be a better way." He became a barber, repaired watches, took up the new field of photography, and sold jewelry. In 1881 he ventured into real estate. He married Florence Terry, who like her mother Caroline, was born in slavery. Florence and James Engham had three daughters, although the youngest died tragically at age eighteen. With Florence, James continued to expand his business. He purchased Old Totten Mill, which ground grain into flour and bottled soft drinks—most memorably, strawberry Try Me. Most successful was their real estate venture, which Florence continued after James's death. Florence helped seven people become homeowners by allowing them to pay over time.

James Arthur and Florence Engham's home on Main Street in Sperryville. Note the barber pole in the right foreground. *(Courtesy James D. Russell)*

"J.A." Engham's grandson, James Russell, recalled one particular lesson from this successful entrepreneur. As a boy he rode with his grandfather in his fine Graham Touring Car to a local apple orchard, where they met Mr. Hisle. Engham gave James a large flour sack and asked him to gather apples for Hisle while the two men talked. James did so, exerting as little effort as possible. Many of the apples he put in the bag were past ripe, much to his grandfather's dismay. "I would like to … see what you are going to do in later life," he told the boy. "Are you going to gather the bad apples, when you have an absolute opportunity to gather the good ones?" James Russell later published fond recollections of his ancestors.

Resources

Russell, James D. *Beyond the Rim: From Slavery to Redemption in Rappahannock County, Virginia.* [Sperryville, Va.: James D. Russell], 2003.

Rappahannock County
Courthouse

Washington Historic District
(Little Washington)

68

E nslaved African Americans suffered through annual hirings and auctions at county seats across Virginia, surrounded by the very buildings they helped to construct and maintain. During the 1860s, the decade of the Civil War and

HISTORIC SITE	Open to the public
THINGS TO DO AND SEE	Stroll through the quiet village. Many of the streets bear the names of the first families to own land on which the town was founded
DESIGNATIONS	National Register of Historic Places
LOCATION	Washington, VA
ON THE WEB	*town.washington.va.us*

emancipation, the black population declined by 766 people or almost 20 percent. In 1876, some of those who remained established First Baptist Church. On one momentous day, all forty-five founding members underwent baptism by immersion in the nearby Rush River. Initially, they worshipped in an old church on Wheeler Street. In 1880 the trustees purchased a lot on Main Street. With the help of the Rising Hope Lodge of the Grand United Order of Odd Fellows, a fraternal organization, they built their own church in 1881, with a meeting hall on the second floor. In 1900, the thriving community founded a second congregation, Promise Land Baptist Church. Both congregations remain active.

Resources

Rappahannock Historical Society. Census records, church files.

Culpeper County
VIRGINIA

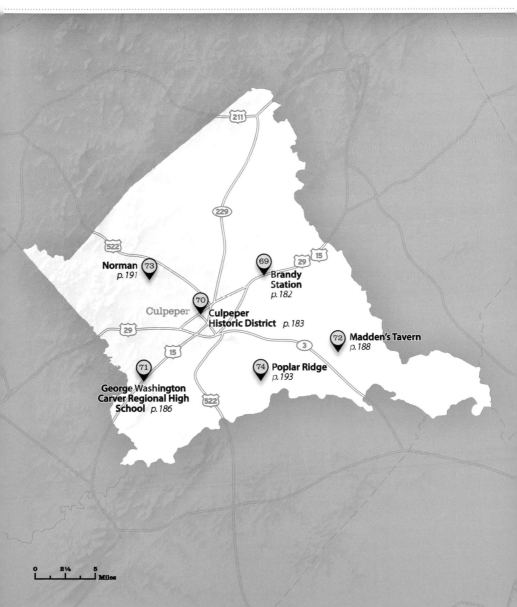

Norman (73)
p. 191

Brandy (69)
Station
p. 182

Culpeper (70)
Culpeper
Historic District   p. 183

Madden's Tavern (72)
p. 188

(71)
George Washington
Carver Regional High
School   p. 186

Poplar Ridge (74)
p. 193

Shiloh Baptist Church
at Brandy Station

(69) | # Brandy Station

For most of its history, inhabitants called this town Brandy, but the railroad played an important

HISTORIC SITE	Viewable from the road
LOCATION	Shiloh Baptist Church, 15055 Stevensburg Road, Brandy Station, VA

role in its economic development. While most known for the famous Civil War cavalry engagement fought there, it had its heyday in the latter half of the nineteenth century. It supported considerable industries, including lumber and flour milling, blacksmithing, wheel, broom, and soap making, and it boasted five stores and three taverns. African Americans worked in and supported these businesses. They established Shiloh Baptist Church in 1867 and built a sanctuary on former battlefield land donated by free black tavern owner Willis Madden. Samuel Gordon served only a short time and the congregation found a powerful leader in Rev. Leland Waring, who had himself known slavery. He served twenty-four years. During Dillard Johnson's tenure, which followed, the congregation built a larger church in 1897. Still in use today, it is the oldest surviving black church in Culpeper. The next two pastors, James C. Colbert and John J. Jackson, were born and raised in Culpeper and were both known for their kindness and integrity. African American children in Brandy attended the first Brandy School in 1891; the third school, which had multiple classrooms, is located on Route 663 and is used as a residence.

Resources

Shiloh Baptist Church 135th Anniversary Booklet, April 25, 1999.

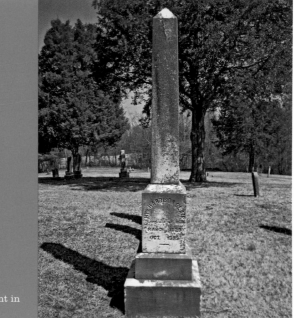

Rev. Blair's monument in Fairview Cemetery.

Culpeper Historic District

70

HISTORIC SITE	Open to the public
THINGS TO DO AND SEE	The Culpeper Visitors Center, located in the historic Train Depot, welcomes local and out-of-town visitors with a wealth of community, regional and state information and is a wonderful resource for maps, brochures, and other guides
DESIGNATIONS	National Register of Historic Places National Historic District
LOCATION	Edmonson, Stevens and West Streets, Culpeper, VA Culpeper Historic District is bounded by Edmonson, Stevens and West Streets
CONTACT INFORMATION	(888) 285-7373, (540) 727-0611
ON THE WEB	www.visitculpeperva.com

In 1859, African American members of Mount Pony Baptist Church established their own "African" church. Although common in cities such as Richmond, their action was unusual in a rural county before the Civil War. In 1867, after general emancipation and Virginia legislature repealed laws that required white ministers, the congregation reorganized as Antioch Baptist Church and called Harrison Blair to be its first pastor. Jack and Maria Madden with Lea Cole, a white woman, and Thomas Faulconer, a former Confederate lieutenant, in concert with the Freedmen's Bureau, soon established a school. Church and school met in the vacated Confederate barracks until the congregation bought land on Locust Street in 1870 and built a sanctuary. In 1886, they built a new church at 202 West Street that still serves its congregation.

Antioch Baptist Church

Fairview Cemetery, on Sperryville Pike one-half mile west of Main Street, has significant African American history. The Town Council passed segregation laws in 1903 that banned black people from burial there. The following year, Antioch Baptist Church, Sunny Fountain Lodge of the Grand United Order of Odd Fellows, and Summers Tabernacle of the Grand United Order of Galilean Fisherman established their own cemetery on adjacent land. A fence separated the black cemetery from the white one. They merged in 1970.

Resources

Eugene M. Scheel. *Culpeper: A Virginia County's History Through 1920*. Culpeper, Va.: Culpeper Historical Society, 1982.

National Register of Historic Places Nomination Form. "Fairview Cemetery, Culpeper County, Virginia." VDHR No. 204-5031, 2004. Available online in PDF format. Some photographs *at: www.dhr.virginia.gov/registers/Counties/Culpeper/NR_Culpeper_FairviewCemetery_photographs_page.htm*

PEOPLE
· IN THE ·
PLACES

Dangerfield Newby   (1820–1859)

D angerfield Newby was the eldest of eleven children who grew up in racially complex world. His father Henry Newby was white and his mother Elsey technically belonged to her husband's friend in Fauquier County, but the couple lived together as husband and wife in Culpeper. She and some of their children became free when most of the family moved to Ohio in 1858. Dangerfield, then age thirty-eight, had married an enslaved woman named Harriet and with her had seven children. He desperately wanted them to join him in freedom. Dangerfield accompanied his parents to Bridgeport, Ohio, where he earned and raised money to purchase his wife. Harriet then lived at Brentsville in Prince William County, Virginia, in the household of her owner, Dr. Louis Jennings. He refused to sell to Newby. Harriet expressed her love and anguish in her letters to her husband *(see p. 140)*.

Dangerfield Newby returned east and joined John Brown in the raid on Harpers Ferry. He was the first of the raiders to die. Three of Harriet Newby's letters to her husband were found and published. Compatriot John Copeland wrote: "And in this commencement of the strugle for the freedom of the negro slave the first blood spilt was that of a Negro (one who had come to free his wife from the cruel hands of her master) Dangerfield Newby." Harriet Newby, along with their children, were sold and taken to Louisiana.

Dangerfield Newby. *(Library of Congress)*

Resources

Sherrie Carter. "Who We Are: A Story of Strong and Lasting Roots of Black Fauquier County Families." Manuscript in possession of the author, 2007.

Philip Schwarz. *Migrants Against Slavery: Virginians and the Nation.* Carter G. Woodson Institute Series in Black Studies. University of Virginia Press, 2001.

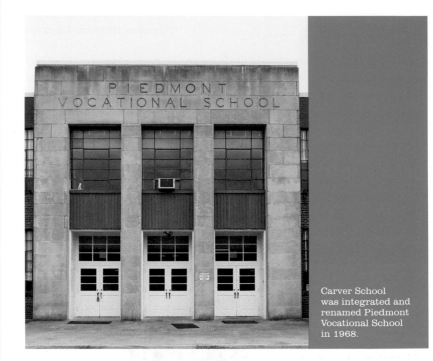

Carver School was integrated and renamed Piedmont Vocational School in 1968.

George Washington Carver Regional High School

(71)

African Americans throughout Virginia lobbied persistently for better education, yet progress came slowly. Even after World War II, few jurisdictions offered public high schools for black students. Culpeper and Orange offered very limited secondary programs, while education in Greene, Madison, and Rappahannock did not extend beyond seventh grade. Some students attended the Manassas Industrial School in

HISTORIC SITE	Viewable from the road
THINGS TO DO AND SEE	Public technical school Historical Highway Marker on Route 15
LOCATION	9432 James Madison Highway Rapidan, VA
CONTACT INFORMATION	(540) 825-2817

Prince William County or the Christiansburg Institute in southwest Virginia, but many families could not afford the cost of tuition, board, and transportation, or endure the separation. In 1946, after an agreement between the two jurisdictions, black students from Rappahannock County could attend high school classes in Culpeper. School officials in all of the counties in the region, however, worried about potential lawsuits charging that they were in violation of the national "separate but equal" policy since this arrangement was still far from equal. Therefore, in 1946, representatives from Culpeper, Madison, Orange, and Rappahannock requested and received funds from the state to build a regional high school. George Washington Carver Regional High School opened in 1948 and quickly earned respect for the quality of the students and the education they received In 1968, after public schools integrated, officials changed the school into Piedmont Technical Education Center. In 1992, members of

Historical Highway Marker on Route 15

the still-active alumni association lobbied to restore the original name. The old high school now serves Culpeper County residents as the George Washington Carver-Piedmont Technical Education Center.

Resources

George Washington Carver-Piedmont Technical Education Center. "About Us: A Brief History." *www.atgwc.org/about/about.html*

Madden's Tavern
(Virginia Department of Historic Resources, photo by Ann Miller)

72 | Madden's Tavern

This simple log structure is a rare relic of pre-Civil War black entrepreneurship in rural Virginia. Completed about

HISTORIC SITE	Not open to the public
LOCATION	VA 610, Lignum, VA East of Culpeper near Lignum on Route 610, north of Route 3 and west of Route 647

1840, the tavern was built, owned, and operated by Willis Madden (1799-1879), a free black man, and was likely the only tavern in the region owned by an African American. Virginia free blacks were able to earn and keep wages and to own and operate a business but were forbidden to vote, bear arms, testify against a white person, or be educated. Madden built the tavern on property purchased in 1835 on the Old Fredericksburg Road. Half of the structure was Madden's family quarters, the other portion consisted of a public room and a loft for overnight guests. A general store and blacksmith-wheelwright shop was also on the property. Union troops sacked the tavern in 1863-64.

The property is still owned by Madden's descendants. It was also known as Maddenville Farm.

PEOPLE
· IN THE ·
PLACES **Sarah Madden**   (1758–1824)

T he daughter of an unmarried Irish woman and a black man, Sarah Madden
was taken from her impoverished mother at age two and indentured until age
31 to a man in Fredericksburg, Virginia. Because of debt, however, his widow transferred the indenture to Colonel James Madison of Orange County. Sarah Madden,
age nine, became a personal servant and learned to sew and launder clothing. One
of the Madisons' several children was James, Jr., later president of the United States.
Sarah had three children while living with the Madisons, and under the law they
too became indentured. They were listed as free negroes in the Madison household. Their indentures were given to Col. Madison's son Francis in Culpeper. He,
however, was in need of funds and sold them to a man in Pennsylvania. Much dis-
traught, Sarah eloped to Fredericksburg to appeal to the court. She was successful but not quick enough—the three oldest children had been taken away by the
time she returned to Culpeper. An infant remained with her, and she had several
more children in the after years. After Sarah's indenture ended in 1789, she moved
to Stevensburg in Culpeper County where she lived for the remainder of her life. She
earned a living as a seamstress and laundress, and over time acquired a dairy herd.
In her later years her son Willis helped to support her. She died in 1824. The family
placed a large boulder to mark her grave.

Resources

T. O. Madden, Jr. *We Were Always Free: The Maddens of Culpeper, Va.: A 200-Year Family History.* New York:
W. W. Norton, 1992.

PEOPLE
· IN THE ·
PLACES **Willis Madden**   (1799–1879)

Willis Madden
(Madden family)

S arah Madden's son, Willis, was ambitious and multital-
ented. He learned many skills, including blacksmithing, shoemaking, distilling; and he did them all while
also working as a teamster. He married Kitty Clark in the
early 1820s. They had two children by 1827 when Kitty's
mother came to live with them, and then had seven
more. In 1835, Willis Madden bought eighty-seven acres
of farmland and a run-down old house where his mother
had once lived as a tenant. It was poor land, he knew, but
it was also located on a well-traveled road midway in the
two-day journey between Culpeper and Fredericksburg. Willis

Madden's Tavern

Madden built a blacksmith shop, a wheelwright shop, and general store. He allowed drovers and other travelers to camp on his property and he provided provisions and services. Then, he and his sons built a house with two sections—one for the family and one for paying guests. By the 1850s, Madden's Tavern was a popular stop for travelers as well as men from the local community. His accomplishments were remarkable by any standard, but they were especially so given the many laws and social customs that restricted free blacks in antebellum Virginia. During the Civil War years, however, Confederate and especially Union troops ravaged Madden's property, reduced him to near-poverty, and drove him into a depression from which he never recovered. He died in 1879.

Resources

T. O. Madden, Jr. *We Were Always Free: The Maddens of Culpeper, Va.: A 200-Year Family History.* New York: W. W. Norton, 1992.

Good Hope
Baptist Church

Norman

HISTORIC SITE	Viewable from the road
THINGS TO DO AND SEE	Properties are privately owned
LOCATION	Good Hope Baptist Church 14123 Norman Rd. Culpeper, VA
CONTACT INFORMATION	Good Hope Baptist Church (540) 825-8670

The black and white communities were particularly intertwined in Norman, first called Stone House Mountain. People of European and African descent had lived in the area for more than a hundred years before the post office took the name Norman in 1873 and again in 1883. One of them, Joseph William Bowen, was a white slaveholder whose wife Sarah became wheelchair-bound and unable to have children. He fathered ten children between 1830 and 1863 by a black woman he owned named Harriet Jackson. The three adults raised the children with care, Sarah making clothes for them and teaching them to read and write. After general emancipation, Harriet and her sons used the surname Jackson, while the daughters chose Bowen. The family remained in Norman and descendants of both white and black branches of the Bowen line still live in the area.

Norman

Beginning in the early 1890s, Lewis H. Tutt, born in slavery, operated a store and blacksmith shop in Norman. His son Ewell took over the store upon his death in 1904, but the store burned down some years

Norman School

later. Lewis H. Tutt's other son, Lewis Tutt Sr., rebuilt the store in 1950 and his son, Lewis Tutt Jr., operates Norman Grocery today. Good Hope Baptist Church continues to serve community. Across the road from the church, community members established Norman School in 1932 with the assistance of the Rosenwald Foundation. It still stands.

Resources

Allison Brophy and Zann Nelson Miner, "Unraveling the Shared Family History of Master and Slave." *Culpeper Star Exponent,* September 23, 2007.

Cruise, Melani T. W. *The Truth Is The Light If It's Told In The Dark*. Loretta Yager Wyatt, ed. M. T. W. Cruise, 2007.

Zann Nelson Miner. "Opportunity for All." *Culpeper Star Exponent,* February 12, 2009.

Eckington School
(Virginia Department of Historic Resources)

Poplar Ridge

74

HISTORIC SITE	Viewable from the road
THINGS TO DO AND SEE	Properties are privately owned Eckington School is on the National Register of Historic Places and Free Union Baptist Church is still in operation.
DESIGNATIONS	Eckington School is on the National Register of Historic Places
LOCATION	Eckington School intersection of routes 658 and 661
	Free Union Baptist Church 21649 Mount Pony Rd. Culpeper, VA
CONTACT INFORMATION	Free Union Baptist Church (540) 825-2269

On a low rise near Eckington, African Americans established Poplar Ridge Baptist Church, later called Free Union, in 1879. The gifted preacher and creative fundraiser Rev. Wanza Tibbs served the congregation until his death in 1919. Rev. Willis J. Madden succeeded him. In 1895, adjacent to the church, Culpeper County's Cedar Mountain School District built Eckington School.

Local residents likely assisted in the construction. At the time, Virginia was encouraging replacement of old log schools—three of which were still in use in Culpeper County—but most new schools had at least two rooms. Eckington had only one. When Culpeper County consolidated its schools in 1941, Free Union Church used the building for a fellowship hall. In 1950 the congregation added a shed, but after a large hall was added to the church in 1987 they used the old school for storage.

Resources

Virginia Department of Historic Resources. Eckington School Nomination Form, File No. DHR 23-5041, 2001. Culpeper/023-5041_Eckington_School_2001_Final_Nomination.pdf

Scheel, Eugene M. Culpeper: *A Virginia County's History Through 1920.* Culpeper, Va.: Culpeper Historical Society, 1982.

Spotsylvania County
VIRGINIA

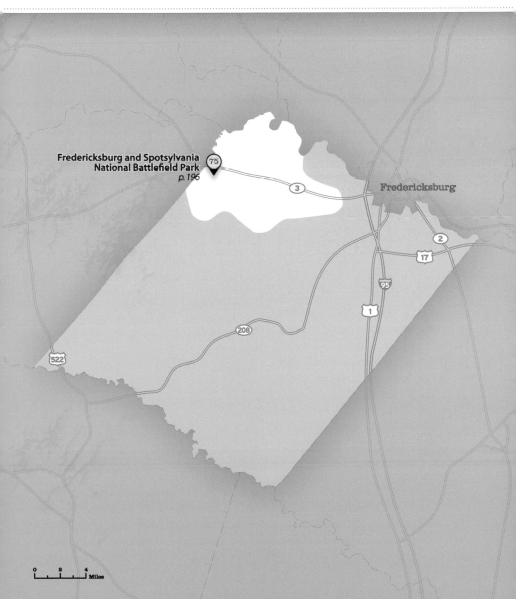

Fredericksburg and Spotsylvania
National Battlefield Park
p. 196

Fredericksburg

At the Battle of
the Wilderness in
1864, U.S. Colored
Troops escorted
Confederate
prisoners to the
rear

*(Frank Leslie's
Illustrated Newspaper,
June 4, 1864)*

Fredericksburg and Spotsylvania National Battlefield Park

75

A fter the Emancipation Proclamation took effect in 1863, President Abraham Lincoln announced that he would allow free black men to enlist in the Union Army.

They served in segregated regiments officially designated U.S. Colored Troops (USCT). Some regiments were assigned to the Army of the

HISTORIC SITE	Open to the public
THINGS TO DO AND SEE	Fredericksburg & Spotsylvania consists of four battlefields and several historic buildings which are widely scattered over a large area. It is best to begin your visit at the Fredericksburg or Chancellorsville Visitor Centers where staff can provide information and maps.
LOCATION	120 Chatham Lane, Fredericksburg, VA
CONTACT INFORMATION	(540) 373-6122
ON THE WEB	*www.nps.gov/frsp*

Potomac and participated in General Grant's Virginia Overland Campaign in spring of 1864—the last major initiative of the Civil War. Two brigades in the Fourth Division led by General Edward Ferrero—part of the Ninth Corps commanded by General Ambrose Burnside—participated at the Battle of the Wilderness. Joshua K. Sigfried commanded the 27th, 30th, 39th, and 43rd USCT regiments, while Henry G. Thomas commanded the 19th, 23rd, and part of the 31st. Being newly organized, they performed rear guard duties such as protecting the numerous and crucial supply wagons and guarding prisoners. After the action at the "Mule-Shoe" Salient on May 14th, for example, Ferrero's Division guarded Confederate prisoners including General Edward "Allegheny" Johnson and General George H. Steuart.

On May 4, 1864, as the army crossed the Rapidan River into Spotsylvania County, the Confederate Army's 9th Virginia Cavalry skirmished along the rear and captured some Union stragglers. One Confederate cavalryman wrote of some black soldiers they captured, "it is needless for me to say what became of them." Another reported "they were taken out on the road and shot, and their bodies left there." At least one black P.O.W. was taken with white prisoners to the Orange County Courthouse but, once there, he was summarily hanged.

Members of the 23rd USCT regiment faced combat in Spotsylvania County. On May 15, 1864, they were called to support the 2nd Ohio Cavalry, which had fallen back after a Confederate assault. They attacked and routed the dismounted Confederate Cavalry. On May 17th, near Old Salem Church, the 23rd regiment repulsed a Confederate attempt to break their lines. While northern and southern whites had formerly expressed doubts about black soldiers' ability to fight effectively, these and many other engagements—such as the assault on Fort Wagner—laid such suspicions to rest. Approximately ten percent of the Union Army during the Civil War was of African descent— more than 180,000 men in 163 units.

Resources

Central Rappahannock Regional Library, "African American History of Spotsylvania, Virginia." In HistoryPoint.org. *www.historypoint.org/af_am_spotsylvania.asp*

James K. Bryant II. "'...That Sable Hero': African-Americans in the Fredericksburg-Area Battlefields," *The Journal of Fredericksburg History* 7 (2003): 37-54.

Wikipedia. "U.S. Colored Troops." Available online at *en.wikipedia.org/wiki/United_States_Colored_Troops*

Orange County
VIRGINIA

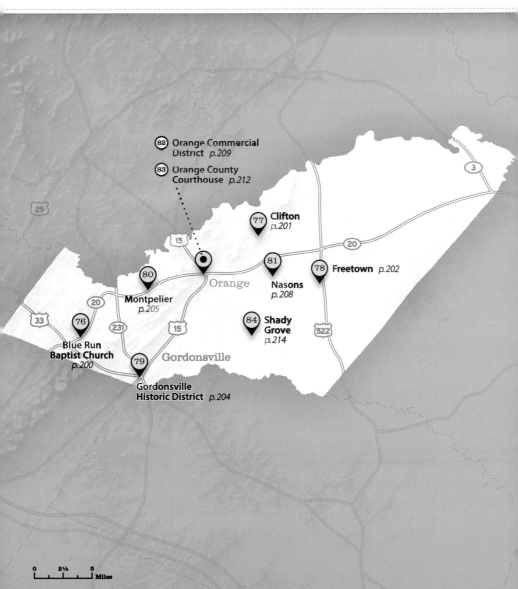

- 82 Orange Commercial District *p.209*
- 83 Orange County Courthouse *p.212*
- 77 **Clifton** *p.201*
- 81 **Nasons** *p.208*
- 78 **Freetown** *p.202*
- 80 **Montpelier** *p.205*
- 76 **Blue Run Baptist Church** *p.200*
- 84 **Shady Grove** *p.214*
- 79 **Gordonsville Historic District** *p.204*

Orange

Gordonsville

0   2½   5
Miles

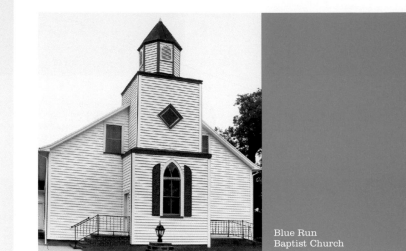

Blue Run
Baptist Church

Blue Run Baptist Church

76

Two black Baptists were among the founders of Blue Run Baptist Church in 1766. In its early years, the denomination denounced slavery and professed brotherhood and

HISTORIC SITE	Viewable from the road
THINGS TO DO AND SEE	Operating church
LOCATION	6435 Constitution Hwy (Route 20) Barboursville, VA
CONTACT INFORMATION	(540) 832-5943

sisterhood in Christ. As churches were built, however, black members were segregated in the balconies and the official leadership was white. Black members could be exhorters, but not ministers. Over the years at Blue Run, however, black membership outstripped white, so that by the time of the Civil War more than eighty percent was black. After the war, African Americans wanted a church with black leadership. The congregation divided along racial lines. The black members bought out the white ones and retained ownership of the building. The congregation remains active.

Resources

Orange County African-American Historical Society. "Street Festival Display."
www.ocaahs.org/streetfestival.pdf

Orange County Historical Society, Inc., 130 Caroline Street, Orange, Virginia 22960-1533, (540) 672-5366,
www.orangecovahist.org

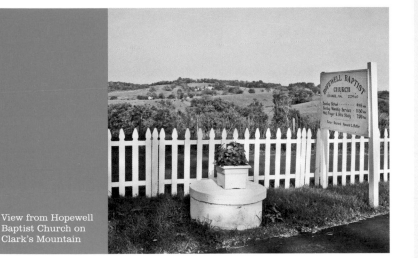

View from Hopewell
Baptist Church on
Clark's Mountain

Clifton

HISTORIC SITE	Viewable from the road
THINGS TO DO AND SEE	Operating church and cemetery; school used as a meeting hall
LOCATION	Hopewell Baptist Church 8566 Clifton Rd., Orange, VA
CONTACT INFORMATION	(540) 672-5757

Many Afritcan American farms and churches in Virginia's Piedmont are found on hilly land that was less expensive to buy and is beautiful to behold. Hopewell Church and Clifton school are especially nicely situated on the southern side of Clark Mountain—the highest mountain in Virginia east of the Blue Ridge. Surnames of students at the school in 1928/29 included Campbell, Davis, Graves, Jackson, Johnson, McDaniel, and Washington. Quite a few African American families made their homes on Clark Mountain. Other children attended schools located at Mountain Level and Bear Pond. In a few unusual cases, black children attended white schools with the children of their parent's employers.

Clifton School and Hopewell Baptist Church

Resources

Patricia J. Hurst. *The History and People of Clark Mountain, Orange County, Virginia.* Orange, Va. [Orange, Va.]: P.J. Hurst, 1989.

Orange County Historical Society, Inc., 130 Caroline Street, Orange, Virginia 22960-1533, (540) 672-5366, *www.orangecovahist.org*

Bethel Baptist Church, Freetown.

78

Freetown

Freetown began after the Civil War when a slaveholder gave grants of land to three people he had formerly held as slaves. Eight other families joined them, with the houses and their separate kitchens radiating in a circle. Chester and Lucindy Lewis, who lived in the center with their many children, established a school in their living room. They first hired a nearby West Indian man and later Isabella Lightfoot, a graduate of Oberlin College, to teach. Students paid one dollar per month and walked as far as eight miles to attend. Lucindy Lewis served lunch each day to the thirty students. One student, with money raised by family members, continued her education at the Manassas Industrial School. In Freetown, residents built Bethel Church and a school that they named for Miss Lightfoot. Except for an early vocational building, the school is no longer standing, but a newer school that bears her name is still in operation today.

HISTORIC SITE	Viewable from the road
THINGS TO DO AND SEE	Operating church and cemetery; burial site of educator Isabella Lightfoot
LOCATION	Bethel Baptist Church 12108 Marquis Rd. Unionville, VA
CONTACT INFORMATION	Bethel Baptist Church (540) 854-5356

Edna Lewis, a daughter of Freetown, fondly recalled sharing work that was close to nature and celebrating culture through plays, poetry readings, singing quartets, and special events such as Emancipation Day and Revival Week. She wrote that the community's adults "showed such love and affection for us as children, at the same time asking something of us, and they knew how to help each other so that the land would thrive for all. Each family had its own talents, its special humor, but they were bound together in an important way." But as adults themselves, most moved away to find suitable employment. Notable among them, Edna Lewis introduced southern cuisine to the elite culinary world in New York City, and Mathew Lewis, Jr. won a Pulitzer Prize for his photography.

Resources

Edna Lewis. *The Taste of Country Cooking: 30th Anniversary Edition.* New York: Knopf, 2006.

Orange County African-American Historical Society, Street Festival Display. *www.ocaahs.org/streetfestival.pdf*

Orange County Historical Society, Inc., 130 Caroline Street, Orange, Virginia 22960-1533, (540) 672-5366, *www.orangecovahist.org/*

PEOPLE · IN THE · PLACES

Edna Lewis   (1916–2006)

Growing up in Freetown in the 1920s, Edna Lewis enjoyed the birth of farm animals in the spring, eating and preserving garden fresh fruits and vegetables in the summer, attending Emancipation Day and Race Day in the fall, and Christmas celebrations in the winter. In the 1930s, however, Edna felt the pull of the bright lights and rode a bus to New York City. She worked first as a seamstress, then as a cook at a friend's new restaurant, Café Nicholson in Manhattan. There she prepared fresh meats and produce in a refined yet traditional southern manner. She once told a reporter,

Edna Lewis. *(Courtesy Knopf)*

"As a child in Virginia, I thought all food tasted delicious. After growing up, I didn't think food tasted the same, so it has been my lifelong effort to try and recapture those good flavors of the past." While recuperating from a broken leg, she handwrote *A Taste of Country Cooking* (1976) that included recollections of rural life in Freetown along with seasonal menus and recipes. With her cookbooks and her growing reputation as a master chef, Edna Lewis helped launch the culinary movement that celebrates regional cooking with farm-fresh seasonal foods. Edna Lewis became known as the "first lady of southern cooking." Throughout her life she was also deeply committed to civil rights and social issues. She found much of value in Freetown that she wanted to share with the world. She wrote, "Although the founders of Freetown have passed away, I am convinced that their ideas do live on for us to learn from, to enlarge upon, and pass on to the following generations."

Resources

Edna Lewis. *The Taste of Country Cooking: 30th Anniversary Edition.* New York: Knopf, 2006.

National Public Radio. "Remembrances: The Life and Legacy of Southern Cook Edna Lewis." *www.npr.org/templates/story/story.php?storyId=5222253*

Eric Asimov and Kim Severson. Obituary. *New York Times,* Feb. 14, 2006.

Fried chicken vendors
in Gordonsville
(Orange County Historical Society)

79

Gordonsville Historic District

In the mid-nineteenth century Gordonsville, with its intersecting rail lines, became a center of transportation. During the Civil War, large numbers of troops passed through and some stayed to recover in Union hospitals in the town. Enterprising African

HISTORIC SITE	Viewable from the road
THINGS TO DO AND SEE	The Exchange Hotel and Civil War Museum has exhibits and interpretive signs about the fried chicken vendors
DESIGNATIONS	National Register of Historic Places
LOCATION	Exchange Hotel and Civil War Museum, 400 South Main St., Gordonsville, VA
CONTACT INFORMATION	(540) 832-2944
ON THE WEB	www.hgiexchange.org

American women prepared fried chicken and biscuits and sold them to hungry travelers. They called themselves "waiter carriers" and later "chicken vendors." The town gained fame as "the Fried Chicken Capital of the World." The income from their business helped women gain autonomy and improve the lives of their families. Second-generation vendor Bella Winston, interviewed for the town's centennial in 1970 related that, "My mother paid for this place with chicken legs." In the twentieth century, with the advent of dining cars, closed vestibules, and finally, air-conditioned trains, the business declined and perished. In 1965, however, Bella Winston still prepared and sold fried chicken in the community.

Churchgoers in Gordonsville attended Union Baptist Church on Cobb Street. Children studied at Gordonsville School, a two-room structure with tongue and groove paneling built in 1925. Classrooms were added in 1928 and 1930 to serve the growing community.

Resources

Psyche A. Williams-Forson. *Building Houses Out of Chicken Legs: Black Women, Food, and Power.* Chapel Hill: University of North Carolina Press, 2006.

Walker, Frank S. *Remembering: A History of Orange County, Virginia.* Orange, Va.: Orange County Historical Society, 2004.

Artist's rendition
of enslaved people
at Monpelier
(By Linda Boudreaux
Montgomery, courtesy
Montpelier)

Montpelier

80

HISTORIC SITE	Open to the public
THINGS TO DO AND SEE	Audio, guided and self-guided tours; Enjoy the landscape walk around the mansion, including the 2-acre formal garden. There are also walking trails to the James Madison Landmark Forest, the Mount Pleasant archaeological site, the Madison Family Cemetery, and the Slave Cemetery.
DESIGNATIONS	National Register of Historic Places National Historic Landmark
LOCATION	Four miles west of Orange on State Route 20
CONTACT INFORMATION	(540) 672-2728
ON THE WEB	www.montpelier.org

Enslaved people owned by Ambrose Madison lived at Montpelier and constructed dwellings and farm buildings even before he moved there with his family in 1732. James Madison Sr. inherited the farm and enslaved people from his father and probably used slave labor to construct the brick manor house in 1760. Slaves at Montpelier operated a blacksmith shop, gristmill, sawmill, and distillery, while still others worked in agriculture, the main house or its dependencies. One man named Sawney served at various times as an overseer and a personal servant to future president James Madison Jr. at the College of New Jersey (Princeton), and cared for "Mother Madison."

To learn more about African Americans at Montpelier you can tour the main house and visit the slave cemetery, where you'll find an illustrated interpretive sign. You can also follow the Confederate Camp and Freedman's Farm Trail, which includes illustrated interpretive signs on Post-Emancipation Life in Orange County and the Gilmore farm, where you can see the restored log cabin. On Saturdays you can take the "Montpelier Enslaved Community Tour." Periodically, Montpelier hosts large descendant reunions.

Resources

Montpelier. *The Montpelier Enslaved Community. www.montpelier.org/history/enslaved_community.cfm*

_____. *Special Tours. www.montpelier.org/visit/special_tours.cfm*

Montpelier: James Madison University Magazine. "Slaves' Descendants Give Voice to Silent History" (Spring 2001). *www.jmu.edu/montpelier/issues/spring01/descendants.htm*

PEOPLE IN THE PLACES — Paul Jennings (b. 1799)

COLORED MAN'S REMINISCENCES

of

JAMES MADISON.

By PAUL JENNINGS.

BROOKLYN:
GEORGE C. BEADLE.
1865.

Title page of Paul Jennings's Memoir, published in 1865.

With his modest and authoritative account of James and Dolly Madison during James's presidency Paul Jennings pioneered the genre of "inside the White House" memoirs. He was born at Montpelier in 1799 when his owner—the future president—was thirty-one years old. In 1809, at the age of ten, he accompanied the Madisons to the White House. In 1814 he watched them flee the capital as the British invaded. Later, as James Madison's valet, he shaved him every other day and attended at his death in 1836. He served Dolley Madison until she sold him in 1846 due to grave financial problems.

Paul Jennings then worked for freedom for himself and others. He persuaded the antislavery senator from New Hampshire, Daniel Webster, to purchase him and allow him to buy his freedom. In 1848 he conceived a way to help enslaved people and their free loved ones escape together to the North. He collaborated with Daniel Drayton, a white sea captain from Philadelphia. Drayton borrowed the schooner Pearl and sailed to Washington. Jennings spread word of his arrival, and freedom seekers boarded the ship at night. Calm winds in the Chesapeake Bay stilled the ship. In the morning, slaveholders noticed absences and a black man with a grudge revealed the conspiracy. A steamer caught up with the schooner and officials arrested the freedom seekers.

In 1865, at the behest of others, Paul Jennings published his memoir of the Madisons. He dispelled the myth that Dolley Madison had cut out the painting of George Washington to save it from the British during the War of 1812. He mentioned the numerous and brave black soldiers in the United States Army during that conflict, and wrote of the Madisons from a black perspective, believing that they earned a high regard.

Resources

Paul Jennings. *Colored Man's Reminiscences of James Madison.* Brooklyn, N.Y.: George C. Beadle, 1865. *docsouth.unc.edu/neh/jennings/jennings.html*

G. Franklin Edwards and Michael R. Winston. "Commentary: The Washington of Paul Jennings – White House Slave, Free Man, and Conspirator for Freedom." *White House History 1,* no. 1 (1983): 52-63.

PEOPLE
· IN THE ·
PLACES

George Gilmore (b. 1810)

A fter the Civil War and general Emancipation, many freedmen elected to remain in Virginia. They often cherished their ties to the land—regardless of ownership—and generations of connections to its people. George Gilmore likely

occupied a favored position at Montpelier, even during slavery. He could read and write and was often hired out for his skills as a carpenter, earning income for the Madisons and likely for himself during his "free" time. Gilmore made saddles as well. He married a seamstress named Polly Braxton in 1850, and together they raised eight children. In 1864, during the Civil War, a federal officer included George Gilmore in a short list of white and "colored" people the Union Army could count on to assist them in their occupation of Orange County.

Rebecca Gilmore Coleman in front of her family's cabin at Montpelier. *(Photo by Kenneth L. Garrett)*

George and Polly Gilmore elected to stay in Orange County after Emancipation. They rented land near the main house from Dr. James Madison, great-nephew of President Madison, tended a farm, and supplemented their income with their trades. An archaeological study suggested that initially the family may have lived in a hut once part of a Confederate encampment. In 1873, they built a more substantial structure using chestnut logs, and later added a frame addition. Descendants of the Gilmores continue to live in Orange County. In 2006 his great-granddaughter, Rebecca Gilmore Coleman, donated land to Montpelier that was had been part of the original farm. Visitors can walk this property and see the restored house.

Resources

James Madison's Montpelier. National Trust for Historic Preservation. "The Gilmore Cabin." *www.montpelier.org/archaeology/gilmore_farm.cfm*

Montpelier: James Madison University Magazine. "Slaves' Descendants Give Voice to Silent History" (Spring 2001). *www.jmu.edu/montpelier/issues/spring01/descendants.htm*

Nasons School

(81) Nasons

In 1878, Reverend Barnett and about sixty members of Hopewell Baptist Church at Clifton organized Mount Calvary Baptist Church. They wanted a church in the valley more conveniently located and built their first church adjacent to Nasons Post Office. The move was auspicious, as

HISTORIC SITE	Viewable from the road
THINGS TO DO AND SEE	Operating church
LOCATION	Mount Calvary Baptist Church 11229 Kendall Rd. Orange, VA
CONTACT INFORMATION	Mount Calvary Baptist Church (540) 672-2848 info@mountcalvary-nasons.org
ON THE WEB	Mount Calvary Baptist Church www.mountcalvary-nasons.org

the congregation soon outgrew not only their first building but their second as well. The third church, built in 1958 on land purchased from Douglas Carter for eight dollars is still standing. The congregation maintains a large cemetery across the street. In 1924, the school board, probably with help from local residents, built Nasons school on a wood post foundation. It has two classrooms heated with separate stoves and two exterior coat closets with an open vestibule between them. The school is now a private residence.

Resources

Mount Calvary Baptist Church. *www.mountcalvary-nasons.org*

Orange County Historical Society, Inc., 130 Caroline Street, Orange, Virginia 22960-1533, (540) 672-5366, *www.orangecovahist.org*

Prospect Heights
School

Orange Commercial District

82

HISTORIC SITE	Open to the public
THINGS TO DO AND SEE	Visitor center and self-guided tours
LOCATION	122 E. Main St., Orange, VA
CONTACT INFORMATION	(540) 672-1653 • (877) 222-8072 info@orangecova.com
ON THE WEB	www.townoforangeva.org

In 1860 Orange County had almost 11,000 people; more than 6,000 were enslaved and only 187 were free people of color. But enslaved people also participated in commerce. Each month on the Sunday before court day, they assembled at the courthouse and sold their produce and other goods. After general emancipation in 1865 quite a few African Americans left the county—the black population had declined 13 percent by 1870, while the white population increased slightly. A considerable number of Freedmen who stayed in the county moved to Orange and Gordonsville where there were more opportunities for employment.

Prospect Heights School, built for black children in 1956, now serves students of all races. It replaced Orange Graded School, erected in 1925 on the same hilltop site. Students who wished to attend high school left the area, studied privately, or earned a certificate at the Lightfoot School that was the equivalent of a high school diploma. In 1948, George Washington Carver High Regional School opened in Culpeper County and served students from Culpeper, Madison, Orange, and Rappahannock counties until desegregation in 1968.

Orange Commercial District

Resources

National Register of Historic Places Nomination Form, File No. 275-5001.
www.dhr.virginia.gov/.../Orange/275-5001_Orange_Commercial_Historic_District_1999_Final_Nomination.pdf

John Schlotterbeck. "The Internal Economy of Slavery in Piedmont Virginia." In *The Slaves Economy, Independent Production by Slaves in the Americas,* Ira Berlin and Philip Morgan, editors. London: Frank Cass, 1995.

Nannie Helen Burroughs   (1879–1961)

Nannie Helen Burroughs.
(Library of Congress)

Nannie Helen Burroughs left a lot of family history behind when, at the age of five in 1884, she and her mother moved away from Orange. Her father's father, a woodworker, had purchased his freedom and a small farm. Her father John aspired to the ministry and studied at the Richmond Institute but couldn't find a church that needed a pastor. Her mother Jennie, born in slavery, supported the family with domestic work and became the only breadwinner when her husband died. Wanting a better education for her daughter than she could get in Orange, they went to live with Jennie's sister in Washington, D.C., and found a church home at 19th Street Baptist. Nannie excelled in school, but upon graduation she was unable to win a teaching assistant job. The color line in D.C. barred black women from jobs in white schools and an entrenched, light-skinned black elite controlled the few positions in colored schools.

Burroughs determined to establish a school that would educate black women of all social backgrounds and prepare them for success. She found work for the Christian Banner in Philadelphia and then, in 1900, with the National Baptist Convention. She delivered an address at the national convention in Richmond, Virginia, "How the Sisters are Hindered from Helping." The speech and her continuing efforts earned her national fame and promoted the formation and growth of black women's organizations, including a Women's Convention auxiliary that grew to 1.5 million members worldwide. By 1909, Burroughs had the support she needed to establish the National Training School for Women and Girls in Washington, DC. In 1926 it became the National Trade and Professional School for Women and Girls, with the motto "We specialize in the wholly impossible." Burroughs was a stirring orator and a tireless civil and women's rights advocate. One supporter observed, "She has dynamic power. Measured, not as a Negro woman, but as a woman, she has extraordinary ability, and her living faith in God and all His children, of whatever race, her spirit of service and sacrifice have energized her gifts as only faith and love can do."

Resources

Library of Congress. "Special Presentation – Nannie Helen Burroughs." In *Discovering Hidden Washington: A Journey Through the Alley Communities of the Nation's Capital. www.loc.gov/loc/kidslc/sp-burroughs.html*

Veronica Davis. "Nannie Helen Burroughs." In *Inspiring African American Women of Virginia*. New York: iUniverse, 2005).

Traki L. Taylor. "'Womanhood Glorified': Nannie Helen Burroughs and the National Training School for Women and Girls, Inc., 1909-1961." *Journal of African American History* (Autumn 2002): 390-402.

PEOPLE IN THE PLACES Andrew Maples, Jr.   (1920–1944)

A World War I veteran from New York with damaged lungs, Andrew Maples Sr. married Julia Michie and moved with her back to her hometown of Orange, where the fresh air would benefit his health. Their son, Andrew Jr., attended the local segregated school, but his parents shared their worldly experiences and high expectations. Although the Orange County then offered black students a certificate at the Lightfoot School equivalent to a secondary school diploma, Maples went to live with a relative in Washington, DC, and attended Armstrong High School. He then studied for two years at Hampton Institute and somehow learned to fly airplanes. He transferred to Tuskegee Institute and enrolled in their rigorous Flying School, authorized by the Army Air Corps in 1941. Andrews graduated in 1942 in a class of forty-three. Each graduate received his diploma, pilot's wings, and commission as Second Lieutenant in the Army Air Corps. They became known as Tuskegee Airmen, famous for their courage and skill in battling foreign enemies and pervasive racism.

Even in this distinguished group, Andrew Maples stood out. After advanced training in Michigan he was promoted to First Lieutenant and deployed overseas with the 301st Fighter Squadron. In 1944 his company flew P-47 Thunderbolts, new high-power, long-range aircraft. Returning from escorting a successful deep-penetration bombing mission over Hungary on June 26, 1944, he radioed over the Adriatic sea within sight of Italy that his engine had quit. Although his compatriots searched extensively, the twenty-four-year-old airman was never found. His family, including five brothers also serving in the military, heard no news until one year after his death when the Army declared him dead on the day of his disappearance and promoted him to Captain posthumously. People in Virginia honored him with the name of the segregated Veterans of Foreign Wars post in Orange and by including his name on a memorial in Richmond for Virginia's WWII airmen killed in action.

Resources

Walker, Frank S. Remembering: *A History of Orange County, Virginia*. Orange, Va.: Orange County Historical Society, 2004.

Orange County Courthouse
(Virginia Department of Historic Resources)

83

Orange County Courthouse

In May of 1864, citizens in Orange County saw African American Union soldiers for the first time. Since their inception in 1863, U.S. Colored Troops serving in the Civil War faced harsher treatment than their white counterparts, especially by

HISTORIC SITE	Open to the public
LOCATION	Madison Rd. and N. Main St., Orange, VA
HISTORIC DESIGNATIONS	National Register of Historic Places
CONTACT INFORMATION	(540) 672-1653 • (877) 222-8072 tourorangeco@firstva.com
ON THE WEB	*www.visitorangevirginia.com*

the enemy. Those serving in General Burnside's Overland Campaign of 1864 were among the first African American soldiers that Army of Northern Virginia soldiers under Robert E. Lee had seen. In Spotsylvania County during the Battle of the Wilderness, Confederate troops captured black and white soldiers. Some black prisoners were executed on the spot. One was spared and brought with white prisoners to an enclosure at the Orange County Courthouse, but there, on May 8, 1964, he was hanged from an oak tree on the courthouse lawn.

Resources

James K. Bryant II. "'...That Sable Hero': African-Americans in the Fredericksburg-Area Battlefields." *Journal of Fredericksburg History* 7 (2003): 37-54.

Frank S. Walker. *Remembering: A History of Orange County, Virginia.* Orange, Va.: Orange County Historical Society, 2004.

PEOPLE IN THE PLACES **John Washington** (1828–1918)

John Washington. *(Courtesy of the Alice J. Stuart Family Trust and the Massachusetts Historical Society)*

Two-year-old John Washington and his mother were hired out to Richard Brown of Orange. The boy treasured his early childhood memories, before he felt the hardships of slavery. A fair-skinned and fair-haired boy, he remembered playing mostly with white children, chasing butterflies in clover-scented fields, fishing with a pin hook and line, watching the moss-covered mill wheel throw sprays of water. His mother taught him to read in the evenings and took him to church on Sundays. Once he rode with the white family to Orange Courthouse to see the circus. They lost him during a thunderstorm and returned home without him, much to his mother's distress. Washington's godmother found the crying boy as the crowd thinned that evening, packed him in "comforts" in an oxcart, and drove him home. He "arrived safe about Sunlite … amidst great rejoicing."

Washington experienced the hardships of slavery as the Brown's fortunes declined. When he was four he awoke to see a line of men, women, and children with bundles on their backs, sold South. "I shall never forget the weeping … among those that were left behind," he wrote. When John was about twelve, he and his mother were returned to their Fredericksburg owner. John grieved when his mother was hired in Staunton. They exchanged letters, monitored by their white owners. Washington was hired to a tobacco factory owner and later a saloonkeeper.

The Civil War found Washington in Richmond in charge of a tavern when, as federal troops approached, white people fled. He gathered the servants and poured them drinks, toasted with them the Yankees' health, and paid them "according to orders." Then, with a cousin, he crossed the river in a boat and went into the Union lines. Soldiers there told him he was free. He was so filled with joy he "could only thank God and laugh." He worked for the Union Army and traveled with them to Warrenton and Culpeper, and eventually made it back to his wife near Fredericksburg. He wrote his reminiscences in 1873, and died in Massachusetts in 1918.

Resources

John Washington. Memoir, "Memorys of the Past," undated. Manuscript Division, Library of Congress. Transcription by history professor Randy Shifflet available online at *courseware.vt.edu/users/shifflet/ hist3205/jwash.htm*

Prince Hall
Freemasons Lodge
in Shady Grove

84

Shady Grove

African Americans in southeastern Orange County established Shady Grove Baptist Church in 1871 and soon purchased land from the Woolfork family. The congregation erected a bush arbor and worshipped there until the church was finished the following year.

HISTORIC SITE	Viewable from the road
THINGS TO DO AND SEE	Operating church, school under restoration, cemetery, Prince Hall Masons lodge hall
LOCATION	Shady Grove Baptist Church 15270 Piney Wood Ln. Orange, VA
CONTACT INFORMATION	Orange Count Historical Society
ON THE WEB	www.orangecovahist.org

No school served the area until 1925 when Orange County built one near the church in the light-filled, airy Rosenwald style. It had two rooms heated by wood stoves vented through a central brick chimney. In the 1930s, not far from the church and school, John Mickey lived in a log cabin with a stone chimney, crafting bushel baskets and caning chair bottoms for fifty cents each. His grave is in the church cemetery. Estelle White lived on a nearby finger ridge but ventured out often to deliver babies. Prince Hall Freemasons gathered in a two-story lodge that still stands. Shady Grove Baptist Church has grown into a large brick building and its members are restoring the old school.

> **Resources**
>
> Orange County African American Historical Society. "The Mickey, White, and Long Families of Shady Grove" in the exhibition, *People, Places, and Memory: African-American Families in Orange County, Virginia.*
>
> Orange County Historical Society, Inc., 130 Caroline Street, Orange, Virginia 22960-1533, (540) 672-5366, *www.orangecovahist.org/.*

Madison County
VIRGINIA

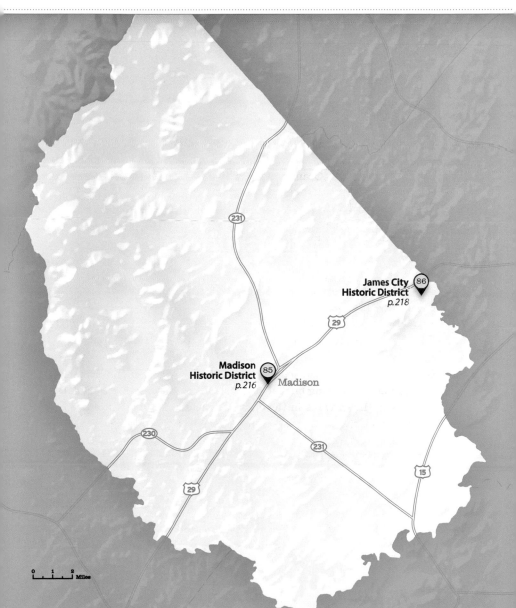

James City
Historic District
p.218

Madison
Historic District
p.216

Madison

Clinton Greaves's tombstone in Green Lawn Cemetery, Ohio

(Photo by Dave & Scooter, FindAGrave.com)

85

Madison Historic District

PEOPLE IN THE PLACES	**Clinton Greaves**	(1855–1906)

This Congressional Medal of Honor recipient was born in slavery on August 12, 1855 in Madison County, Virginia. His father was blacksmith John Greaves; his mother's name is not known. Clinton was seven years old when the Civil War broke out and ten when the Thirteenth Amendment abolished slavery. He made his way

HISTORIC SITE	Open to the public
THINGS TO DO AND SEE	A walking tour of Madison's Historic Homes is availalbe. Homes range in age from the late 1700's through the 1930's
DESIGNATIONS	National Register of Historic Places National Historic District
LOCATION	Madison, VA
CONTACT INFORMATION	(540) 948-4455
ON THE WEB	www.madison-va.com

to Prince George's County, Maryland, where he worked as a laborer in 1872, and made a decision that changed his life. The young man—five-foot-six-and-a-half-inches tall, with dark skin, black hair and black eyes—enlisted in the U.S. Army, signing his consent with his mark since he never learned how to write.

Greaves served in the western United States with Company C of the 9th Cavalry Regiment, one of the black regiments serving in the West. They were called "Buffalo Soldiers," supposedly named by the Indians for their tenacity and bravery. The 9th Cavalry's motto was "We Can. We Will." On January 24, 1877, Corporal Greaves accompanied Lt. Henry Wright, five other troopers and three Navaho scouts to pursue an Apache band who left their reservation without authorization. They found the Apache encampment and ensuing events were recorded in Greaves's Medal of Honor citation. "While part of a small detachment to persuade a band of renegade Apache Indians to surrender, his group was surrounded," it read, "Cpl. Greaves in the center of the savage hand-to-hand fighting, managed to shoot and bash a gap through the swarming Apaches, permitting his companions to break free." Five Apaches died and the rest retreated. With only minor wounds, all ten of the 9th Cavalry party—with several captured ponies—returned to Fort Bayard. Greaves reenlisted in Santa Fe in December 1877, that time signing his name. He served more than twenty years in the Army and died in 1906 at age 51. He was buried in Green Lawn Cemetery in Franklin County, Ohio without a marker. In 1998, at the initiative of the Medal of Honor Historical Society, local veterans' organizations installed a marker and dedicated it with full military honors.

Resources

Wikipedia, "Clinton Greaves." *en.wikipedia.org/wiki/Clinton_Greaves*

Buffalo Soldiers, Washington DC Chapter, 9th and 10th (Horse) Cavalry Association, *www.9thcavalry.com/greaves.htm*

Find a Grave. "Clinton Greaves." *www.findagrave.com/cgi-bin/fg.cgi?page=gr&GRid=8204863*

James Kuschel. "Clinton Greaves."

www.geocities.com/Pentagon/9904/greaves.html

www.geocities.com/Pentagon/9904/bio.html

Jennifer Logan. "We Can. We Will." *Texas Parks and Wildlife Magazine* (April 2006). *www.tpwmagazine.com/archive/2006/apr/legend*

Abandoned buildings in what was once James City

James City Historic District

86

The James City Historic District contains a group of unused commercial, residential, and agricultural buildings and is

HISTORIC SITE	Viewable from the road Properties are privately owned
LOCATION	East of state U.S. Routes 29 and State Routes 716 and 631, now called Leon

located on a 280-acre tract of land to the east and south of U.S. Route 29 on the Madison-Culpeper County line. The commercial buildings include two stores, a tavern and a blacksmith shop. There are two houses, one of which was used as a school. The farm lane was once the main road from Fredericksburg to Madison County, and the tavern at James City was a stop on a stagecoach line.

It appears that the first buildings date from the late 1700s and that the last ones were built in the 1940s. The buildings are all wooden structures and, while some of the buildings are in disrepair and additions have been made over the years, the basic integrity of each one has remained intact.

As the commerce moved out of the buildings in town and the town slowly died, agriculture took over and the James City property continued as a farming community. Finally in the 1980s the Bruce store closed and the family stopped farming, leaving James City stopped in time.

Resources

National Register of Historic Places Nomination Form. VDHR File No. 056-5011. "James City Historic District, Madison County, Virginia. Prepared by Roberta C. Kerr and Christopher C. Kerr, 2000. Available online in PDF format.

PEOPLE
· IN THE ·
PLACES

Noah Davis

(c. 1804–?)

REV. NOAH DAVIS,
PASTOR OF THE
Saratoga Street African Baptist Church,
BALTIMORE.

Until he was twelve years old, Noah Davis lived near a busy merchant mill on Crooked Run in James City (now Leon), Madison County, Virginia. His father John Davis was the head miller. Noah recalled that "in this responsible station he was much respected." Fredericksburg attorney and businessman Robert Patten owned the family as well as a share of the mill, but he allowed his slaves, especially the Davises, more privileges than most. John and his wife Jane kept livestock of their own and their children remained with them until they were old enough to learn a trade. Noah's oldest brother assisted their father in the mill. Both parents were pious Christians. On Sundays, John Davis sat in a bush arbor with his children and their black neighbors and read from a Bible that an older son sent from Fredericksburg. Before Noah left James City he resolved to be as much like them as he could.

In 1816 the owners decided to sell the mill. Robert Patten moved the enslaved people to his Culpeper farm near Stevensburg, where John and Jane Davis were freed and allowed to farm part of the property. Sometimes John put Noah and his brother in charge of the farm while he worked at another mill or sold farm produce. But when Noah turned fourteen, he was sent to Fredericksburg to learn a trade. He chose shoemaking in the same shop as an older brother.

In Fredericksburg, as a young man, Davis experienced a religious conversion and became a Baptist. He married a young woman who was baptized at the same time; together they had nine children. Davis felt called to become a minister. His owner allowed him to travel to the North to raise money with which to purchase his freedom. White Baptists in Baltimore invited him to become a minister among people of color there and said they would help him raise the balance. He accepted their offer and attended a growing congregation while continuing to raise money to purchase his wife and children. He published his autobiography in an effort to purchase their last two sons. During the Civil War, he and other black Baptist clergymen met with President Abraham Lincoln and went to minister to U.S. Colored Troops and southern countrymen who flocked to Union lines.

Resources

Davis, Noah. *A Narrative of the Life of Rev. Noah Davis, a Colored Man. Written by Himself, at the Age of 54.* Baltimore, Md.: J.F. Weislampel, Jr., 1859. Available online at *docsouth.unc.edu/neh/davisn/davis.html*

Albemarle County
VIRGINIA

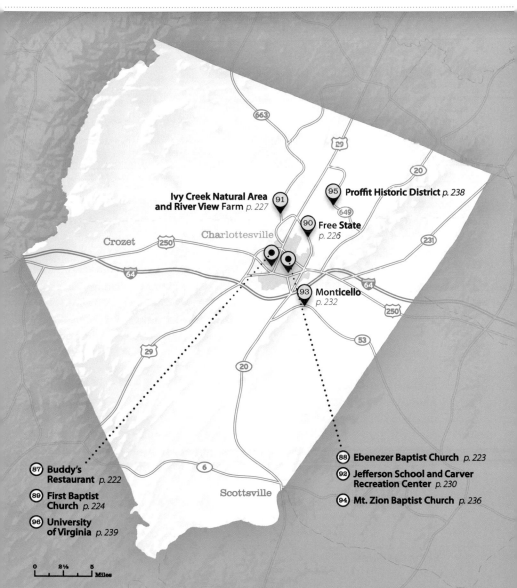

Ivy Creek Natural Area and River View Farm *p. 227* — 91

Proffit Historic District *p. 238* — 95

Free State *p. 226* — 90

Monticello *p. 232* — 93

Crozet

Charlottesville

Scottsville

0   2½   5 Miles

Former site of
Buddy's Restaurant,
Charlottesville

87 | Buddy's Restaurant

HISTORIC SITE	Viewable from the road
THINGS TO DO AND SEE	Now the Institute for Environmental Negotiation, University of Virginia
LOCATION	104 Emmet St., Charlottesville, VA
CONTACT INFORMATION	(434) 924-1970
ON THE WEB	*www.virginia.edu/ien/contact.htm*

White restaurant owner Buddy Glover refused to serve African Americans. In 1963, he unwittingly played a pivotal role in desegregrating Charlottesville. On Memorial Day weekend, black and white members of the Human Relations Council and NAACP branch, formed to support civil rights locally, decided to seek service at two segregated restaurants. The first group encountered no difficulty, but the ones who went to Buddy's—among them black community leaders Floyd and William Johnson and white University of Virginia professor Paul Gaston—did. They sat ignored at their table until they were ushered out at closing time, and were denied entry the next morning. As they stood outside, two white men struck a black minister in the group. When Gaston entered a phone booth to call the police, he was punched four times in the face. The Johnson men were also beaten and police then arrested the protestors. This violent incident confirmed that racial tensions and the Civil Rights Movement were not confined to the lower South. Averse to the storm of negative publicity that followed the incident, Charlottesville's restaurants, theatres, and motels dropped their barriers. Buddy's restaurant remained an exception. When the Civil Rights Act outlawing segregation passed on July 2, 1964, Buddy Glover shuttered his business. The building now houses the Institute for Environmental Negotiation at the University of Virginia.

Resources

Lisa Provence. "Brown's Birthday: The Road to Equality in Charlottesville" in *The [Charlottesville] Hook*, May 6, 2004. *www.readthehook.com/Stories/2004/05/06/COVERcivilrightslandmark2.html*

_____. "A Long and Winding Road: City Residents Recall Integration Battles" in *The [Charlottesville] Hook*, issue no. 0314, April 8, 2004. *www.readthehook.com/Stories/2004/04/08/COVER%20massive%20resistance3.2.html*

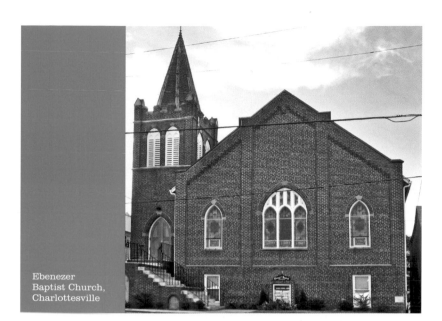

Ebenezer
Baptist Church,
Charlottesville

Ebenezer Baptist Church | 88

HISTORIC SITE	Viewable from the road
THINGS TO DO AND SEE	Operating church
LOCATION	113 Sixth St., NW Charlottesville, VA
CONTACT INFORMATION	(434) 296-7032 ebc113@comcast.net
ON THE WEB	www.ebc113.com/Index.htm

Members of Mount Zion Baptist Church who lived in and around the African American neighborhood of Vinegar Hill founded Ebenezer Baptist Church on March 25, 1892. They first worshipped at the Daughters of Zion Hall at 4th and Commerce Streets in Vinegar Hill, then bought a lot and built a church in 1907 on Sixth Street in adjacent integrated Starr Hill. The current brick building dates to 1908. In the 1920s, the growing congregation purchased a lot at 411 8th Street and built a parsonage. Despite urban renewal that destroyed much of the Vinegar Hill neighborhood in the 1960s, many former residents continue to attend church there.

Resources

Ebenezer Baptist Church. "The History of Ebenezer Baptist Church." www.ebc113.com/Index.htm

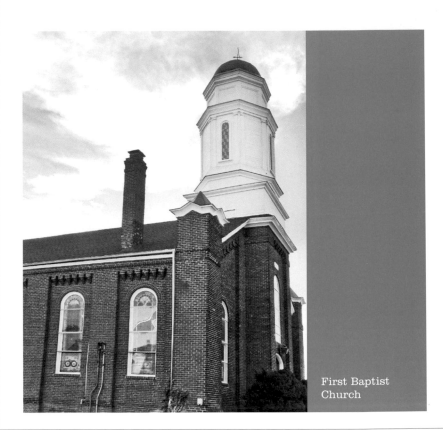

First Baptist
Church

89 First Baptist Church

Empowered by the Emancipation Proclamation, which freed slaves in the states in rebellion effective January 1, 1863, around 800 black members of Charlottesville's biracial First Baptist Church (1833) in essence declared independence. On March 6, 1863, they petitioned to separate and establish their own church, where they could worship on the main floor and participate in decision-making. In 1864, church leaders consented and allowed the new black congregation to use the same building. As

HISTORIC SITE	Viewable from the road
THINGS TO DO AND SEE	Operating church and historical highway marker
DESIGNATIONS	National Register of Historic Places
LOCATION	Transformation Ministries First Baptist Church 632 West Main St., Charlottesville, VA
CONTACT INFORMATION	(434) 979-0952 churchoffice@ntelos.net
ON THE WEB	www.transminfbc.org

still required by Virginia law, they hired a white minister. Before long the new congregation met in the basement of the Delevan Hotel, which served variously since the 1820s as a temperance hotel for college students, a classical academy, a military hospital, a Freedmen's Bureau school, and the site of the city's first biracial political meeting (1867). In 1868 the fledgling congregation—then called "Delevan Church of Charlottesville"— purchased the deteriorating building and called their first black minister in 1870. When Delevan Church was condemned in 1876, they demolished the building and laid the cornerstone for a new sanctuary in 1877. When completed in 1884, the congregation changed its name to First Colored Baptist Church of Charlottesville and their home is now considered one of the city's "premier Victorian churches." Currently named Transformation Ministries First Baptist Church, it has continued its tradition of activism over time, with members involved in formation of the local NAACP branch and integration of public schools and the University of Virginia hospital. The church motto is "Where God is Praised and Disciples Are Made."

Resources

Transformation Ministries First Baptist Church. "A Brief History of First Baptist Church" www.transminfbc.org

City of Charlottesville. Architectural and Historic Survey. "Delevan/First Baptist Church." (1982) www.dhr.state.va.us/registers/Cities/Charlottesville/104-0376_Delevan_Baptist_Cthurch_surveys.pdf

Headstone from the
Bowles family cemetery.
*(Steven Thompson/Rivanna
Archaeological Services for
Stonehaus, Inc.)*

90 | Free State

F ree State was one of the earliest free black communities in central Virginia. It traces its origins to 1788, when Amy Bowles Farrow, a free woman of color, purchased 224 acres of Albemarle County land

HISTORIC SITE	Private. Now part of the Belvedere development
THINGS TO DO AND SEE	Family cemeteries on both sides of Free State Rd. will be preserved and will feature an interpretive kiosk
LOCATION	Free State Rd. near Belvedere Dr.
CONTACT INFORMATION	Belvedere: (434) 951-0988

from William Johnson. Her son Zachariah Bowles—born free because his mother was free—inherited half of the property upon her death. Documentary records indicate that he worked occasionally at Monticello as a wage laborer, and that he married Critta Hemings, an enslaved woman there and the sister of Sally Hemings. Emancipated in 1827 after Thomas Jefferson's death, she joined her husband and lived out her life on their farm. During the antebellum period, various members of the Bowles family farmed and practiced various trades there. The community grew during the late 19th century but had been largely abandoned by the end of the 20th. Beginning in 2005, when the land was planned for a development (named *Belvedere* for a nearby manor house), Rivanna Archaeological Services began documentation of the community. Further archaeological and historical studies were completed in 2009, and two historic cemeteries will be preserved. The largest, the Bowles family cemetery, contains about 60 graves. Only one of several gravestones is legible, that of Mary Bowles who died in 1882. Across the road, the Brown family cemetery will also be preserved.

Resources

Stephen M. Thompson. "The Archaeology of the Bowles' Lot: ... A Late 18th-19th Century Free African-American Rural Domestic Site in Albemarle County, Virginia." Prepared for Stonehaus, Inc. by Rivanna Archaeological Services, 2009.

African-American Cemeteries of Albemarle and Amherst Counties. *www2.vcdh.virginia.edu/cem/db/cemetery/details/BWL*

The barn at
River View Farm
*(photo by
Mathias Tornqvist)*

Ivy Creek Natural Area and River View Farm

91

HISTORIC SITE	Open to the public
THINGS TO DO AND SEE	7:00 a.m. to sunset. Six miles of walking trails, educational activities, guided walks and nature programs.
LOCATION	Six miles north of Charlottesville on Earlysville Rd.
CONTACT INFORMATION	(434) 973-7772 icf@ivycreekfoundation.org
ON THE WEB	*ivycreekfoundation.org/ICNA.html*

The Ivy Creek Natural Area (ICNA) is a 215-acre preserve with six miles of walking trails through a mix of pine and hardwood forests, old fields, streams, natural springs, and two miles of shoreline on the South Fork Rivanna Reservoir. ICNA is an official site on the Virginia African American Heritage Trail in recognition of its rich social and agricultural history as a Freedman's farm dating back to 1870. Hugh Carr, born in slavery, was in his early twenties in 1865 when the Civil War ended and the Thirteenth Amendment abolished slavery. Over the next decade, Carr worked on white men's farms, saving enough to buy, expand, and build on this property he named River View Farm.

Nearby stood the community of Hydraulic, a thriving mill village dating back to the early 1800s. After the Civil War, Hydraulic became the center of the free black community of Union Ridge of which Hugh Carr was a prominent member.

After Hugh Carr's death in 1914, his oldest daughter Mary and her husband Conly Greer, carried on the farming tradition, expanding the farm to more than 200 acres. Mary Carr Greer's death in 1973 marked 100 years of ownership by the Carr-Greer family. Shortly afterwards, The Nature Conservancy bought the property, subsequently selling it to the City of Charlottesville and Albemarle County with the help of the Ivy Creek Foundation, who manage the nature preserve today. Visitors can take a walking tour and see the farmhouse (a private residence), family cemetery, barn, and a new education center.

Hugh Carr (c. 1843–1914)

Hugh Carr
(Ivy Creek Foundation)

Hugh Carr was born into slavery between 1840 and 1843 in Albemarle County, Virginia. First Baptist Church records note his baptism in 1860 "belonging to R.W. Wingfield." On Christmas Day, 1865, newly freed Hugh married Florence Lee at her parent's home. In the next five years, he worked for local farmers and saved $100 to put down on a 58-acre tract that would become Riverview Farm. By 1880, now widowed, Carr lived on his own 83-acre farm growing oats, wheat and corn with a half acre orchard. He also raised livestock for milk, meat, and eggs. In 1883 he married Texie Mae Hawkins and together they raised six daughters and a son at Riverview Farm, cultivating in them a high regard for education.

Mary Louise Carr Greer (1884–1973)

Mary Carr grew up at River View Farm, the eldest child of Hugh and Texie Mae Carr. She and her five sisters—Fannie, Emma, Peachie, Hazel, and Virginia—and brother Marshall attended school at Union Ridge Graded School in their African American community of Union Ridge. Their mother died in 1899, when

Ivy Creek Natural Area and River View Farm

Mary Carr Greer
(Ivy Creek Foundation)

Mary was fifteen years old, but the family held fast to their educational goals. At the age of 16, Mary Carr began a life-long career dedicated to the education of African American children by earning a certificate from Charlottesville's Piedmont Industrial Institute which qualified her to teach. Several years later, she continued her education at Virginia Normal and Industrial Institute in Petersburg, now Virginia State University. On return from college, she married fellow VSU graduate Conly Greer and joined the faculty at Albemarle Training School, located near her home at Riverview Farm. When Mary's father died in 1914, Conly Greer took over the management of River View Farm, eventually expanding it to more than 200 acres. Renowned for his agricultural knowledge, Conly became the first African American extension agent In Albemarle County, helping black farmers learn modern farming practices. River View Farm became a model in the county and farmers, both black and white, visited frequently to observe Greer's methods.

In 1931, Mary Carr Greer became the third principal of Albemarle Training School, leading the school to improve and expand its curriculum from a two-year vocational training program to a full four-year high school. In 1974, one year after Mary Carr Greer's death, Albemarle County honored her dedication to education with the opening of the Mary Carr Greer Elementary School, located on Lamb's Road, not far from Riverview Farm.

Resources

Ivy Creek Foundation. "History and Heritage: The Carr Family and African American History "Hugh Carr Family History," *ivycreekfoundation.org/FamilyHistory.html*

_____. "The Life and Legacy of Hugh Carr: River View Farm." (Brochure).

Jefferson
High School

92

Jefferson High School & Carver Recreation Center

efferson High School is part of a larger story of African American education in Charlottesville. In 1865, just after the Civil War and the end of laws that prevented African Americans from obtaining an education, black and white citizens with

HISTORIC SITE	Open to the public
THINGS TO DO AND SEE	Carver Recreation Center is open M-F 5 to 9 and S 9-3
DESIGNATIONS	Virginia Historic Landmark and National Register of Historic Places
LOCATION	223 4th St. SW, Charlottesville, VA
CONTACT INFORMATION	(434) 293-2259

the Freedmen's Bureau established a school in the Delevan Hotel that had served as a hospital for wounded Confederates. Anna Gardner, a Massachusetts abolitionist supported by the New England Freedmen's Aid Society, became the first teacher and named the school for the third president, whom she admired. Hundreds of pupils—some over sixty years old—attended. Other schools and teachers, some of them local African Americans, followed. By 1869 the Delevan building was no longer adequate, and a school with the same name opened near the train station. It served the community until 1894 when the larger Jefferson Colored Graded/

Elementary School on Fourth Street replaced it. Fourth Street was the western edge of a largely black residential and business community called Vinegar Hill. In 1924, eighty-six parents and community members petitioned the school board for a high school. In 1926, Jefferson High School opened on the same parcel of property. After the Supreme Court called for integration in the Brown versus the Board of Education decision of 1954, black parents, students, and community leaders, with the NAACP, pushed for change. Charlottesville achieved city-wide integration in the fall of 1965. That academic year, Jefferson High School accommodated all of Charlottesville's middle school students. Around the same time, the city demolished most of the historic buildings in the Vinegar Hill community. The Jefferson School building remains and now serves as the Carver Recreation Center, with plans for an African American Heritage and Cultural Center there.

Resources

National Register of Historic Places Nomination.
www.dhr.virginia.gov/registers/Cities/Charlottesville/104-5087_JeffersonSchool_NRdraft_2005_Oct.pdf

Kenneth A. Schwartz. "Vinegar Hill." Institute for Advanced Technology in the Humanities, University of Virginia. *www3.iath.virginia.edu/schwartz/vhill/vhill.html*

Joinery chimney
on Mulberry Row
at Monticello
*(Thomas Jefferson
Foundation/Bill Moretz)*

93

Monticello

An entire community of enslaved people—around 120 individuals in several family lines—lived at Monticello and its affiliated farms. Some worked in the main house and their lives were closely intertwined with those of Thomas Jefferson and his family. Along Mulberry Row and elsewhere on the plantation skilled workers shaped wood, metal, wool, and linen into useful products. Most of the others in their laboring years worked in agriculture at Monticello and affiliated farms.

HISTORIC SITE	Open to the public
THINGS TO DO AND SEE	Plantation Community Tours visit Mulberry Row and other plantation-related sites near the mountaintop and focus on the African-American community at Monticello and the economic operation of the plantation.
DESIGNATIONS	National Register of Historic Places National Historic Landmark Unesco World Heritage Site
LOCATION	931 Thomas Jefferson Parkway Charlottesville, VA Two miles south of Charlottesville on VA 53
CONTACT INFORMATION	(434) 984-9800
ON THE WEB	*www.monticello.org*

For the past fifteen years, Thomas Jefferson Foundation historians have investigated and reconstructed the lives of enslaved people at Monticello and traced their descendants. Among them they discovered: emigrants to Liberia and the western United States; Underground Railroad activists;

Union soldiers and their wives, and founders of churches. In a project called "Getting Word," they interviewed living descendants. One interviewee recalled her grandmother telling her "about the beauty of Monticello and the ugliness of slavery."

Today, visitors can easily learn more about African Americans at Monticello including Sally Hemings, a slave who lived in Paris and Monticello with Jefferson and two of his daughters and had at least six children. Docents include African Americans in the historical interpretation of the main house. Guided tours of Mulberry Row, where enslaved people lived and worked, include stories of their lives. The Monticello website contains information about Mulberry Row, biographical sketches, an interactive database on more than 600 enslaved people at Monticello, and information about descendants and their reunions.

Resources

Thomas Jefferson Foundation. *A Day in the Life of Thomas Jefferson.* "To Labour for Another." *www.monticello.org/jefferson/dayinlife/plantation/home.html*

_____. Getting Word: The Monticello African American Oral History Project. *www.monticello.org/gettingword/index.html*

_____. Monticello: The Home of Thomas Jefferson. The Plantation. *www.monticello.org/plantation/index.html*

_____. Monticello Plantation Database. *plantationdb.monticello.org/nMonticello.html*

Lucia Stanton. *Free Some Day: The African American Families of Monticello.* Monticello Monograph Series. Charlottesville, Va.: Thomas Jefferson Foundation, 2000.

_____. *Slavery at Monticello.* Monticello Monograph Series. Charlottesville, Va.: Thomas Jefferson Foundation, 1996.

PEOPLE IN THE PLACES **Wormley Hughes**   (1781–1858)

Rev. Robert Hughes *(1824-1895),* son of Wormley Hughes. *(Union Run Baptist Church)*

Even as a boy, born and raised in slavery at Monticello, Wormley Hughes demonstrated versatility and diligence. He worked in the house and yard and, at age thirteen, was the second highest producer in Thomas Jefferson's prized and profitable nailery on Mulberry Row. At nineteen, Hughes blasted rock for Jefferson's canal. He learned gardening, probably from Scotsman Robert Bailey, whom Jefferson hired in 1794 to help establish the ornamental gardens at Monticello. Afterward, Hughes's work was cited often in Jefferson's journal, as he prepared beds, planted seeds, bulbs, and shoots, and prepared the beds for winter. In between he performed a wide variety of other tasks. His passion for horses was foremost, however, and eventually Jefferson appointed him head hostler. As such, he managed the stables at Monticello. Hughes enjoyed the deep trust of Jefferson and his family and was "given his time," or unofficially freed after his master's death, apparently at his behest. His wife and children were sold, but by their efforts and those of sympathetic whites, most of the family reunited at Edgehill, the home of Thomas Jefferson Randolph.

Wormley Hughes's wife was Ursula, a member of another enslaved family at Monticello. She was a farm laborer and cook who studied under French chef Honoré de Julian for a year in Washington, D.C. while Jefferson served as president. Wormley and Ursula Hughes had at least thirteen children. One son, Rev. Robert Hughes, established a church in Albemarle County, and Robert's son Rev. Wormley Hughes founded churches in Fauquier and Loudoun counties. Karen Hughes White, a descendant, co-founded the Afro-American Historical Association of Fauquier County in 1992 (see p. 152).

> ### Resources
>
> Thomas Jefferson Foundation. "Robert Hughes" in *Getting Word: The Monticello African American Oral History Project*. www.monticello.org/gettingword/index.html
>
> _____. "The Plantation: Wormley Hughes (1781-1858)." *Monticello: The Home of Thomas Jefferson*. www.monticello.org/plantation/lives/wormley.html
>
> _____. Monticello Plantation Database. *plantationdb.monticello.org/nMonticello.html*
>
> Lucia Stanton. *Free Some Day: The African American Families of Monticello*. Monticello Monograph Series. Charlottesville, Va.: Thomas Jefferson Foundation, 2000.

  Edith Hern Fossett   (1787–1854)

Peter Farley Fossett *(1815-1901)*, son of Edith and Joseph Fossett. *(Wendell P. Dabney, Cincinnati's Colored Citizens, 1926)*

Edith Fossett contributed notably to rich culinary traditions in the mid-Atlantic region. Born at Monticello, Edith was among the enslaved servants who accompanied Thomas Jefferson to the White House in Washington, D.C. There she received a small monthly stipend and trained for 6 ½ years under French chef Honoré de Julien. Dinner guests raved about the food, especially a dessert of ice cream "inclosed in covers of warm pastries." When Jefferson retired at Monticello, he installed her as head cook. Guests there continued to record their compliments. Daniel Webster, who visited

Monticello in 1824, noted that "dinner is served in half Virginian, half French style, in good taste and abundance."

Edith Fossett's tenure in Washington entailed hardship for her and her family, as her husband Joseph Fossett remained in Charlottesville. He managed the blacksmith shop at Monticello. Jefferson did not acknowledge their marriage, although her first child was born a few months after her arrival in Washington. About midway in her tenure, possibly after receiving distressing news about his family, Joseph left Monticello and hastened to Washington without permission. He was captured there and returned to Charlottesville the following day. Joseph Fossett was one of the few bondmen whom Jefferson freed in his will.

Edith Fossett and the couple's eight children were sold at auction in 1827. With the help of free family members, Joseph managed to purchase Edith and some of children out of slavery. The family moved to Ohio around 1840. Their son Peter's owner refused to sell and he was left behind. Ten years later, after two foiled escape attempts, he was put on the auction block and bought out of slavery through the combined efforts of family and friends. Peter Fossett settled in Cincinnati where he became a caterer, minister, and Underground Railroad agent.

Resources

Thomas Jefferson Foundation. "Peter Farley Fossett" in *Getting Word: The Monticello African American Oral History Project. www.monticello.org/gettingword/GWpeter.html*

Lucia Stanton. *Free Some Day: The African American Families of Monticello.* Monticello Monograph Series. Charlottesville, Va.: Thomas Jefferson Foundation, 2000.

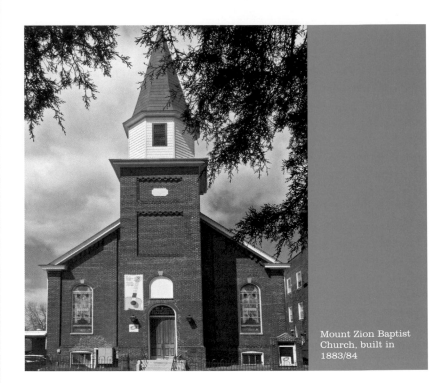

Mount Zion Baptist Church, built in 1883/84

Mount Zion Baptist Church

94

In 1863, in the midst of the Civil War, African American members of the Baptist Church on Park Avenue successfully petitioned to form their own congregation. Still prevented by Virginia law from worshipping together without a white minister, they nonetheless established The Delevan or First Colored Baptist Church in 1864. In 1867 some members of that body organized

HISTORIC SITE	Contact site before visiting
THINGS TO DO AND SEE	The building now holds the Music Resource Center
DESIGNATIONS	Virginia Historic Landmark National Register of Historic Places
LOCATION	105 Ridge St. Charlottesville, VA
CONTACT INFORMATION	Mount Zion First African Baptist Church: (434) 293-3212 Music Resource Center: (434) 979-5478
ON THE WEB	Mount Zion First African Baptist Church: www.mtzionfabc.com Music Resource Center: www.musicresourcecenter.org

Mt. Zion Baptist Church and called "the horseback preacher," Reverend Spottswood Jones, to become the first African American pastor in Charlottesville. They met in private homes and built a small frame church on Ridge Street in the 1870s. The growing congregation replaced it with a large brick structure in 1883/84 and added the steeple, stained glass windows, and a pipe organ in the 1890s. On Easter Monday, 1905, an overflow crowd witnessed the mortgage burning ceremony. When the church was built on Ridge Street, Charlottesville—like many southern towns—was residentially integrated, but during the twentieth century neighborhoods became segregated. Not far to the north of Mt. Zion an Irish neighborhood evolved into the center of black social and business activity in Charlottesville, known as Vinegar Hill. The Mount Zion congregation continued to thrive and eventually outgrew the old church. They moved in 2003 to a large new building at 105 Lankford Avenue.

Resources

Mt. Zion First African Baptist Church Website. *www.mtzionfabc.com/history.html*

National Register of Historic Places Registration Form. "Mount Zion Baptist Church, Charlottesville, Virginia." VDHR File No. 104-0181, 1992. Available online in PDF format.

Evergreen (formerly Bethel)
Baptist Church

95 ## Proffit Historic District

T wo and one-half miles east of Route 29 on VA 649 lies the remnant of a Freedmen's village called Proffit. The community began in the early 1870s when John Coles and Benjamin Brown purchased land from their former owner W. G. Carr in

HISTORIC SITE	Viewable from the road
THINGS TO DO AND SEE	Properties are privately owned
DESIGNATIONS	National Register of Historic Places
LOCATION	2309 Proffit Rd., Charlottesville, VA
CONTACT INFORMATION	www.vcdh.virginia.edu/afam/proffit/ community
ON THE WEB	www.vcdh.virginia.edu/afam/proffit

exchange for labor. Ned Brown then bought seventy-five acres and divided it into small lots that other freed people could afford. He named the community Egypt. Virginia Midway Railroad boosted the local economy and attracted white residents when it built a railroad station in 1881 on land purchased from white landowner Samuel Proffit. The station and a subsequent post office were called Proffit, eclipsing earlier names. Black residents organized a Baptist congregation in 1881 and built Bethel Baptist Church, later called Evergreen, in 1891. During the 1920s, some of the men worked at a local sulphur mine. The community declined after Route 29 was finished in the early 1930s and automobiles and trucks overshadowed railroads. The church and a historical highway marker placed in 2000 identify Proffit. Nearby are a reconstructed one-lane wooden bridge and the remains of six dwellings, post office, and sulphur mine.

Resources

Carter G. Woodson Institute for Afro-American and African Studies, Proffit Historic District Online Resource Archive. *www.vcdh.virginia.edu/afam/proffit*

Virginia Foundation for the Humanities, African American Heritage in Virginia, Heritage Site database. "Proffit Historic District." *www.web.virginia.edu/vfhdb/AAHV/sites.asp?MailingListID=548*

Luther P. Jackson
(1892-1950)

University of Virginia

HISTORIC SITE	Open to the public
THINGS TO DO AND SEE	Conducted tours of the Rotunda are offered daily at 10 AM, 11 AM, 2 PM, 3 PM and 4 PM. No admission charge. Closes for 3 weeks at Christmas time and during graduation in May.
DESIGNATIONS	National Register of Historic Places National Historic District
LOCATION	Charlottesville, VA Bounded by University and Jefferson Park Avenues, Hospital and McCormick Roads
CONTACT INFORMATION	(434) 924-7969
ON THE WEB	www.virginia.edu/academicalvillage

Enslaved and free laborers and craftsmen together shaped the landscape and constructed the buildings that transformed Thomas Jefferson's visions of an academical village into reality. University policy forbade students from bringing enslaved servants with them, but each scholar was assigned to a hotel for meals and support services that depended heavily upon slave labor. Although Virginia law tried to prevent people of color from obtaining an education, some managed anyway. Isabella Gibbons, for example, owned by Professor Francis H. Smith, taught her children to read and later instructed others at a Freedmen's Bureau school. A few faculty members or relatives taught Sunday school, and at least one professor's daughter gave individual instruction.

University of Virginia

After the Civil War and the Thirteenth Amendment to the Constitution ended slavery, people of color continued to play the same support roles at the university. In 1870, despite concerted opposition, Virginia law mandated separate schools for white and black students. The law took a century to overturn.

In the twentieth century, people of color intensified efforts to desegregate higher education. In 1935, Virginia Union University professor Alice Jackson applied to graduate school at the University of Virginia and was denied admission. The state legislature, worried about an NAACP-backed lawsuit, offered to pay out-of-state tuition for graduate education for black students. After World War II the university began inviting black lecturers such as historian Dr. Luther Porter Jackson, who delivered a conference paper in 1949 entitled, "Virginia and Civil Rights."

Stimulated by national challenges to *Plessy v. Ferguson,* the University admitted its first black student, Gregory Swanson, to its law school in 1950. Others followed. In 1955, the year following the *Brown v. Board of Education* decision, black undergraduate students were admitted for the first time. Undergraduate women had to wait until 1970.

Today, the University of Virginia enjoys the highest African American graduation rate of any public university. The Office of African-American Affairs, based in a building named to honor Luther P. Jackson, supports their success.

Resources

University of Virginia. "The First Generation: Thirty Years of the Office of African-American Affairs at the University of Virginia," by Ervin L. Jordan. *www.virginia.edu/oaaa/history.html*

Schulman, Gayle M. "Slaves at the University of Virginia." Available as a PDF file at *home.ntelos.net/~gayles*

Atima Omara-Alwala. *Trailblazing Against Tradition: Desegregation at the University of Virginia* 1955-75. *xroads.virginia.edu/~UG03/omara-alwala/Harrison/Trailblazing.html*

Conclusion

I t is not uncommon to view history in fairly defined and sometimes stark terms. However, when we experience history by walking in the footsteps of those who went before us, we see that our American Story is, in fact, richly varied and full of complex human struggles, harsh decisions, tragedies, and achievements both small and grand. By switching the lens through which we view history, we not only honor those who went before us, but by literally following their paths, we enrich our own lives.

The research represented within this book has already inspired some to do just that. For example, descendants of Catherine "Kitty" Payne *(see profile on p. 35)* visited the Journey Through Hallowed Ground in 2007 to understand their American Story. Payne's great-great granddaughter, Sandy Kasabuske, was contacted during our

research and in the process became better acquainted with her own ancestor. In response, she organized a family reunion that began in Gettysburg. One of our local advisors, Debra McCauslin, responded by having the day of the reunion officially-declared *Kitty Payne Day* in Gettysburg, PA and led a tour of sites significant to this family's story in Adams County including Payne's headstone at Lincoln Cemetery, her original burial place at the site of the black community called Yellow Hill, and the house on Cemetery Hill at Gettysburg National Military Park that once belonged to Payne's second husband Abraham Brian. These same family

Kitty Payne descendants in April 2007 at the Rappahannock County farmhouse of their ancestor.

members traveled to Rappahannock County, where they were joined by members of the Rappahannock County Historical Society and together they visited the jail where Payne and her children were held for months as they awaited the outcome of their freedom suit. Finally, they visited the farmhouse where Payne was raised in slavery. For these descendants, and for the people in Adams and Rappahannock County who joined in the commemoration, it was a deeply moving experience.

In 2008, Kasabuske made two additional trips to continue her genealogical research and exploration. She visited Loudoun County, Virginia, where her ancestors stayed on their journey back to Pennsylvania. She returned to see an exhibition of historic Quaker friendship quilts, one containing a signed block made by Kitty Payne's daughter, Mary. The connections from the past seemed alive again in the collected group who was sharing research and interest in Kitty Payne and the antislavery networks that helped her regain her freedom.

While Kitty Payne's life and contributions are notable for their dramatic consequences and for the number of communities she touched, this book demonstrates that there are many other individuals with similarly powerful stories, and compelling historic sites that anchor them.

We hope you have enjoyed this book, and that it will launch a larger journey of discovery—one that will last a lifetime. By exploring, remembering, and sharing the stories of our ancestors, we keep their ideals alive and weave their sense of individual duty into our own lives. There is no more meaningful way to honor the paths of those who trod this hallowed ground, and in the course, made our way so much richer.

Sandy Kasabuske, Debra McCauslin, Mary Robare, Deborah Lee, Elaine Thompson, and Judy Tole at the Virginia Quilt Museum during the 2008 exhibition, *Quilts and Quaker Heritage,* curated by Mary Robare. Kasabuske is pointing to Mary Payne's signed quilt block. *(Sandy Kasabuske)*

Acknowledgments

This project and publication were made possible by grants from the Virginia Foundation for the Humanities, the Pennsylvania Museum and Historical Commission, the Loudoun Restoration and Preservation Society, the Virginia Department of Historic Resources, and individual supporters including Mr. and Mrs. James Moorman, Mr. and Mrs. Donald Pongrace, and Mr. and Mrs. David Williams. We deeply appreciate their financial support, as well as the help of a legion of individuals and organizations that helped us shape the project, conduct research, document sites, select sites to interpret and people to profile, and who reviewed and commented on drafts of the text. Some are named below.

Core Project Advisors

Karen Hughes White • Director, Afro-American Historical Association of Fauquier County, The Plains, VA

Jenny Masur, PhD • National Capital Regional Coordinator, Underground Railroad Network to Freedom Program, National Park Service, Washington, DC

James K. Bryant II, PhD • Associate Professor of History, Shenandoah University, Winchester, VA

Support and Editorial Assistance

Beth Erickson • The Journey Through Hallowed Ground Partnership

Subject Matter and Content Advisors

Harry Bradshaw Matthews • (USCT, UGRR, AME Church, Free Masons) United States Colored Troops Institute for Local History & Family Research, Hartwick College, Oneonta, NY

Denise Oliver-Velez, PhD • (Loudoun County and Family Research) AfriGeneas Surnames and Family Research Forum

Ronald Palmer • (UGRR, AME Church, Free Masons) George Washington University, Washington DC

Dr. Robert K. Sutton • Chief Historian, National Park Service

Elaine Thompson • Black History Committee, Friends of Thomas Balch Library, Leesburg, VA

Marie Tyler-McGraw, PhD • Independent Historian and Public History Consultant, Washington, DC and Shepherdstown, WV

Regional Advisors

PENNSYLVANIA, ADAMS COUNTY

Norris Flowers • Gettysburg Convention & Visitors Bureau

Charles Glatfelter, PhD • Adams County Historical Society

Jean Green • Third Ward Concerned Neighbors and Black History Museum Project, Gettysburg

Scott Hancock, PhD • Professor of History and African Studies, Gettysburg College

Carol A. Hegeman • Eisenhower National Historic Site, Gettysburg

John Latschar, PhD • Gettysburg National Military Park

Debra McCauslin • For the Cause Productions, Gettysburg

Wayne Motts • Adams County Historical Society

Lincoln Cemetery Project Association • Gettysburg

Alisha Sanders • Gettysburg

Timothy Smith • Adams County Historical Society

MARYLAND

Charles (Sonny) Doleman • (Washington County) Doleman Black Heritage Museum, Hagerstown

Chris Haugh • (Carroll County, MD) Tourism Council of Frederick County

Mary Harris • (Frederick County) AARCH (African American Resources – Cultural and Historic) Frederick

Dean Herrin, PhD • (Maryland) Catoctin Center for Regional Studies, Frederick

Belva King • (Frederick County) AARCH (African American Resources – Cultural and Historic) Frederick

VIRGINIA

Roxanne Adams • (Prince William) Manassas Museum and Jennie Dean Memorial

Black History Committee • Friends of Thomas Balch Library, Leesburg

David Blake • (Buckland) Buckland Preservation Society, Gainesville

Jane Butler • (Fauquier County) Afro-American Historical Association of Fauquier County, The Plains, VA

Phyllis Cook-Taylor • (Loudoun County) Friends of the Slave Quarters, Middleburg

Rebecca Gilmore Coleman • (Orange County) Orange County African American Historical Association

Lee Langston-Harrison • (Culpeper County, VA) Museum of Culpeper History, Culpeper

Ann L. B. Miller, PhD • (Virginia) Virginia Transportation Research Council, Charlottesville

Robert Orrison • (Brentsville Courthouse Historic Centre) Prince William County

Matthew Reeves, PhD • (Orange County) Montpelier Foundation, Montpelier Station and Orange County African American Historical Association

Dede Smith • (River View Farm) Ivy Creek Foundation, Charlottesville

Leni Sorensen, PhD • (Monticello, Albemarle County) Monticello Foundation, Charlottesville

Lucia Stanton, PhD • (Monticello, Albemarle County) Monticello Foundation, Charlottesville

James Russell • (Rappahannock County) Sperryville

Elaine Thompson • (Loudoun County) Hamilton

Judith Tole (Rappahannock County) • Rappahannock County Historical Society, Washington

Dorothy Warner • (Rappahannock County) Scrabble School Preservation Foundation Scrabble

Karen Hughes White • (Fauquier County) Afro-American Historical Association, Fauquier County, The Plains

WEST VIRGINIA, HARPERS FERRY

Melinda Day • Harpers Ferry National Historical Park

Dennis Frye • Harpers Ferry National Historical Park

James Taylor • Jefferson County Black History Preservation Society, Ranson, WV

Index